Praise for
Fake Science

"Have you ever noticed how selectively science is worshipped by the Left? Liberals love to use 'science' as an argument-ender for every question under the sun. But they don't like scientifically modified food, for some reason. And they *really* don't like what science has to say about gender. Or sexuality. Or demographics. For some reason, the Left only seems to be interested in 'science' when it tells other people how to live their lives. *Fake Science* is a smart, encyclopedic collection of all the ways the Left professes to love 'science' while rejecting actual, you know, science."

> —Jonathan Last, senior writer at *The Weekly Standard* and author of *What to Expect When No One's Expecting*

"With verve and vivid examples, Austin Ruse dissects the Science Bluster, a dance of two steps. First progressives call their politics science. Then, in step two, they dismiss real science as politics. It's no wonder the Left keeps tripping over itself."

> —William Briggs, Ph.D., adjunct professor of statistical science at Cornell University and author of *Uncertainty: The Soul of Modeling, Probability & Statistics*

"If his pen were a scalpel, Austin Ruse would be a brain surgeon. In *Fake Science*, he exposes the lobotomy the progressive Left has attempted to perform on America's brain. One of the most courageous and cogent writers today, Ruse demonstrates how thoughtless one would need to be to accept the unreality proffered by the forces of unreason. To use another medical analogy, he lances the boils of pseudoscience—transgenderism, "born that way" homosexuality, abortion, global warming, and others. Each of these has, in fact, become its own religion, which is why its adherents cleave to it *against all the facts of real science.* You will be entertained and enlightened by Ruse's demolition of these false gods."

> —Robert R. Reilly, author of *Making Gay Okay: How Rationalizing Homosexual Behavior Is Changing Everything* and *The Closing of the Muslim Mind: How Intellectual Suicide Created the Modern Islamist Crisis*

"For decades, the Left has claimed the mantle of science, and accused conservatives of being 'anti-science.' But in most of the big debates about science that rise to the level of public debate, the Left has taken the side of bad politics rather than good science. Whether the subject is climate, sex, life-saving technology, and even human nature itself, many on the Left invoke the name of science but reject its substance. Austin Ruse does a masterful job of exposing this hypocrisy. He offers a delightfully readable survey of today's science wars and defends real science from its detractors."

> —Jay Richards, Ph.D., executive editor of *The Stream* and author of the *New York Times* bestseller *Indivisible: Restoring Faith, Family, and Freedom Before It's Too Late*

Fake Science

Fake Science

Exposing the Left's skewed statistics, fuzzy facts, and dodgy data

Austin Ruse

REGNERY
PUBLISHING
A Division of Salem Media Group

Regnery® is a registered trademark of Salem Communications Holding Corporation

Cataloging-in-Publication data on file with the Library of Congress

First e-book edition 2017: ISBN 978-1-62157-614-3
Originally published in hardcover, 2017: ISBN 978-1-62157-594-8

Published in the United States by
Regnery Publishing
A Division of Salem Media Group
300 New Jersey Ave NW
Washington, DC 20001
www.Regnery.com

Manufactured in the United States of America

10 9 8 7 6 5 4 3 2 1

Books are available in quantity for promotional or premium use. For information on discounts and terms, please visit our website: www.Regnery.com.

Distributed to the trade by
Perseus Distribution
www.perseusdistribution.com

For my wife, Cathy, and our children, Lucy and Gianna-Marie

CONTENTS

Spit-Balls across the Public Square

This is not a book of science. You will find no quarks here, no third law of thermodynamics, no E = mc².

This is a book about fake science.

There's real science, and then there's "science," or what passes for it these days. And there's a big difference.

Real science is about data that can be measured, about facts and biological processes that can be established by observation and experiment, about results that can be replicated. Science has enormous credibility in our society. And for very good reason. Over the past couple of centuries, science—real hard science—earned its well-deserved reputation by exploding harmful myths, discovering life-saving medicines, and enabling the invention of hitherto undreamt-of technologies. Real science has cured epidemic diseases, given us cars and airplanes and computers and cell phones, taken us to the moon, and, perhaps most significantly, allowed the Earth to house seven billion people—the vast majority of whom would quickly starve to death if modern scientific advances were reversed—in a state of health and prosperity undreamed of by our ancestors.

But that reputation has been hijacked by a cause that's anything but scientific. "Science" is now a cover for the leftist agenda.

The Democrats are "the party of science"—even as they refuse to acknowledge basic biological facts. Late-breaking news: A man isn't really a woman just because he "identifies" as female. Unborn babies are living human beings.

If we object to wrecking the world economy to cure the supposedly planet-destroying threat of global warming, we're told that "the science is settled"—though there is hardly any less scientific statement than that. Science is about free inquiry, which is the very opposite of conformity to an existing "consensus."

Which in any case is always changing—for the activists' convenience. The sea level is going to rise twenty feet and everyone will starve because of catastrophic global warming. But when those disasters fail to materialize, no, wait, it's not warming at all, it's "climate change."

And when the real, hard science actually is settled, it's ignored, even if that means that people suffer and die unnecessarily. Rice genetically modified to produce beta-carotene could have saved the vision—and in some cases the lives—of literally millions of poor people across the globe if the anti-food activists on the Left hadn't kept it off the market for more than twenty-five years.

Humility—the willingness to submit your opinion to the real facts of the matter, wherever they may lead—is the hallmark of real science. But the purveyors of leftist pseudoscience are anything but humble. No matter how often their predictions fail to pan out, how often they reverse their advice, or what obvious facts contradict their theories, they're never deterred. They go on making absurd, unscientific assertions and issuing new recommendations with absolute assurance, all on the authority of "science." Being wrong—even laughably wrong—doesn't even slow them down.

The reputation of real science has been stolen by its evil twin, a fake "science" that's really just an ideology and a narrative. That ideology is simply masquerading in the credibility that rightfully belongs to real science. As David Burge (@iowahawkblog on Twitter) has pointed out, this is the standard modus operandi of the Left:

1. Identify a respected institution.
2. Kill it.
3. Gut it.
4. Wear its carcass as a skin suit, while demanding respect.[1]

That's exactly what the leftists have done with science. They've distorted, faked, misreported, and skewed the real science, all the while claiming its mantle for their highly unscientific political agenda. And dangerously, the fake, politicized "science" is undermining our faith in the real thing. Whole disciplines have become profoundly degraded and therefore increasingly worthless—except as a source for political propaganda.

Real science does not rely on the argument from authority—which even St. Thomas Aquinas, back in the Middle Ages, knew was the weakest argument. Real scientists present the evidence and let it do the persuading. They don't attempt to impose their opinions—much less their pre-existing political assumptions—by the weight of their authority.

In any case, the "authority" of many of the "experts" trotted out by the Left is dubious at best. Scientists from one field wander into another field where they have no genuine expertise. A Ph.D., no matter what discipline it is in, seems to qualify any leftists to warn laymen off hallowed "scientific" ground.

One such "expert" sniffed at me, "Why not leave those questions"—he was referring to the highly unscientific born-that-way doctrine about homosexuality—"to those who are trained in the human sciences?" The problem is, plenty of people "trained in the human sciences" have held irrational and very unscientific beliefs over the years—often for political reasons, and sometimes with horrific results. Fully trained doctors experimented on Jews in Nazi Germany, carried out frontal lobotomies and sterilized the mentally "unfit" in the name of eugenics right here in

America, and subjected African-Americans to excruciating and preventable death from tertiary syphilis at Tuskegee. Will our modern "transgender" science one day seem just as barbaric? After all, today fully qualified and thoroughly respectable doctors are castrating little boys on the pretense that they can turn them into women. In fact, it's becoming hard to be a respectable scientist if you raise scientific objections to this truly evil project. As we shall see, one scientist who brought up inconvenient evidence that casts doubt on the wisdom of surgically mutilating "transgender" children was recently hounded from a medical conference.

And the fake science doesn't just affect scientists and the tiny minority of disturbed people whose delusions they are enabling. With the full authority of "science" behind them, the leftists are imposing their agenda on the rest of us, backed by the crushing power of the state. You can now be fined up to $250,000 by the New York City government if you're a shopkeeper and you persistently refuse to use someone's preferred gender pronoun. In other words, you will be bankrupted if you don't go along with the fiction that a person with XY chromosomes and male genitalia is really a woman.

And if you're a scientist, you'll discover that vital funding, opportunities for publication, and the other necessary accoutrements of a successful career are difficult to come by if your research challenges the leftist narrative.[2] As we'll see in chapters six and ten, research results that tell against the global warming scare, for example, or the lie that same-sex-couple parenting is good for children, can be highly dangerous to your scientific career. The Left controls what counts as "science" by excluding not just inconvenient facts but inconvenient fact-finders. Any scientist whose work turns up evidence that calls the program of the Left on any issue into question is inevitably said to be "discredited."

But it deserves repeating: fake science is not just a problem for scientists. The fact that science has become so degraded by ideology does not give any of us an excuse to simply ignore it. We're not off the hook; it's too important. The current state of the debate requires that we evaluate the "scientific" claims made by the other side. A surprising amount of them are junk science—while real science often backs up conservative claims.

That is the reason for this book. Public policy issues—which in the current political climate covers not only the direction of our country but the intimate details of our lives—are too important to be left to ideologues, even if they call themselves "scientists."

Even now, your local school board is probably debating what to do about the transgender issue, inviting so-called experts into their meetings and into the halls of your schools to spout the latest nonsense. Will you simply stand aside and let them have the field uncontested? There is plenty of hard science that debunks "transgenderism." Boys are boys and girls are girls; science confirms what we all know is common sense. But to fight the crazy ideology you need to have the real science at your fingertips—so that you can engage at all levels of the public policy debate, from the dinner table, to the school board, to your college campus, to the U.S. Congress, to the United Nations.

This book comprises eleven issues where the science is "settled"—squarely on the side of the Left and their agenda. You are just supposed to take their word for it, to sit down and shut up.

But why should you trust them?

The experts told us repeatedly through the 2016 campaign season that Donald Trump had no chance to win the presidency, that he had no path to 270 electoral votes, and there was no way Hillary Clinton would not be the next president of the United States. In chapter one we examine how the actual polling data told the truth, but the pollsters and pundits still somehow managed to get the story terribly wrong.

Chapter two addresses perhaps the hottest "scientific" topic in America right now: "transgenderism." Practically overnight, a "consensus" that some boys are really girls and some girls are really boys has emerged. In fact, there is no truly scientific evidence for this preposterous belief. A "transgender woman" looks at his male body in the mirror and sees a woman in just the same way as an anorexic girl looks in the mirror and sees her skeletal self as fat.

It's equally "settled" that homosexuals are "born that way." Except that all the science purporting to prove that is in one way or another phony. We examine it in chapter three.

Abortion may be the most lied-about topic of any public policy issue in history. Almost every "scientific" claim that abortion advocates make is wrong, misleading, or even an outright lie. The unborn child is a human being alive from the moment of conception. She does feel pain, and abortion does hurt her mother. Real science backs up these claims; we show how in chapter four.

In chapter five we look at the scientific experts of the Sexual Revolution who told us—and they still tell us, *ad nauseam*—that we will be happy only once we break the shackles of traditional morality, marriage, the family, and the Church. Starting with the French Revolution right down to the present day, even at meetings happening right now at the UN, we have been told that sexual pleasure without limits is the way to true enlightenment and happiness. True science tells another story: the Sexual Revolution leads to disease and death.

In chapter six, we look at "scientific" claims, from the 1960s onward, that portrayed divorce as a panacea—both liberation for women trapped by traditional marriage and a positive benefit to children. True science shows the divorce culture has been a disaster for men and women, and especially children, but also for society at large. The grand experiment on children continues today with same-sex marriage.

There is no scare quite like a good food scare; no scam quite like a food scam. People are downright obsessional about what they put in their mouths. California now requires the labeling of more than six hundred chemicals that you might meet in your food. The creation of true miracle foods by genuine scientists has been met with leftist hysteria, scientific fraud, threats, and lawsuits. For example, as we'll see, a new strain of rice that could save hundreds of thousands of children from blindness has never gone to market. We look at this disaster in chapter seven.

There is a poverty racket that is alive and well in this country. Hunger hucksters are raising hundreds of millions with their dire claims that children are going to bed hungry. In fact, it is the hucksters themselves who are keeping children and their parents below the poverty line. The poverty line, by the way, is not what it used to be. We examine this issue in chapter eight.

For decades, we have been told that we were running out of fossil fuels, the kind that heat our homes and make our cars go. But then we discovered the United States was sitting on the world's largest reserves of natural gas, lying in massive lakes hundreds of miles across and two miles below the surface of the earth, under almost impenetrable rock—and we discovered a method to get it out of the ground: hydraulic fracking. The radical environmentalists, who were counting on the decline from "peak oil" to persuade the world to return to a pre-modern economy, have been driven just about around the bend. They have cooked up all manner of phony science to stop fracking. We tell the truth in chapter nine.

Global warming is one of the great scientific frauds of our time. Not that the world hasn't been warming these past hundred and fifty years. It has—and that's a good thing. The fraud comes in with the dire warning that this gradual warming will end life as we know it. The seas will rise and engulf Manhattan. The polar bears will all die. We will be swept away by an increasing cacophony of catastrophic storms. Almost all the "scientific" claims related to catastrophic climate change are phony. We explore the real science in chapter ten.

In the 1960s Dr. Paul Ehrlich told us the planet was about to have a massive die-off due to starvation caused by overpopulation. His dire predictions did not come true, nor have any of the other predictions of catastrophe related to so-called overpopulation. In fact, because of advances in health and medicine and a dropping birth rate, the world faces the opposite threat—a demographic winter, life on a graying planet. In chapter eleven, we look at the phony science related to the "population explosion."

We can't let ourselves be intimidated by "science." What purports to be science is often really leftist narrative, skewed statistics, or simply wrong. Touted experts are frequently ideologues twisting the real facts to fit their agenda. Sadly, it is up to laymen to fight back, and perhaps in the process save science from itself.

Real science improves all our lives exponentially because it tells us the truth about the world we live in. The fake "science" that the Left is pushing does just the opposite. It establishes fraud, propaganda, and even (see "transgenderism") literal insanity as the basis of our public policy, with disastrous results. We can't concede science to the Left. It's too important. We have to fight to take the mantle of science back from the leftists who have appropriated it for their very unscientific agenda. This book will arm you for the battle.

CHAPTER 1

Pollsters' Waterloo

F or months, the experts had told us that it was nigh impossible for Donald Trump to win the presidency. Hillary Clinton was basically a shoo-in. Clinton and her cronies actually popped champagne corks as they flew across the country to New York and her all-but-inevitable election-night celebration.[1]

But we all know it didn't turn out that that way. And Hillary wasn't the only one humiliated by the actual election results. The experts in the media, the professional consulting class, and especially the pollsters emerged from the 2016 election with egg on their faces.

Nourishing the Narrative, Dissing the Data

So how did "modern scientific polling" go wrong? Oddly, many of the polls got the national vote nearly exactly right, predicting that Hillary would win the popular vote by a few percentage points. But we don't have national elections, and many of the key battleground polls got the story completely wrong. Moreover, when the pollsters put on their pundit hats, they were hugely wrong, reporting that Trump had no chance, literally no chance. As *New York Times* media critic Jim Rutenberg wrote the day after the election, "All the dazzling technology, the big data and the sophisticated modeling that American newsrooms bring to the fundamentally human endeavor of presidential politics could not save American journalism from yet again being behind the story, behind the rest of the country."[2]

To understand how they could have been so wrong, you have to understand "the narrative"—a phenomenon that goes a very long way to explaining how so much skewed and even fake science is accepted as fact in twenty-first-century America.

I spent years writing culture-war stories for *Breitbart News*, where our marching orders were to "change the narrative." It was obvious to us that "the narrative" followed by news outlets all across the country was driven by the *New York Times*, the famed "paper of record." Two days after the 2016 election, longtime *New York Times* reporter Michael Cieply revealed how that narrative is created by a few editors from whom even experienced all-star reporters at the *Times* take their narrative orders. One senior reporter played solitaire on his computer in the morning, waiting for his marching orders. He overheard a national staff reporter "more or less" tell a source, "My editor needs someone to say such-and-such, could you say that?"

In his column about his twelve years with the *Times*, Cieply explained how shocked he was on day one on the job, when he discovered that the *Times* was a completely editor-driven paper. At other papers, he said, editors ask reporters what's going on, what's the news. That's how reporting is supposed to work. The reporters have their sources. They follow up on the stories and bring them to the editors. But at the *Times*, "by and large, talented reporters scrambled to match stories with what internally was often called 'the narrative.' We were occasionally asked to map a narrative for our various beats a year in advance, square the plan with editors, then generate stories that fit the pre-designated line."[3]

The narrative in the 2016 presidential race was very clear: Donald Trump had no chance. Hillary Clinton would win in a walk. Trump was—take your pick—racist, misogynist, xenophobic, authoritarian, or the second coming of Hitler. The Republican candidate was fomenting violence, and racial violence at that. (Much of the violence, it would turn out, was deliberately sparked by Democratic provocateurs getting into the faces of Trump supporters. If it was between a black or brown person and a Caucasian, so much the better.)[4]

Sticking to their narrative, reporters didn't seem to see the massive numbers turning out for Trump or how motivated they were. The intensity factor of the Trump voter seemed to escape them. He was turning out ten or twenty thousand people consistently at a time when Hillary could only muster a few hundred. Keep in mind that Trump was holding these rallies several times a week—toward the end of the campaign, several times a day. People traveled hours to get into the venue and then waited hours longer for the event to start. These were some very motivated people. But somehow this phenomenon did not raise the curiosity of the reporters. It was not part of the narrative. The narrative was that Trump had no chance.

I live in Fairfax County, Virginia, and one of the early rallies after the GOP convention was at a school in Ashburn in nearby Loudoun County, not far from the West Virginia border. My wife and I foolishly decided to show up half an hour early for a noon rally. What we found was astonishing. The line to get in stretched across the front and down the side of the school, then along the back, where the line doubled upon itself and continued to the football field. Perhaps five thousand people were waiting in the hot sun, and none of us got in because the venue had filled hours before.

The numbers were startling. Even more startling were the demographics. There were plenty of white folks but also a remarkable number of blacks, Hispanics, and Asians. And everyone was happy, celebratory even.

My wife and I ended up standing in a small group near where Trump would arrive. Next to us were people of every color and three college-age white girls who, upon Trump's arrival, began shouting anti-Trump slogans. No one hassled them. It was such a polite and happy crowd. At one point, I leaned over and congratulated them on their courage and commitment. They smiled and laughed. I also said, "Aren't you shocked at the number of people of color?" And they agreed, eyes wide, vigorously nodding, obviously shocked at how the evidence before their eyes contradicted the narrative.

It would be nice if journalists would report the facts, however inconvenient they may be to their preferred narrative. But at least nobody claims reporters are scientists. Polling, on the other hand, is actually supposed to be a science. That's why they call it "modern scientific polling"—in contrast to just spit-balling about how you guess people might vote.

Evading the Evidence

What happened in presidential polling in 2016 is characteristic of how fake science happens: the statistics themselves were accurate, but the experts wouldn't follow the evidence because they didn't like where it was leading them. Hillary led the national polls by a few percentage points—a result that was borne out by the election results. In fact, Hillary did win the popular vote by 2.1 percent. Sure, some polls had her up 5 percent. Some crazy polls had her up 12 percent. But for the most part, the polls had her up 4 to 5 percent, with the race tightening as election day neared.

Look at the RealClearPolitics final average: 3.2 percent in favor of Clinton nationally.[5] Bloomberg had her up 3 points; IBD/TIPP Tracking had her up 1; *Economist*/YouGov gave her a final 4-point lead; ABC/*Washington Post* gave Clinton a 3-point nod; Fox News had Clinton up by 4; Monmouth had Clinton up by 6; NBC/*Wall Street Journal* had her up 5; CBS up 4; and Reuters/Ipsos up 5. The only national poll that gave the election to Trump was the *Los Angeles Times*/USC poll, which had him up by 3 and they were wrong. Though Trump won the election, he lost the popular vote nationally.

Yet the pollsters who got the popular vote numbers right completely missed the Electoral College results—in other words, who would actually win the election. They gave Hillary virtually no chance to lose and

Trump no chance to win. The mantra was that Trump had "no path to 270." If you heard it once, you heard it a million times.

As *The Hill* reported the day after Trump's win, "Going into Election Day, a strong majority of pollsters and election modelers forecast that Democrat Hillary Clinton would coast to victory, with many predicting she would sweep the battlegrounds and win north of 300 electoral votes."[6]

The respected University of Virginia Center for Politics predicted Clinton would win a whopping 322 electoral votes to Trump's 216, and that she would win Florida, North Carolina, Pennsylvania, and Wisconsin—each of which she ended up losing.[7]

The *New York Times* Upshot blog never gave Trump more than a 42 percent chance of winning until election night. That high came in June 2016. After that his trend line trended downward. He was back up to 31 percent in July and again in October, but on election day the *New York Times* gave him no better than a 15 percent chance of winning the presidency.[8] They also gave him only a 35 percent chance to win North Carolina, 33 percent to win Florida, 11 percent to win Pennsylvania, and 6 percent to win Michigan—all states he ended up winning. It was a thrill "running right up your leg"[9] to watch the *New York Times* eat crow in real time on Election Night. Their percentage chance of Trump winning eventually went to 95 percent and then stopped.

Wünderkind prognosticator Nate Silver at *FiveThirtyEight* did only slightly better. On October 20, he reported that "Clinton probably finished off Trump last night." He said in that kind of snotty elite media tone, "I'm not sure I need to tell you this, but Hillary Clinton is probably going to be the next president." He reported that she had gone into that final debate with a seven-point lead and won it, which could only mean she had finished Trump off. "[Trump] doesn't have an obvious—*or even a not-so-obvious*—path to the presidency," said Silver.

On October 20, Silver had given Trump just a 14 percent chance of winning. That went up to 15 percent on October 24. Silver caused quite a stir among the cognoscenti when on election eve he boosted Trump's chances to 28.6 percent and dropped Clinton's chances to 71 percent, even though he was still betting heavily on her: "There's a wide range of outcomes, and most of them come up Clinton." Silver said his forecasting model suggested an Electoral College landslide for Clinton at 323, "including all the states President Obama won in 2012 except Ohio and Iowa, but adding North Carolina." He did forecast a fairly accurate national vote in favor of Clinton at 3.6 percent and said that her chances of winning the popular vote stood at 81 percent.

There were two wild cards: the states and the undecideds. As the day of the election approached, there still remained a large percentage of undecideds. According to Silver, 12 percent were undecided or leaning third party. This number was declining, but it remained higher than in previous elections. Only 3 percent had remained undecided on election day in 2012. Both candidates were polling low for undecideds; Clinton at 46 percent and Trump at 42 percent, "the lowest of any candidate since Bob Dole in 1996," according to Silver. If two-thirds of the undecideds went for Trump there would be a popular vote tie. If Clinton took them by that same margin, she'd win the popular vote by 7 or 8 percent.[10]

And then there were the states. The state pollsters really blew it.

The Marquette University Law School poll—which "nailed the results of the 2012 and 2014 elections" and is considered the gold standard for Wisconsin polling—released its final election numbers on November 2, six days before the election. Marquette announced that Hillary Clinton would win the state by seven percentage points, 44–37. Hillary canceled a planned trip to Wisconsin, and Nate Silver gave Trump only 16.5 percent chance of winning the Badger State. Trump ended up winning by 0.78 percent.

While Ohio seemed to have drifted from Clinton over the summer, the *Columbus Dispatch* mail poll reported the Sunday before the election that the race was basically tied. Trump won by 8.54 percent, the biggest GOP win in the state since 1988.

It was the same story in Michigan. The final EPIC-MRA poll had Clinton up by 4 points though she had been up by 11 after the debates. The lead shrank with WikiLeaks and with FBI Director James Comey's letter about Clinton's possible ill-doings. Still she held on. But in the actual election, though it took a few weeks to call, she lost by 0.25 percent.

Two state polls in Pennsylvania—Susquehanna and Morning Call/ Muhlenberg College—released final numbers that showed a 3–6 percent margin of victory for Hillary Clinton. Trump won by 1.14 percent.[11]

And so a number of things conspired to make fools of modern scientific pollsters including the fact of their built-in bias against the candidate they viewed as a clown.

The general disdain for Donald Trump, prevalent even in GOP circles, extended to his aides, including the one pollster who wasn't blinded by the prevailing narrative. While Clinton, lulled into overconfidence by the pollsters, was giving short shrift to the Rust Belt states that turned out to be crucial—even cancelling a scheduled campaign trip to Wisconsin just a few days before the election—Donald Trump was benefiting from the advice of Kellyanne Conway of The Polling Company and campaigning in the states that would actually decide the election. When Conway and Steven Bannon of *Breitbart News* stepped in to take over the Trump campaign in mid-August, Politico reported, "GOP leaders in key battleground states aren't buying it. Fewer than a third of Republican members of the Politico Caucus—a panel of activists, strategists and operatives in 11 key battleground states—believe Trump's reshuffling will move the campaign in the right direction."[12] One Virginia Republican said, "You can keep moving people in and out of the car, but so long as the drunk guy is driving it while blindfolded, the ride probably isn't going to get any smoother."[13]

And yet it was Donald Trump who managed to hire the pollster with her finger on the pulse of the electorate and her eyes open to the actual data—while the Left-leaning pollsters' bias blinded them to the facts. So in this case, the skewed statistics didn't even help the Left, in the long run. The pollsters' breathtakingly wrong prognostications, their absolute certainty that Trump had no chance, actually hurt Hillary. And it wasn't only a case of the misallocation of her campaign resources. Throughout the much-touted early voting, all you heard was that Trump had no chance. This may have had the unintended effect of lulling Democratic voters into a false sense of security and at the same time further angering and therefore energizing those huge Trump crowds the news media was refusing to report on.

Media critic Jim Rutenberg got it just right. It was "a Dewey defeats Truman lesson for the digital age," and how sweet it was.

CHAPTER 2

The Transgender Moment

In September 2016, a man in Ecuador gave birth to a child. Or so the news media reported.[1] The media reported this without question, with a totally straight face and all the proper pronouns. Oddly, the person who gave birth looked nothing like a man and the person who was supposed to be "his" wife looked nothing like a woman. Because—as the news reports helpfully explained—the new mother used to be a man, and he had married a man who used to be a woman. Got that?

Around the same time, Brown University announced the installation of tampon dispensers in men's bathrooms. The reason? As *Newsweek* reported, with a totally straight face, "Not all people who menstruate are women."[2]

A few years earlier, the *Washington Post* had published "Transgender at Five," the story of Kathryn, who at the age of two announced (somehow) to her parents that she was a boy. She rejected girly things. She wanted to wear pants. She wanted short hair. She wanted trucks and swords. Her parents, Maryland liberals both, checked in with "expert" Stephanie Brill, who had published *The Transgender Child: A Handbook for Families and Professionals*, and not surprisingly, decided their daughter should be raised as a boy. Kathryn's eight-year-old sister helps us understand, "It's just a boy's mind in a girl's body." Kathryn is now Tyler.[3]

If you think this all seems to have happened very quickly, you would be right. It did, practically overnight.

Gerrymandering Gender

Transgenderism had long nestled quietly and often ignored at the tail end of the now-ubiquitous acronym "LGBT." Gay men, who had the political power, were the main focus, followed distantly by lesbians. Transgenders were the neglected stepchildren.

No longer. Though LGBT has now grown to include Q and I, transgenders have taken center stage.

In 1995, the *New York Times* published a grand total of two mentions of the word "transgender," and one was not even in a story but a letter to the editor. The other was in a story about the gay pride parade in San Francisco.

The paper of record eventually paid more attention to transgenders, but at first the rate of change was glacial. In 2000, the *Times* ran only twenty-four stories that included the word "transgender," nearly all of them in the context of LGBT.

By 2005, there were fifty-four stories. That grew to 190 stories in 2010. And then came the big jump. The year 2015 saw 752 stories that mentioned "transgender," and by 2016, the *Times* published a whopping 1,166 transgender stories, an average of more than three every single day of the year. That is a jump of more than 26,000 percent in twenty years, a 420 percent increase in the last six years alone. What on earth is the explosion of attention to the transgender issue about?

It is likely that the needs of gay men were thought to have been finally and totally met by the Supreme Court's June 26, 2015, *Obergefell* decision declaring same-sex marriage a constitutional right. After *Obergefell*, gay leaders pivoted to two issues: destroying Christian businesses that resisted catering gay weddings—and promoting transgenderism, usually while hiding behind the skirts of "transgender" kids.

The most famous transgender teen is undoubtedly sixteen-year-old "Jazz Jennings." Jaron Seth Bloshinsky (his original name) was immediately "assigned" to the male sex at his birth on October 6, 2000—a practice that is now frowned upon, as it relies on the observation of genitalia, not taking into account the gender identity decisions that the baby may go on to make later. While even advocates agree that most gender assignments at birth comport accurately with the later gender identity, they argue that such assignments should not be forced on babies.

Jaron's parents, Greg and Jeanette, insist that their son asserted his female "identity" as soon as he was able to talk. They told ABC News in 2007 that their fifteen-month-old baby would unsnap his onesie to make it look like a dress.[4] They do not say how they discerned their toddler's intentions. (And the fact is, any parent will tell you that children that age love to unsnap snaps.) Later, when they praised him as a "good boy," he would correct them; he was a "good girl." They claim that at two years old he said, "Mommy, when's the good fairy going to come with her magic wand and change, you know, my genitalia?" What strikes you about all of these claims is the reporter's gullibility. A baby designing dresses out of onesies? A two-year-old talking about his "genitalia"?

Jeanette Bloshinsky consulted her copy of the *Diagnostic and Statistical Manual of Mental Disorders* (*DSM*), the volume used by mental health professionals. Yes, Jaron's mom had her very own copy; she didn't even have to go to the library. She diagnosed her son with what the professionals now call "gender identity disorder"—a mismatch between a person's genital and DNA sex and how they "identify"—in other words, their feelings.

Naturally, Dr. Marilyn Volker, a gender specialist, confirmed Jaron's mother's diagnosis. Jaron was really a girl. At some point, Jaron Bloshinsky became Jazz Jennings.

Jazz's parents let him grow "her" hair long, get pierced ears, wear dresses, and pack "her" room with girly things, girly colors, dolls, and mermaids. Trans kids love mermaids, according to Jazz's mom, because they are different, you know, down there. In short order, Jazz went on *20/20* with Barbara Walters and *The Rosie Show*, where he appeared with Chaz Bono, Sonny and Cher's cute little daughter, Chastity, now "presenting" as a chunky hirsute "man."

Jazz Jennings became a breakout star. He was featured in the documentary *I Am Jazz* on the Oprah Winfrey Network. He started a YouTube channel, published a book—also called *I Am Jazz*—that school districts now require children to read, and has a reality show—yet again *I Am Jazz*—on The Learning Channel. In June 2016, Crown Books for Young Readers published his memoir, *Being Jazz*. It was announced early in 2017 that a Jazz Jennings doll was in the offing.

Jazz has received a boatload of awards, from GLAAD (the Gay and Lesbian Alliance against Defamation), *Time* magazine, *The Advocate*, OUT, and the Human Rights Campaign (HRC).

Six-year-old Jazz told Barbara Walters that he was attracted to boys, but two years later on his YouTube channel he said he was "pansexual." Jazz says he wants to become a mother.

Jazz isn't the only trans kid taking a star turn.

An eight-year-old named Jackson Millarker, a girl who identifies as a boy, is set to play a boy named Tom in the hit TV show *Modern Family*. She is being called "the first transgender child actor."[5]

Rapper R. Kelly's fifteen-year-old daughter Jaya came out as Jay in 2014 and says she has identified as a boy since she was "6 or 7." Revealingly, Jaya said her famous father was not aware of her new gender identity for months after her transition.[6] Of course coming out as the opposite sex couldn't have anything to do with trying to get daddy's attention.

Largely under the radar, the daughter of Warren Beatty and Annette Bening has gone by the name of Stephen Ira since her early teens. She is a lively blogger on all things trans. She got into a dustup with Chaz Bono, who made the mistake of saying there was simply a disconnect between her boy brain and her girl body. Ira was having none of that, and a quite comical trans slap fight broke out. Transgenderism is not a mistake in any way, shape, or form, Ira insists, and Bono is nothing more than a self-hating bigot.

It makes sense that trans kids would be the shock troops for the transgender movement. After all, most trans "women" look very much like Corporal Klinger from the old television show *MASH*—a hairy man with an enormous Adam's apple dressed as a woman in hopes of getting a Section 8 mental health discharge and being sent home from the Korean War. Like Corporal Klinger, most trans "women" look nothing like a woman. Little boys and little girls can plausibly pass for the opposite sex. Adult men, not so much.

Laws have been changed around the country in the name of kids who think they are the wrong sex, that their "gender assignment" was wrongly chosen for them at birth. And the battleground chosen by the gay establishment was the bathroom. Put "bathroom bill" into Google and fifty-seven million plus hits appear.

In the spring of 2016, a girl who goes by the male name of Gavin Grimm sued the Gloucester County School Board in Virginia because the school district required girls to use the girls' bathroom and boys to use the boys' bathroom. Then sixteen, Gavin insisted she was a boy and demanded access to the boys' bathroom. Notice that it is the bathroom that is usually invoked in these debates rather than the locker room or shower room. Bathroom stalls afford a measure of privacy and therefore mixed-sex bathrooms are less offensive to the general public than mixed-sex showers or changing rooms. Putting a naked anatomically correct boy in the girls' shower room might be more upsetting to little girls and their moms and dads.

Gavin Grimm argued that bathroom "discrimination" by sex is a violation of Title IX regulations that forbid it. In fact, Title IX does allow for discrimination by sex for bathrooms and shower rooms. The school board allowed Grimm the use of a private bathroom in the nurse's office, but that was not good enough. The school offered to build single-stall unisex bathrooms. Grimm rejected the offer, saying she was not unisex. Grimm was determined to squat in the boys' room.

Grimm and her allies in the American Civil Liberties Union (ACLU) demanded relief from the courts, invoking a 2015 letter that Barack Obama's Department of Education had sent to all school districts in the United States. The letter admitted that discrimination based on sex is allowed in restrooms, locker rooms, shower rooms, housing, and on athletic teams but went on to say that when such sex discrimination comes into play, schools must "treat transgender students consistent with their gender identity."[7]

Edward Whelan, formerly clerk to Supreme Court Justice Antonin Scalia and currently president of the Ethics and Public Policy Center, pointed out the incoherence of this ruling: "If the majority and the Obama administration are right that a boy who identifies as female has a right under Title IX to use the girls' bathrooms, locker rooms, and shower facilities, then it would be discrimination on the basis of gender identity to bar a boy who identifies as male from having the same access." So if "transgender girls" cannot be barred from using the girls' bathroom, neither can any other boys.[8]

Gavin Grimm became a celebrity, the latest civil rights hero. In a fawning interview posted on the CNN website, Grimm explained that she is not a predator and that no one has anything to fear from her. She said, "The bottom line is I'm a boy just like anybody else."[9] Well, except for her vagina and her two X chromosomes, sure she is.

The Fourth Circuit Court of Appeals ordered the school district to allow Grimm to use the boys' room. The case was slated to be heard by the Supreme Court in late March, but Donald Trump was elected, his Department of Education withdrew the guidance letter on transgenderism, and the Supreme Court kicked the case back to the lower courts. At this time, it is unclear what will happen.

But the little trans heroes kept coming.

Nine-year-old Stormi,[10] a "transgender girl," tried to sell Girl Scout cookies in his neighborhood and accused a mean man of saying, "Nobody wants to buy cookies from a boy in a dress." Stormi took to the Internet, and BuzzFeed made him a star. Stormi got even with the "bully" by selling three thousand boxes of cookies to folks who were cheering him on.[11]

In January 2016, a video of eight-year-old Ethan Wilwert having an elaborate makeup session with openly gay makeup artist Joey Killmeyer went viral. Ethan is shown with long false eyelashes, purple lipstick accentuating pouty lips, dark eye shadow, and a pink streak in his hair. His mother, Season, said, "He's a normal eight-year-old boy who likes to do makeup." Ethan explained that he wanted to learn drag makeup after watching videos of YouTube sensation Jeffree Starr.[12]

The Transgender Moment could never have happened without heavy-handed support from a number of power players in our society. First there was the unbridled enthusiasm of the news media—and Hollywood. When North Carolina passed a statewide law mandating that you had to use the public bathroom corresponding with your birth sex unless you had a sex change reflected on your state-issued identification, Hollywood threatened to boycott. They did the same in Georgia. Both states faced the reality that they could lose millions in film and television revenue.

Big business also got involved. Salesforce backed out of an expansion in North Carolina, costing the state several hundred jobs. North Carolina was denounced by Tim Cook of Apple, and many other major CEOs.

Big-time sports put their thumbs on the scale, too. The National Basketball Association pulled the All-Star Game from North Carolina. Rock stars canceled concerts. Even the porn peddlers got involved. Porn site HamsterX blocked all IP addresses from that beleaguered state—and claimed that transgender porn was very popular with North Carolina IP addresses.

Blotting Out Biology

But what about science? Aren't male and female basic facts of biology? As it happens, "scientific" claims have been crucial to the Transgender Moment.

The very phrase "gender identity" was coined by Dr. John Money, who founded the Johns Hopkins University's sex-change clinic.

Money had long studied hermaphroditic children. Called "intersex" today, these are kids who have been born with indeterminate secondary sexual characteristics: enlarged clitorises that resemble penises, or stubby penises that resemble clitorises. Money and others postulated that these kids had received conflicting doses of male and female hormones in utero.

But Money further postulated that parents and doctors could make a decision about the sex of the child, and that given surgery and socialization, the child could be happily raised as either a boy or a girl. And he didn't apply that principle just to children whose biological sex was ambiguous. Money claimed that "gender identity" in general was caused less by nature than by nurture.

Money's most famous case was the "John-Joan case"—a textbook example of the human tragedies that result when science is dragooned into the service of ideology. It involved a baby boy whose penis had been burned off in a routine circumcision. The distraught parents saw Money on television talking about his successful experiments with intersex children—how they were never the wiser about their sex at birth, provided they were socialized in the right way.

Money was overjoyed to hear from the Reimer family because they came to him with identical twin boys, who would make the perfect test subjects for his theory. The two boys had identical DNA, but one would be raised as the boy he was and the other would be raised as a girl that he wasn't.

Money had the penis-less boy castrated and a rudimentary vulva created. The boy's parents renamed him Brenda, put him in dresses, and began raising him as a girl.

The experiment went on for years, with Money dutifully reporting to peer-reviewed scientific journals, to the media, and in bestselling books that the experiment was a ringing success. The boy without a penis was now a girl who preferred to wear dresses, played with dolls, and demonstrated a strong maternal instinct.

In reality, the experiment was a failure from the very beginning. The boy's parents reported that when first put into a dress "Brenda" tore at it and tried to rip it off. Brenda refused to play with dolls, preferring trucks and guns. Rather than being a prim, proper, feminine little girl, he was dirty and aggressive. He loved to fight.

Money knew all this; the disastrous results of his experiment were clear from annual visits Brenda and his family made to Money at his clinic in Baltimore.

For years Money pressured a reluctant Brenda to begin hormone treatments to grow breasts and shift fat to the lower body. Brenda finally agreed and was horrified when breasts began to bud. All along Money pushed Brenda to undergo a full sex-change operation: the excavation of a rudimentary vagina and lowering of the vulva, so the mutilated boy would be forced to urinate sitting down—something he was refusing to do.

Frustrated with Brenda's failure to acclimate as a girl, Money began ordering him and his brother to take their clothes off, explore each other's genitals, and simulate copulation during their annual sessions. He forced them to watch hard-core pornography. Brenda later referred to Money as a pervert.

Meanwhile, Money's twins experiment was heralded around the world as a smashing success. But when he pushed Brenda—bullied him, really—to have a full vaginal excavation, Brenda balked. In a scene right out of a Woody Allen movie, Brenda's last visit with Money ended with Brenda being chased down the hospital hallway by a transsexual and doctors in lab coats. Not long afterwards, Brenda's family came clean with him and told him the whole story of his life. His first question: "What was my name?"

Money continued to report that the twins experiment was a success, and it became a key piece of "scientific" data supporting all manner of irresponsible social experiments—right up to our own Transgender Moment.

Men dressing as women is nothing new. Transvestitism has been the subject of great mirth in popular culture. Long before Corporal Klinger in *MASH*, Milton Berle was a big 1950s television star who often dressed in drag. To hide from gangsters, Tony Curtis dressed as a woman opposite Marilyn Monroe in *Some Like It Hot*. Johnny Carson often did drag. Dressing in drag was always played for laughs.

The psychological sciences traditionally viewed transvestitism as a form of sexual perversion, lumping it in with homosexuality and fetishism.

Once John Money began promulgating his gender theories, though, psychiatrists discovered a psychopathological condition called "gender identity disorder." This diagnosis entered the third edition of the psychiatrists' diagnostic manual (*DSM-III*) in 1980 and remained unchanged until *DSM-5*, when it was changed to "gender dysphoria." Of course, transgender advocates—and psychiatrists who are increasingly caving to pressure from those advocates—believe it should not be considered a disorder.[13] If your DNA and genitalia say you're one sex, but your mind says you're the opposite, there's nothing wrong with your mind—right?

Meanwhile, psychologists who want to get around the obvious biological facts rely on a spurious distinction between people's biological "sex" and their "socially constructed" "gender."

A pamphlet published by the American Psychological Association explains,

> *Sex* is assigned at birth, refers to one's biological status as either male or female, and is associated primarily with physical attributes such as chromosomes, hormone prevalence, and external and internal anatomy.
>
> *Gender* refers to the socially constructed roles, behaviors, activities, and attributes that a given society considers appropriate for boys and men or girls and women. These influence the ways that people act, interact, and feel about themselves. While aspects of biological sex are similar across different cultures, aspects of gender may differ.[14]

Apparently, boys play with trucks only because we teach them that. They could just as easily play with dolls. It is our choice as parents and society to impose such binary gender roles.

This was a central tenet of John Money's "gender identity" theory. Of course, the feigned success of the "gender reassignment" in the twins case was an enormous boon to radical feminists in the 1960s. But more recent years have seen the exponential growth of gender identities.

Judith Butler, author of the influential 1990 book *Gender Trouble*, described gender as "a free-floating artifice, with the consequence that man and masculine might just as easily signify a female body as a male one, and woman and feminine a male body as easily as a female one."[15]

By 2014, Facebook was offering users fifty-eight different possible genders, to allow the user to "feel comfortable being your true, authentic self," an important part of which is "the expression of gender."[16] And they came under attack for not offering more.

A young man recently attending a conference on political correctness at the UN Commission on the Status of Women sported a luxurious beard but also a pair of quite fetching dangly earrings. Asked about his gender, he said he was "gender non-binary." Though he appeared to be a man, he insisted he was not—since gender is socially constructed. He admitted to being a male but did not identify as either gender. He was "male gender-non-binary."

Manipulating Medicine

The young man *might* have "gender dysphoria," which is defined in the *DSM-5* as an "incongruence between one's experienced/expressed gender and assigned gender." But only if he was also experiencing "clinically significant distress or impairment in social, occupational, or other important areas of functioning."[17] That's the out the experts have left in the diagnosis—to protect themselves from the wrath of the advocates. Because not all men who wear dresses feel bad about it. Some are homosexuals catering to the tastes of some heterosexual men. Still others are heterosexual men who simply like to wear dresses but still consider themselves heterosexual men.

So in order to meet the diagnostic criteria, one must identify as a sex separate from the one assigned at birth *and* experience distress because of it. If the young man was as happy with his dangling earrings and a big beard as he seemed to be, there's nothing wrong with him. All right, then.

On the other hand, the *DSM-5*'s description also spreads too wide a net—which could cover any typical tomboy with "a strong preference for the toys, games, or activities stereotypically used or engaged in by the other gender."[18] As a result, perfectly normal little girls who play truck games with their brothers are in danger of being caught in the Transgender Moment—urged by parents, teachers, and even doctors to explore the possibility of "transition" to boys. As Mayer and McHugh point out, the persistence of gender dysphoria in children is quite rare. Even according to the *DSM-5*, "in natal [biological] males, persistence [of gender dysphoria] has ranged from 2.2% to 30%. In natal females, persistence has ranged from 12% to 50%."[19]

Dr. Kenneth Zucker, who was the longtime editor-in-chief of the *Archives of Sexual Behavior* and psychologist-in-chief at Toronto's Centre for Addiction and Mental Health, does not deny transgenderism. But he has studied and worked with gender-confused children for years, helping them become more comfortable with their biological sex. And this is where he ran into trouble. He and his team found that of twenty-five girls they treated for gender confusion, only three still had gender identity disorder later in life. For this, Zucker came under fire from the transgender community, he was fired, and his clinic was closed.[20]

Early in 2017, Zucker was slated to appear on several panels of the inaugural scientific conference of the U.S. Professional Association for Transgender Health. His was the lone voice making the case that people's feelings should be conformed to the biological reality of their bodies. Trans-bullies invaded his first panel and disrupted it. Afterwards they demanded that conference organizers remove Zucker from his other panels, and the organizers caved to their demands.[21]

The new regime for treating such children is to give them drugs to slow or halt puberty so they have more time to decide what gender they want to be—with the future possibility of irreversible mutilating surgery that will remove their own sex organs without giving them functioning organs of the opposite sex. As Mayer and McHugh argue, "there is relatively little evidence for the therapeutic value of these kinds of puberty-delaying treatments."[22] And yet, they report with alarm, the United

Kingdom has seen a 50 percent increase in the number of children referred to gender dysphoria clinics.

In the summer of 2016, an academic associated with the University of Michigan reported that her autistic daughter had been convinced by a gender therapist that she was not a lesbian, as the girl had thought, but rather a transgender man. The girl, whose autism precluded her from handling her own finances, was allowed to undergo a double mastectomy and enter into an aggressive treatment of hormones against the objections of her mother. The poor girl was convinced that the hormones would help her to grow a penis.[23]

Running Away from the Research

But what does science—real, hard, honest science, in contrast to the unethical experiments of charlatans like Dr. Money and publications from groups subject to massive political pressure—say about gender identity and transgenderism?

The most recent, most thorough, and most objective analysis of the existing "science" of transgenderism and transsexuality is a review of the entire scientific literature on the subject published by Lawrence Mayer and Paul McHugh in the Fall 2016 issue of *The New Atlantis*.

Mayer and McHugh are disinterested scientists. For many years, McHugh was head of psychiatry at Johns Hopkins School of Medicine. Mayer has held a dozen prestigious academic posts in science, including at Johns Hopkins, the University of Pennsylvania, Stanford University, and Princeton.

The bona fides of these men are vitally important because of the tendency of the Left to avoid engaging in the issues under discussion by attacking the individuals making the arguments.[24]

It should also be noted that neither Mayer nor McHugh has ever shown any animus toward the transgendered or transsexuals, though of course the Left dismisses their work as "anti-LGBT."[25]

After examining literally hundreds of studies and citing a representative few, Mayer and McHugh conclude, "The studies presented above show inconclusive evidence and mixed findings regarding the brains of transgender adults."[26] They say the results are "conflicting and confusing."

So let's take a look at some of the confused results purporting to find some basis for transgenderism in science.

A team from the Mayo Clinic looked at the case of an intersex person born with "ambiguous genitalia who was operated on and raised as a female."[27] After admitting "some adult patients with severe dysphoria—transsexuals—have neither history nor objective findings supporting a known biological cause of brain-body disjunction," the authors nonetheless concluded, "Absent psychosis or severe character pathology, patients' subjective assertions are presently the most reliable standards for delineating core gender identity."[28] But this is a classic example of "hard cases make bad law." The fact that a minuscule number of individuals are, tragically, born with indeterminate or otherwise literally deformed genitalia—and that surgery to correct that disability can be helpful to them—hardly proves that the lives of people without any such deformity would be improved by surgery to remove their normal sex organs.

So the race is on to find something, anything, in their actual biology that differentiates "transgender women" from ordinary men, and "transgender women" from men who are comfortable with their masculinity.

A team from the Medical University of Vienna, including one of John Money's former students, claim to have found a "polymorphism of the CYP17 gene related to sex steroid metabolism is associated with female-to-male but not male-to-female transsexualism."[29] The *Journal of Biological Psychiatry* published a report issued by seven geneticists who had examined 112 male-to-female transsexuals and hypothesized "that male-to-female transsexualism is associated with gene variants responsible for undermasculinization and/or feminization." They found "a likely genetic component to transsexualism, and genes involved sex steroidogenesis."[30] The official journal of the International Society of Psychoneuroendocrinology published a paper from the Max Planck Institute of Psychiatry in Munich that found male-to-female transsexuals have similar second and fourth finger lengths to biological women.[31]

In their *New Atlantis* paper, Mayer and McHugh cite several similar studies, including one by Stanford professor of biology Robert Sapolsky, who claims that neuroimaging shows the brains of transgender adults are similar in small but important ways to those whose gender identity matches their biological sex. Sapolsky argues that some males may have female brains.[32]

In 2011 Giuseppina Rametti and her Spanish colleagues "used MRI to study the brain structures of 18 female-to-male transsexuals who exhibited gender nonconformity early in life and experienced sexual attraction to females prior to hormone treatment."[33] The goal was to discover whether brain structures corresponded more to their biological sex or their sense of gender identity. A control group of twenty-four male and nineteen female heterosexuals was used for comparison. Researchers looked specifically at "white matter microstructure of specific brain areas"[34] and claim to have found that female-to-male transsexuals, those who've not yet been treated with testosterone, had brain structures more similar to those of males than females in three of four areas of the brain.

In 2013, a group of scientists from the Taipei Veterans General Hospital showed films to groups of transsexuals (male-to-female and female-to-male) with matched groups of non-transsexuals and measured their brain reaction to both erotic and non-erotic films. Their brain activity was measured, and they were asked to give a "selfness" score—that is, they were asked who in the films they most identified with. The report claims that in both neural imaging and in selfness scores, transsexuals are more closely related to their desired sex than their biological sex. "Collectively, these findings indicate that GID is characterized by structural and functional alterations in the brain," the study reports.[35]

There are dozens of such studies purporting to prove that transgenderism is in the brain or the genes.

But, as Mayer and McHugh point out, the studies purporting to show that transgenderism is inborn are methodologically unsound.

None of the studies is serial, longitudinal, or prospective. They are all simply snapshots in time taken of very small groups that may or may not have any relationship to the larger population. These studies are on tiny numbers of people. And they don't look at their subjects at regular intervals using the same criteria over the lifetime of the subject.

The fact that there may be a difference in brain morphology or functioning at one moment in time does not prove innateness or causality. Mayer and McHugh point out, "There are inherent and ineradicable methodological limitations of *any* neuroimaging study that simply associates a particular trait, such as a certain behavior, with a particular brain morphology."[36] Scientists and neurobiologists generally agree on this.

Are any differences in brain structure or functioning the cause of transgenderism or the *results of it*? We know the brain is plastic and is capable of change based on behavior. Neural pathways are changed by the things we do and the things we see. Researchers have established that London cabbies' brains are physically altered by their profession: "London taxi drivers had more gray matter in their posterior hippocampi than people who were similar in age, education and intelligence, but who did not drive taxis.... MRIs showed that the successful [cab-driving] trainees' hippocampi had grown over time."[37] And brain studies demonstrate that watching large doses of pornography can also physically alter the brain. Can this same thing happen to a man who has fantasized about being a woman and dressed and acted that way for years? Have his thoughts and behavior changed his neural pathways?

As Mayer and McHugh point out, "To support a conclusion of causality, even epidemiological causality, we need to conduct prospective longitudinal panel studies of a fixed set of individuals across the course of sexual development if not their lifespan."[38] This would entail "serial brain images at birth, in childhood and at other points along the developmental continuum to see whether brain morphology findings were there from the beginning. Otherwise, we cannot establish whether certain brain features caused a trait, or whether the trait is innate and perhaps fixed."[39]

Sampling Selectively

And then there is the problem of sample size. In order for the study to be methodologically sound, the sample size must be large enough to project across the transgender population as a whole. And it's a challenge to find a large sample of transsexuals—the population of such individuals is vanishingly small. Even the trans-friendly Williams Institute at UCLA puts the total population of transgendered individuals at only seven hundred thousand out of a national population of 318 million—two *tenths* of a percent.[40] The real number is probably much, much smaller.

So scientists eager to find a biological basis for transgenderism are naturally limited to studying small groups. They tend to use "convenience samples" that aren't random. Conclusions from such studies simply cannot be considered methodologically sound—no matter what claims are made in the public policy debate, on television, or in your children's grade school. These findings are no more than ideological journalism masquerading as science.

Mayer and McHugh convincingly argue that the claims of certitude made by transgender advocates cannot be supported with any scientific rigor: "The consensus of scientific evidence overwhelmingly supports the proposition that a physically and developmentally normal boy or girl is indeed what he or she appears to be at birth. The available evidence from brain imaging and genetics does not demonstrate that the development of gender identity as different from biological sex is innate. Because scientists have not established a solid framework for understanding the causes of cross-gender identification, ongoing research should be open to psychological and social causes, as well as biological ones.[41]

So in their *New Atlantis* report, Mayer and McHugh look into the psychological issues attendant on gender dysphoria, something that transgender advocates gloss over, or when they acknowledge them, blame them on what they now call "transphobia."

Mayer's original intention had been simply to review existing studies for statistical accuracy, and no more. But after closely studying five hundred scientific articles and "perusing hundreds more," Mayer became "alarmed to learn that the LGBT community bears a disproportionate rate of mental health problems compared to the population as a whole."

Covering Up the Craziness

In his previous psychiatric work, McHugh has compared transgenderism to anorexia. He says a man looking in the mirror and seeing a woman is similar to a skeletal person looking into the mirror and seeing a fat person. He has pointed out that treating gender dysphoria with castration or mastectomy and hormones does virtually nothing to help patients with the underlying psychiatric issues.[42] After surgery, the person still possesses the same original troubles, only they are exacerbated by irreversible surgery.

Science does not show that transgenderism is from the genes, or brain structure, or brain function, but because the psychological and psychiatric establishments have been captured by the transgender advocates, they do not view transgenderism as a psychological problem. So virtually no one suffering from the belief that he really belongs to the opposite sex will ever get treatment for this obvious delusion. Sadly, this door is being closed to anyone who needs help with the discordant feeling that her vagina should be a penis. It is already illegal in many states for psychologists to treat children with unwanted same-sex attraction, and Kenneth Zucker's clinic in Canada was shuttered because he was trying help children embrace their biological sex. How long before laws are passed to forbid therapists from treating patients for the transgender delusion?

That treatment could save lives. Even trans advocates admit that the transgendered have mental health issues at far higher rates than the general population.

A 2015 study conducted by Harvard epidemiologist Sari Reisner studied male and female transgender individuals aged twelve to twenty-nine and found an "elevated risk" for depression, anxiety, suicidal ideation, suicide attempts, and self-harm without lethal intent.[43]

The trans-friendly Williams Institute at UCLA has conducted the largest study of transgendered individuals and found 41 percent had at one time attempted suicide, which compares to 4 percent of the overall U.S. population.[44] Suicide attempts by transgendered people eclipse even the very high rates among lesbians, gays, and bisexuals.

A 2001 study published in the *American Journal of Public Health* found that 62 percent of male-to-female transsexuals and 55 percent of female-to-male transsexuals "were depressed at the time of the study, and 32% of each population had attempted suicide."[45]

Supposing Social Stress

LGBT advocates insist that the elevated levels of mental health problems are the result of homophobia and transphobia and that reducing the amount of discrimination and prejudice would inevitably result in better mental health. This is the "social stress theory." Mayer and McHugh agree that the social stress model "probably accounts for some of the poor mental health outcomes experienced by sexual minorities, though the evidence supporting the model is limited, inconsistent, and incomplete." But they insist that it cannot be counted as the dominant reason.

One way to test the social stress model is to look at studies conducted among post-op transsexuals living in indisputably trans-friendly environments. Researchers from the Karolinska Institute and the University of Gothenburg in Sweden did just that. Cecilia Dhejne and colleagues studied 324 transsexuals (191 male-to-female, 133 female-to-male) who had undergone sex-change surgery and found that they had roughly "three times higher risk for psychiatric hospitalization than the control group, even after adjusting for prior psychiatric treatment."[46] Post-op transsexuals had "a nearly three times higher risk of all-cause mortality...increased risk of being convicted of a crime...were 4.9 times more likely to attempt suicide...and 19.1 times more likely to die by suicide."[47] There is likely no place on earth that is more trans-friendly than Sweden, yet even there post-op transsexuals are still at massive risk for mental health problems.

Transgender individuals who *aren't* post-op have one big advantage—they can still change their minds. According to researchers,[48] upward of 80 percent of adolescents who claim to be transgender are no longer claiming that by their twenties. Changing your mind is exponentially more difficult if you have undergone sex-change surgery. But even then, there are those who admit to regretting the life-altering decision to "transition."

Dragging the Dissenters through the Mud

In 2004, *The Guardian*, not a conservative paper by any means, commissioned a review of existing research on whether sex-change surgery has improved the lives of transsexuals. The newspaper hired the aggressive research intelligence facility (ARIF) at the University of Birmingham to look at one hundred international medical studies of post-op transsexuals and found "no robust scientific evidence that gender reassignment surgery is clinically effective."

Chris Hyde, the director of ARIF, told *The Guardian*, "There is a huge uncertainty over whether changing someone's sex is a good or a bad thing. While no doubt great care is taken to ensure that appropriate patients undergo gender reassignment, there's still a large number of people who have the surgery but remain traumatized—often to the point of committing suicide."[49]

And then there is the sad true story of Walt Heyer, a senior executive of a major car company who had sex-change surgery in 1983, at the age of forty-two. He was castrated, received breast implants, underwent treatments to remove hair, and began an aggressive course of hormone treatment to last for the rest of his (now "her") life.

Immediately after the surgery, he was euphoric. At long last he could live as he wanted, and all his problems would be over. Within a few years, however, Heyer discovered it was all a sham. Looking like and living as a woman turned out not to cure his deep-seated psychological problems. In fact, he came to realize that his desire to be a woman had come from early childhood trauma. His grandmother had dressed him like a girl, and his stepfather had sexually abused him. Heyer says he should never have been allowed to transition to a "woman." He goes so far as saying there is no such thing as a transgender individual.[50] He coined a term for his situation: "sex-change regret."

Heyer now runs a website that has become a home to the increasing numbers who regret their sex-change operations. There is a growing body of men and women who are willing to tell the story of how they were lied to by doctors and other "scientific" authorities so that they made drastic changes to their bodies, changes that are now irreversible.

Naturally, Heyer has come under severe attack from trans advocates, as have any medical and scientific experts who question the dominant narrative. Scientists and doctors who challenge the dominant gender ideology are finding their academic freedom and even livelihood threatened. This is now part and parcel of the modern "scientific" debate.

Dr. Kenneth Zucker was unceremoniously fired from the University of Toronto for helping children come to embrace their biological sex. His clinic was closed by the Canadian government. Early in 2016, liberal *New York Magazine* ran a long piece about the firing of Zucker, one of the world's leading authorities on "gender dysphoria." In fact, he was on the team that altered the *DSM-5* on its diagnosis. He also helped write the standards of healthcare for the World Professional Association for Transgender Health. But Zucker's pro-trans bona fides did not protect him from the wrath of the trans advocates out to enforce their rapidly evolving beliefs. Zucker was charged with the crime of conversion therapy, the attempt to help those with unwanted sexual desires change.

The advocates have succeeded in keeping the real science out of the public conversation. What we're left with is phony "science." As *New York Magazine* argues, "There's fairly solid agreement about the proper course of treatment for otherwise healthy, stable young people who have persistent gender dysphoria, and who are either approaching puberty or older than that: You help them transition to their true gender."[51] Forget that upward of 80 percent of adolescents who claim gender dysphoria later recant.

The magazine does admit that there is at least a controversy about what to do in the case of younger children. Some argue for "gender affirmation" now, surgery and hormones later. Anyone, like Zucker, who attempts to help the child accept and even embrace his biological sex, is run out of town on a rail. That's the one option that cannot be tolerated.

Mayer and McHugh have come under a similar political attack. The HRC, a $50-million-a-year gay advocacy group, went to Johns Hopkins University and demanded the university denounce the Mayer and McHugh report, even though the report was not issued under the Johns Hopkins name.

HRC made several spurious claims about the Mayer and McHugh report, saying it "falsely implies...that young transgender children undergo medical interventions as part of their gender identities." There's nothing false about that claim. In fact, the report establishes that gender-confused children are given puberty-blocking hormones and that children as young as five are given psychotherapeutic "gender-affirming" therapies. This is all quite well known.

HRC also condemned Mayer and McHugh for suggesting "that being lesbian, gay, bisexual or queer is caused by childhood sexual abuse." In fact, Mayer and McHugh report, "The idea that sexual abuse may be a causal factor in sexual orientation remains speculative" and a proper area of enquiry.

HRC attacked Mayer and McHugh for supposedly saying that "LGBTQ people have inherent psychological difficulties." The report by Mayer and McHugh makes no such claim that the psychological problems are "inherent" but does point out the "well-established scientific literature showing higher rates of mental health problems in LGBT subpopulations compared to the general population." In fact, it was his concern for LGBT people and their mental health that brought Mayer into this project.

HRC threatened that if its demands were not met Johns Hopkins's ranking in the HRC Foundation Health Care Equality Index, which is a ranking of the LGBT-friendliness of hospitals and research institutes, would suffer.[52] *The New Atlantis*, quite properly, pointed out that such threats called into question the supposed objectivity of the HRC rankings and was also a direct assault on academic freedom.[53]

Shutting Down Safe Spaces

The Left is not completely united on the question of transgenderism. Second Wave feminists and some gay men are reacting against this new development, rejecting the ideological "science" being foisted upon the American public.

In the *New Yorker* in 2014, leftwing writer Michelle Goldberg told the story of how feminist gatherings are rejecting the participation of men in dresses. They view this incursion as yet another attack by the patriarchy on the protected spaces of women.[54]

Every year at something called the Michigan Womyn's Music Festival, MichFest for short, several thousand women set up shop in the woods to listen to music and celebrate the sisterhood. They live "the matriarchy," according to Goldberg. Women wear elaborate costumes or nothing at all. MichFest does not allow men in dresses. They say men in dresses make them feel less safe.

And if "transgender women"—that is, men—are allowed to compete in women's contact sports, they will be. It's already happening. There is the story about the Mixed Martial Arts fighter, a man now supposedly a woman who was allowed to fight women and sent his first female opponent to the hospital.[55] A boy was allowed to compete as a girl in an all-state track meet and won.[56] *Glamour* magazine named Bruce Jenner "Woman of the Year." These are all male incursions into the female domain. But if you complain, you're a bigot.

Even some male homosexuals and lesbians are upset that boyish girls and girlish boys are now pushed into the transgender category when they just might be happy to be gay or lesbian. Noted gay author Daniel Harris, writing in the prestigious *Antioch Review*, said, "The whole phenomenon of switching one's gender is a mass delusion. More and more, parents are encouraging their sons and daughters to transition when they spot even the slightest hint of effeminacy or boyishness on the grounds that such behaviors indicate desires to be the opposite sex when in fact their desire to play with dolls and throw footballs may reflect the desire to be something less exotic, even banal, namely gay."[57] Harris came under massive attack for his heresy.

Transgenderism is just one area where science has been brought into the service of ideology. It always works the same way: Dozens of dubious "scientific" studies are fed into the public, academic, media, and political debates. The studies' methodology is highly questionable, and then even wilder claims are extrapolated from them. The authors of any studies that challenge the propaganda are attacked by the Left. Their jobs are threatened and sometimes—as in the case of Kenneth Zucker in Canada—lost. The same script, as we shall see throughout this book, plays out in all the issues related to human sexuality, marriage, and family— but also in other issues: the environment, energy, and practically every controversial area of political discourse.

On all these issues of real importance to the health, safety, and happiness of the human race, we have a choice: swallow the unscientific ideology masked in the garb of fake "science," or put up a fight. For more ammunition, keep reading.

CHAPTER 3

Not Born That Way

Everything you know about homosexuality is fake science.

Gays are 10 percent of the population, right? Wrong.

That's a completely spurious number derived from the phony research of Alfred Kinsey, whose "studies" were riddled with scientific fraud—and worse, involved the sexual abuse of children, including even infants. Judith Reisman has almost singlehandedly dismantled the once sterling reputation of Alfred Kinsey. She looked deeply and reported upon Kinsey's odd and even sick private life and sexual practices and also reported on his slipshod, criminal research methodology.[1] The notorious Table 34 in Kinsey's book on male sexuality cites the sexual responses of children. One five-month-old infant is reported to have had three orgasms. An eleven-month-old had ten in one hour. Another eleven-month-old had fourteen in thirty-eight minutes. When the babies cried, Kinsey called it a typical orgasmic response. And these observations and experiments—torture, really—were carried out by adults, both men and women.

Skewing the Sex Statistics

Kinsey's 1948 book on male sexuality used skewed statistics to convince the public that homosexuality was common.[2] The one in ten number became a kind of giddy gospel and played a huge role in "making gay okay," to quote Robert Reilly.[3] And strangely—or perhaps not so strangely, given how both our news media and our entertainment relentlessly celebrate gay individuals and gay issues—that percent only seems to grow in the public's imagination. Recent polls by Gallup show that the general public now believes 23 percent of the population is gay. A crosstab for millennials shows they think the percentage is even higher. The average American now believes there are between 58 and 63 million adult homosexuals in this country.[4]

In fact, the number is much, much smaller than that. The gay world was rocked a few years ago when the Centers for Disease Control issued a survey that demonstrated the most accurate number is no more than 1.6 percent of adults.[5] This would total roughly four million adults who identify as either gay men or lesbians. There are almost twice that many Methodists in the United States.[6]

Gays push the line that attitudes about them changed as Americans came to know them and become friends with them personally. If that were true, then every single one of the roughly four million gays would have to be friends with an average of eighty heterosexuals.

In reality, most—if not all—of homosexuals' political and legal gains in recent years can be chalked up to such phony ideological science as that one in ten estimate. Equally powerful phony "scientific" claims have been accepted by the highest court in the land: that homosexuality is inborn (innate) and that homosexuality can never ever change (immutable).

Inventing "Innate" and "Immutable" Homosexuality

Gays and lesbian advocates have sold the Supreme Court justices, and the country, on the fishy proposition that their sexual and romantic attractions, their sexual behavior, and their identity are inborn and can never, ever change.[7]

These two propositions were the basis of their public arguments going back a quarter-century or more, which succeeded definitively when the Supreme Court imposed same-sex marriage across all fifty states on June 26, 2015.

How could anyone possibly object to same-sex attraction if it's not anyone's fault, if it's inborn, and if it can never change? Only bigots. That is the basic pitch. We do not punish anyone based on inborn and unchangeable attributes like race or sex. In the same way, we cannot discriminate against those who were born same-sex attracted and whose gayness is set in stone.

In this scientific age, these arguments came with supposed scientific proof, souped-up science with a decided ideological flavor. Just about every bit of it is utterly false. What is most interesting is that even gay-friendly scientists cannot agree on who might qualify as LGBT or what a lesbian or gay might be. How can something be inborn and unchangeable if advocates cannot agree on what the thing is?

What most people don't know is that even the very concept of a "homosexual" was invented no more than 150 years ago.

Of course, before the nineteenth century there were men who acted in a homosexual manner, that is, committed sodomy. In fact, there were some societies in world history where homosexual behavior was widely accepted. But sodomy was a behavior, not a person. It was an act that an individual person committed, but it did not define that individual. The Greeks, for instance, were fine with sodomy, considering it part of a young man's initiation to adult life. They didn't see homosexuals as a special class of persons, and they would have scoffed at the notion that men could marry each other. The Jews and Christians took a somewhat different view, and over time the belief that sodomy is a sin—harmful both to the participants and to society at large—became the dominant view. Still, whether acts of sodomy were accepted or condemned, those who committed them were never seen as a separate class of persons until the nineteenth century.

It was German psychiatrist Richard von Krafft-Ebing who first cooked up the "homosexual" label. Sodomy is an act, but a homosexual is a person. This was a massive change in how we viewed the issue—and even the human person. Now someone who committed a particular sexual act was an entirely different class of person. In his *History of Sexuality*, gay philosopher Michel Foucault explained that with this shift, the homosexual had become a personage, a type of life, a morphology: "The homosexual was now a species."[8]

Michael W. Hannon has argued in *First Things* that the new understanding promoted by the German psychiatrist replaced a robust natural law tradition on human sexuality.[9] But even psychiatrists never fully agreed on the topic, and their views have changed profoundly over time.

Oxford University professor Daniel Robinson points out, "Two of the legendary theoreticians in psychiatry were scarcely of one mind in this area. Both Havelock Ellis and Sigmund Freud rejected the 'disease' theory of homosexuality. Ellis regarded homosexuality as innate and Freud as an expression of the essential bisexuality of human beings."[10]

Robinson, no academic slouch—besides Oxford, he has also held faculty positions at Georgetown, Princeton, Brigham Young, Hofstra, and City University of New York—calls the change in the understanding of homosexuality a mere "shift in fashion" with no basis in actual science.

But though there was no real scientific basis for the change in thinking, and prominent scientists disagreed, the new understanding of homosexuality came to dominate psychiatry and psychology—or at least their professional guilds and associations—and the public discourse. Eventually, homosexuality came to be seen as just a different kind of normal, and homosexuals as a special class of people persecuted for an innate and immutable characteristic that is no choice (much less fault) of their own.

And of course, the mental health professionals' normalization of homosexuality as inborn and unchangeable has been a huge boon to the advocates. But just how the professional mental health guilds changed their tune on homosexuality—from viewing it as a treatable mental disorder to seeing it as benign, innate, and immutable is yet another demonstration of how "science" has been corrupted by politics and ideology.

The story begins with a psychologist named Evelyn Hooker. Psychiatrist Jeffrey Satinover describes her as "a lifelong hard-left political activist" who is "more than anyone else credited by believers with having demonstrated that homosexuality is normal."[11] Satinover writes, "Even today, after almost fifty years after its publication in 1957...her 'The Adjustment of the Male Overt Homosexual' is the only paper referenced in detail on the main website of the American Psychological Association in its discussion of Gay and Lesbian issues, as it attempts to make the case that there is no evidence for an association between homosexuality and psychopathology." [12]

Hooker's 1957 study was one of only two referenced by the American Psychological Association when it delisted same-sex attraction as a mental disorder. It was the only study discussed in the organization's brief to the Supreme Court in *Lawrence v. Texas*, the case that declared homosexual sodomy a constitutional right. And it was the lead study mentioned in 2016 when the American Psychological Association and a dozen other professional guilds in psychology and psychiatry submitted a brief in the Supreme Court's consideration of same-sex marriage.

Hooker's must be the definitive scientific study on homosexuality, right?

Hooker claimed that "homosexuals were not inherently abnormal and that there was no difference between homosexual and heterosexual men in terms of pathology."[13] Up to that time, she explained, the psychological profession and all society had viewed homosexuals as little more than perverts and criminals. Thus the studies prior to hers had found their homosexual subjects in prisons, insane asylums, and the punishment barracks of military facilities. These were in fact the types of places where Alfred Kinsey had found most of his subjects. But Hooker argued that men like these were not normal homosexuals. She believed that normal homosexuals were no different from normal heterosexuals, in terms of mental illness and criminality, and she set out to prove it.

Collecting Convenience Samples

Hooker found her homosexual subjects with the help of activist groups such as the Mattachine Society, one of the first gay rights group in the country.[14] It was a typical "convenience sample"—the opposite of the random sample that's necessary for a study to yield genuinely scientific results. But the scientific fraud didn't stop there. Then she screened the men in the original sample for normality, excluding men who were in therapy or showed any signs of neuroses or instability. In other words, she gamed the study in advance. On top of using a skewed "convenience" sample in the first place, she jiggered that group further so she would get the results she wanted. (She found her heterosexual control group randomly on the street, asking construction workers, firemen, policemen, and so on.)

It should be noted that Hooker was not professionally qualified in this area. She was literally an expert on mice, not men. What's more, she was an advocate and not a scientist—as is evident in how she ran the tests and reported the results.

Hooker used three tests on her subjects; the Rorschach (ROR) or inkblot test, the thematic apperception test (TAT), and the make-a-picture-story test (MAPS). She aimed to prove that there was no difference between the homosexual and the heterosexual groups, that the homosexuals did not present any homosexual markers or pathologies, and that those judging the tests could not even tell the difference between the two groups.

Hooker reported results that are even now repeated ad nauseam. She found no differences at all. Homosexuals are exactly the same as heterosexuals. It is not just the American Psychological Association and the other professional guilds that repeat her findings; any gay blogger worth his salt knows Hooker.

But Hooker's study is classic fake "science."

Begin with her cherry picking the subjects of her study and screening them for any signs of mental issues. Hooker even said, "I knew the men for whom the ratings were made, and I was certain as a clinician that they were relatively free of psychopathology."[15]

Follow this with the fact that she created her own "norms" for the study. Rather than rely on established national baselines for each test, established with massive numbers of test subjects, Hooker decided for herself what was a normal response.

And then consider that Hooker changed her experimental procedure mid-stream, when her test group had the temerity to disprove her theory. She claimed in advance that the three tests would be incapable of determining who was homosexual and who was not. In fact, when taking the TAT and MAPS test, the homosexual group could not refrain from fantasizing about—you guessed it—homosexual sex. What did Hooker do with these results? She threw them out.

Even the editors who published this study knew it wasn't ready for prime time. When Hooker's results were published in *Projective Testing*, the editors affixed a cautionary footnote: "If some of Dr. Hooker's comments, as cautiously presented as they are, seem premature or incompletely documented, the blame must fall on the editors who exercised considerable pressure on her to publish now."[16]

This is the study they relied upon to change the *Diagnostic and Statistical Manual of Mental Disorders*, the psychiatric profession's standard textbook. This is the study cited by the American Psychological Association on their website, even today. This is the study they led with in their brief to the Supreme Court in *Lawrence v. Texas*. And finally, this is the lead study the same group used to persuade the Supreme Court to declare gay marriage a constitutional right in the *Obergefell v. Hodges* decision.

Hooker was a leftist who visited the Soviet Union, and it was mostly leftists who waged the fight to get rid of homosexuality as a mental disorder in the *Diagnostic Manual*. The big story of that change is not Hooker's phony study but the completely unscientific threats, intimidation, and politics of closeted gay psychiatrists.[17]

As we have seen leftists do today, organized gays began invading the annual meetings of the American Psychiatric Association. They began making threats against the members. There were demonstrations. At the 1971 annual meeting of the American Psychiatric Association, Frank

Kameny, a federal worker who had lost his job because of lewd behavior in a public bathroom and who was later honored by President Obama, grabbed the microphone and shouted, "Psychiatry is the enemy incarnate. Psychiatry has waged relentless war of extermination against us. You may take this as a declaration of war against you." Under such pressure, including death threats, noted Columbia University professor Robert Spitzer was given the task of brokering a new deal with gays. This was achieved at a tiki-bar gathering with closeted gay psychiatrists (being gay was grounds for losing your psychiatrist's license in those days) and was based upon not a bit of science, only political pressure.[18] Getting rid of homosexuality as a mental disorder was the key to all that followed, that is, the key to convincing the public that homosexuality is inborn and unchangeable and an utterly normal expression of human sexuality.

Guessing Who's Gay

But that proposition is phony science, as is clear from the fact that pro-homosexual advocates cannot agree on who qualifies as a homosexual. Lady Gaga's anthem "Born This Way," which has been viewed 197 million times on YouTube as of this writing, makes no sense when you realize that Lady Gaga, let alone gay-friendly experts, can't even answer the question, "Born what way, exactly?"

Are you a homosexual if you think you are? Are you a homosexual if you have certain sexual urges? How strong are those urges? Do they happen every day? Or only every year or so? Or only when you're doing crystal meth, part of a new gay trend called "chem-sex"? What if you don't have sexual desires but romantic desires only? Are you gay then? Are you homosexual if you have sex with men? That might be a pretty clear marker until you consider that sometimes men in prison go for that—only for the time they're in prison. Gay advocates don't believe males having sex with males is necessarily a marker for homosexuality: they insisted that priests who sexually abused teen boys weren't really gay and that their assaults were merely "opportunistic."[19] Nothing gay to see here; move along.

On the one hand the American Psychological Association tells us, "Sexual orientation refers to an enduring disposition to experience sexual, affectional, or romantic attractions to men, women, or both. It also encompasses an individual's sense of personal and social identity based on those attractions, behaviors expressing them, and membership in a community of others who share them."[20]

On the other hand, other gay-friendly scientists say, "There is currently no scientific or popular consensus...that definitively 'qualif[ies]' an individual as lesbian, gay, or bisexual."[21] This is from gay advocate Dr. Lisa Diamond of the University of Utah, author of the highly influential book *Sexual Fluidity*. She is not the only one. A study funded by the National Institutes of Health found, "There is no standard definition of lesbian. The term has been used to describe women who have sex with women, either exclusively or in addition to sex with men (i.e., *behavior*); women who self-identify as lesbian (i.e., *identity*); and women whose sexual preference is for women (i.e., *desire* or *attraction*).... The committee strongly believes that there is no one 'right' way to define who is a lesbian."[22] "Scientists" advocating for homosexuality regularly tell us—per Alfred Kinsey's now widely adopted theory—that sexual orientation falls along a continuum from exclusively heterosexual to exclusively homosexual. Each person may have a bit of everything.[23]

The Social Organization of Sexuality by Edward Laumann is considered the gold standard in this type of research. Perhaps the most thorough study ever done on sex in America, it was created to counter the deeply flawed and even criminal Kinsey study. The Laumann study concludes, "This preliminary analysis provides unambiguous evidence that no single number can be used to provide an accurate and valid characterization of the incidence and prevalence of homosexuality in the population at large. In sum, homosexuality is fundamentally a multidimensional phenomenon that has manifold meanings and interpretations, depending on context and purpose."[24]

Even gays aren't always sure of their gayness. Gay writer Benoit Denizet-Lewis wrote a piece for the all-gay-all-the-time *New York Times* exploring "The Scientific Quest to Prove Bisexuality." He went to Cornell

University and sat through tests that included watching pornographic films of women masturbating. He was surprised by his own sexual arousal. Denizet-Lewis rejected the conclusion that he might not be gay. He's not even willing to say that he's bisexual because "it doesn't feel true as a sexual orientation, nor does it feel right as my identity." If he was born that way, and that way can never change, then what was he feeling that day?

And yet the Supreme Court has decided that this group called "gays and lesbians" is an easily identifiable group entitled to special protections along the lines of race and sex—when even the experts can't agree on who belongs to it! The Court fell for phony science in thrall to ideology.

Bolstering the "Born This Way" Myth

Bizarrely, the members of this group that no one can define have not only been born this way, they can never change. "This way" is apparently set in genetic stone never, ever to change, though scientists and advocates alike still cannot define exactly what "this way" is.

Dozens of scientific studies have been published over the years purporting to prove that homosexuality resides somewhere in the genes or in some part of the brain or in the way hormones flooded the unborn child's body. And the results have so seeped into the public consciousness that almost any high-school kid will tell you, *Sexual orientation is in the genes; it's been proven*. But it hasn't. Not even close.

Neuroscientist Simon LeVay led the way with his 1991 study finding that the tiny cluster in the brain called the hypothalamus "is deeply involved in regulating male-typical sex behavior."[25] LeVay argued that the area known as INAH3 was larger in straight men than in gay men. Gays had INAH3s roughly the size of women's. And yet LeVay himself denied he had found a genetic cause of homosexuality. He vociferously denied he could show gay men were "born that way." Even so, his results caused quite a stir.

Quite correctly, LeVay pointed out that he was unable to determine whether the difference he found in the brain had been present at birth or if it developed later, through behavior. This is one of the massive problems of these kinds of studies. Did the brain difference develop because of homosexual behavior? Or was the difference inborn, something that caused the behavior or condition? This was an especially salient question for LeVay because his study was conducted on cadavers—there was no other way to explore the brain that deeply—and the cadavers were of gay men who had died of AIDS. But those on the political hustings for homonormativity were entirely uninterested in that question. They were off to the races. LeVay became a rock star overnight.

Following LeVay, in 1993 geneticist Dean Hamer surveyed the male family members of homosexuals and claimed to have found that homosexuality tended to be inherited. He reported that 13.5 percent of the brothers of gay men were also gay. He also claimed the inheritance came through the maternal line.[26] This meant the X chromosome, the one men inherit from their mothers. So he followed up with another study that examined the X chromosome of forty pairs of homosexual brothers and claimed to have found a common genetic marker on the Xq28 region of the X chromosome. Bingo. Gay gene.

The problem was that Hamer's study has never been replicated, though not for want of trying. The hallmark of true science is replication. If a claim about biology is an actual fact, it will be observable by more than one scientist, in more than one study. No replication, no science. Even a much ballyhooed 2014 study by Alan Sanders did not replicate Hamer. He and his colleagues studied 409 pairs of homosexual brothers and claimed to have identified "two regions of linkage." They say their research "supports the existence of genes...influencing development of male sexual orientation." But even they do not claim "cause."[27]

In recent years, the quest for a biological cause for homosexuality has taken scientists into spaces even tinier than genes, indeed into the spaces between genes where chemical switches turn certain characteristics on and off—an area of study called "epigenetics." Check into political gay blogs and you'll see anonymous commenters rapidly getting into epigenetics. Everyone's suddenly an expert on gene expression.

Researchers at the National Institute for Mathematical and Biological Synthesis have run computer models purporting to show how "epi-marks that influence testosterone sensitivity in the womb might contribute to homosexuality." Note that "might"; even the authors of the study are skeptical. In any case, studies using computer models should immediately be suspect, as they rely on the inputs of the ideologues looking for their favored conclusions. As Professor Sergey Gavrilets has said, "Nobody has been able to present solid experimental evidence for this in spite of significant effort."[28]

Touting Twin Studies Too Good to Be True

And then there are twin studies, lots and lots of twin studies. If identical twins, who share the same DNA, exhibit the same trait, then it can be assumed that genetics play a role. Scientists call this the "concordance rate." If that is similar for identical twins and fraternal twins, who share no more than half their genes, then a shared environment is considered the culprit for that trait.

Psychiatrist Franz Josef Kallmann produced a landmark study in 1952 purporting to show that the concordance rate for homosexuality among identical twins was an astonishing 100 percent. No one believes that now, but it made huge splash at the time. An early example of ideological "science," Kallmann's study presented no evidence that his subjects were identical twins, and his sample group was drawn from psychiatric patients, prisoners, and the "clandestine homosexual world."[29]

In their *New Atlantis* paper debunking most of the modern scientific claims for sexual orientation and gender identity, Lawrence Mayer and Paul McHugh nonetheless assert, "Well-designed twin studies examining the genetics of homosexuality indicate that genetic factors likely play some role in determining sexual orientation."[30] Mayer and McHugh cite a 2000 study carried out using the large twins registry of the Australian National Health and Medical Research Council, which estimated "for males 45% of the differences between certain sexual orientations could be attributed to differences in the genes."[31] But even the authors of that study say that "any major gene for strictly defined homosexuality has either low penetrance or low frequency."[32]

Advocates are fond of citing animals as proof of the innateness of homosexuality. After all, wildebeests presumably do not make a choice to be gay; sometimes they just are. Interestingly, one animal study published at the University of Frankfurt in 2012 claimed that homosexual behavior among fish called "Atlantic mollies" actually resulted in the mollies getting an increased amount of heterosexual action.[33] Female mollies, it seems, found homosexual mollies more attractive than heterosexual mollies. This finding has never been replicated in human populations, with the possible except of certain fashion shows on Bravo.

The thing about gay fish and gay cows and all the rest is that the most common identifiers of homosexuality are attraction, identity, and behavior. Take a male wildebeest humping another male wildebeest. Is he demonstrating homosexual behavior or alpha male dominance? Does he self-identify as homosexual? Is he really exhibiting sexual attraction?

One could go on and on with the studies that supposedly show that being gay is in the genes, or in the brain, or in the hormones. The gold standard Laumann study, also known as the Chicago Sex Survey, demonstrated that men were twice as likely and women a whopping nine times as likely to identify as gay or bisexual if they had completed college. Presumably the correlation is even higher for alumnae of the Seven Sisters. And then there is the phenomenon known as "lesbian until graduation," which suggests that lesbianism is a choice—but is really more likely to be about women avoiding the predatory messiness of the college hook-up scene.

Going for Gay by Choice

One startling recent development in the gay world is the re-emergence of gay as a choice. In what turned out to be an explosive 2012 interview, *Sex and the City* actress Cynthia Nixon told the *New York Times* that she's been straight and she's been gay and gay is better. She said it was a choice and so what? Ceding choice was giving ground to the bigots, she said.[34] Samantha Allen wrote in the *Daily Beast* in 2014 that gays were pooh-poohing the new gay genes studies in 2014 for the same reason—"rolling their eyes." These stories are a measure of gays' new public policy muscle: now that they have persuaded society at large to accept homosexuality as normal on the theory that it is a natural, innate, and immutable condition, they don't need the gay gene any more.

Admittedly, only a tiny minority of gays evoke the choice model. Most gays still want you to believe that their sexuality is beyond their control. Most of them, and I dare say most of the general public, see gayness along the lines of the Brezhnev Doctrine. Once a country went Commie, it could never go back. Similarly, once a person has gone gay, his "identity" is permanent and unchangeable. After all, you were born that way—even if it took you a while to figure it out, even though you may have a wife and children, once your innate gayness is revealed, it is immutable and you can never ever go back.

The notion that sexual identity cannot change, was a vital part of the gay marriage legal battles because it justified the Court in considering LGBTs as an identifiable class facing discrimination for immutable characteristics, just like racial minorities and women.

Persecuting Professionals Who Dissent

Gays insist that they can't change their desires, attractions, or even their actions because their gayness is part and parcel of "who they are." How can anyone change who they are? Any gay who wants to change his gayness clearly hates himself, and anyone who wants to help him is a bigot, a religious whack-job who must be stopped.

As of this writing, several states—California, Illinois, New Jersey, Oregon, and Vermont, plus the District of Columbia—have outlawed professional help for minors who seek help dealing with unwanted same-sex attraction. Gay delegations have visited the United Nations in New York and Geneva demanding that "sexual orientation change efforts" become human rights violations.

So incensed are the advocates about the very possibility that anyone gay could change that the Southern Poverty Law Center funded a multimillion-dollar lawsuit in New Jersey to shut down a Jewish group that helped the same-sex attracted find help. The group, called Jonah, was sued under New Jersey's consumer protection laws for "false advertising." Jonah lost and is on the hook for millions in legal fees and millions more in punitive damages.[35] As of this writing, gay groups are targeting a similar group in Virginia. And they're just getting started.

In its amicus brief in the *Obergefell* gay marriage case, the American Psychological Association cites its own "task force" to the effect that "sexual orientation change efforts are unlikely to succeed and can be harmful."[36]

And when one of the most influential psychiatrists in the country had the temerity to question the dogma that gays can't change, he was bullied into submission. Dr. Robert Spitzer, longtime member of the psychiatric faculty at Columbia University in New York, was instrumental in getting homosexuality as a mental illness out of the *Diagnostic and Statistical Manual of Mental Disorders*. In fact, he wrote the new language when the change was made.

But in 2001, Spitzer delivered a shocking paper that was later published in the peer-reviewed *Archives of Sexual Behavior.*[37] It showed that certain highly motivated men and women could successfully change their sexual orientation from homosexual to heterosexual. His study indicated "66 percent of the men and 44 percent of the women had arrived at good heterosexual functioning," that is, "being in a sustained, loving heterosexual relationship within the past year, getting enough satisfaction from the emotional relationship with their partner to rate at least seven percent on a 10-point scale, having satisfying heterosexual sex at least monthly and never or rarely thinking of somebody of the same sex during heterosexual sex."[38] He found that "89 percent of men and 95 percent of women said they were bothered only slightly, or not at all, by unwanted homosexual feeling."[39]

Professional hell rained down on Spitzer. He and his paper were denounced by his own American Psychiatric Association. When asked if he would do a follow-up study, Spitzer said no, he felt "a little battle fatigue." And finally, after more than a decade of opprobrium being heaped upon him, Spitzer recanted. At the age of eighty, he asked the publisher to take the study down. Interestingly, the publisher refused. Spitzer said his critics were correct, that the study was flawed because he could not know with any certitude that the subjects were telling him the truth. This is a position strangely at odds with the entire psychiatric endeavor, which relies on listening to what your patient tells you.[40]

According to Dr. Paul McHugh, longtime head of psychiatry at Johns Hopkins University, before it became political dogma that gays can't change, it was standard practice for psychiatrists to treat men and women for unwanted same-sex desire. They would not have even considered turning away anyone who wanted help.[41] But these days, any psychiatrists or psychologists who treat people for unwanted same-sex attraction risk their very livelihood. Schools of psychiatry, psychology, and even social work no longer allow students who do not accept the gay ideology of innateness and immutability into their programs. In most states, you can no longer get licensed if you do not believe these two dogmas about homosexuality.

Even so, no matter what the gay rank and file insist on, no matter what everyday Americans have been led to believe, major researchers in the field—who are almost universally gay-friendly—do not really believe in immutability. They may not believe in *therapy* to change same-sex attraction, they may believe that efforts to change sexual orientation are nothing short of human rights abuses, but they do recognize that change is possible, if only organically or by accident.

Hiding Homosexuality's Mutability

The National Longitudinal Study of Adolescent to Adult Health (Add Health) follows a nationally representative sample of students who were in grades 7–12 during the 1994–1995 school year. So far there have been four follow-up interviews of the subjects, the most recent of which were carried out in 2007–2008, when the interviewees were aged twenty-four to thirty-two. The study shows a massive drop in homosexual interest between adolescence and adulthood.

Same-sex and both-sex romantic attractions were quite high in Wave I of the study. Seven percent of males and 5 percent of females reported same-sex attraction during high school. But these numbers dropped precipitously over time. By Wave IV, 80 percent of males who had self-identified as same-sex-attracted no longer did. And women lost sexual interest in other women, too. Among the 5 percent who had self-identified as same-sex attracted in grades 7–12, only half still did by their twenties and early thirties. So much for immutability.[42]

University of Utah professor of psychology Lisa Diamond, the author of *Sexual Fluidity*, points out, "Contrary to the notion that most sexual minorities undergo a one-time discovery of their true identities, 50% of respondents had changed their identity label more than once since first relinquishing their heterosexual identity."[43] Diamond found that "half of the young women…relinquished the first sexual-minority identity they adopted." Additionally, a ten-year study of seventy-nine non-heterosexual women reported that 67 percent changed their identity at least once, and 36 percent changed their identity more than once.[44]

Diamond is not the only one to point this out. Researchers Linda Garnets and Letitia Anne Peplau found, "Female sexual development is a potentially continuous, lifelong process in which multiple changes in sexual orientation are possible…. Women who have had exclusively heterosexual experiences may develop an attraction to other women, and vice versa."[45]

And Dr. Joseph P. Stokes reported in the *Journal of Sex Research*, "Homosexuality is not some monolithic construct one moves toward or from in a linear way; movement toward homosexuality fails to capture the fluid and contextual nature of sexuality. We also acknowledge that changes in sexual feelings and orientation over time occur in all possible directions."[46] In his study, he found "34% of respondents moved toward homosexuality, 17% moved away, and 49% did not change."[47]

A 2003 study by Nigel Dickson in New Zealand "reported a surprising degree of change over time. Ten percent of men, and nearly a quarter of women, reported same-sex attraction at any time, but this nearly halved for current attractions at age 26."[48]

The research abundantly demonstrates that homosexuality—desire, behavior, identity—can and does change over time. But gay advocates aren't willing to admit this dirty little secret. They ridicule anyone claiming to have given up homosexuality as simply white-knuckling it, in the parlance of Twelve Step Programs. The gay lobby would never publically admit that change is possible. Instead they meet any suggestion of professional help for people who want to leave homosexuality behind with white-hot hatred. This is always wrong, harmful, a form of abuse. They derisively refer to such efforts as "praying away the gay."

Despite the abundant and robust science showing that sexual orientation and identity are highly fluid, the American Psychological Association claims that any efforts to change are harmful.[49] Gay advocates tell horror stories about the coercive methods purportedly used in such efforts—hooking homosexuals' genitals up to electrodes, and so forth. None of these wild charges has ever been substantiated, but they get repeated ad nauseam.[50]

So while the real, hard science says that homosexuality is not immutable, the activists have closed the door to help for anyone who wants to escape from homosexuality—which, as we will see below, brings enormous amounts of suffering and dysfunction to the lives of homosexuals.

But what makes people gay in the first place? If there's no "gay gene," what causes homosexuality?

Trashing the Traditional Understanding

Before the change in the *Diagnostic and Statistical Manual*, it was thought that homosexuality was caused environmentally, by a boy's failure to bond with his father and therefore to develop a masculine self-image. With the onset of puberty, this failure manifests as an attraction, eventually sexual, to the missing masculinity. One psychologist asked his gay patients when they last felt like a man. The unanimous answer: "Never."

Richard Fitzgibbons, MD, the director of the Philadelphia-based Institute for Marital Healing, said,

> Those with deep-seated homosexual tendencies identify themselves as homosexual persons and are usually unwilling to examine their emotional conflicts that caused this tendency. Strong physical attraction is present to other men's bodies and to the masculinity of others due to profound weakness in male confidence....
>
> The most common origins of these emotional weaknesses in men arise from a lack of closeness and affirmation in the father relationship and with male peers. These emotional conflicts result in weaknesses in male confidence, sadness, loneliness, anger and often a poor body image. In addition, those from divorced family backgrounds have major trust weaknesses.[51]

Psychiatrist Jeffrey Satinover explains the highly complex nature of the condition. He describes a boy who is born with certain gifts that are seen as problems: "a sensitive disposition, a strong creative drive, a keen aesthetic sense." The boy may display a "greater-than-average anxiety response to any given stimulus."

Satinover says these traits are not in themselves homosexual, but they could set the boy apart as "different," and alienate him from his father and his peers. The boy still "carries silently within him a terrible longing for the warmth, love, and encircling arms of the father he never did or could have."[52] As a result, he develops "intense, nonsexual attachments to older boys he admires—but at a distance.... When puberty sets in, sexual urges—which can attach themselves to any object, especially in males—rise to the surface and combine with his already intense need for masculine intimacy and warmth." The adult homosexual will likely recall that his first sexual longings were for boys and not girls, and thus he will conclude—not unreasonably—that he was gay from childhood.

According to Satinover, "Thus, by the time the boy becomes a man, he has pieced together this point of view: 'I was always different, always an outsider. I developed crushes on boys from as long as I can remember and the first time I fell in love it was with a boy not a girl. I had no real interest in members of the opposite sex. Oh I tried all right—desperately. But my sexual experiences with girls were nothing special. But the first time I had homosexual sex it just "felt right." So it makes perfect sense to me that homosexuality is genetic. I've tried to change—God knows how long I struggled—and I just can't. That's because it's not changeable. Finally, I stopped struggling and just accepted myself the way I am.'"[53]

This traditional understanding of homosexuality is now anathema. Indeed, the National College of Pediatricians has been branded a "hate group" by the Southern Poverty Law Center for espousing this once-common theory.

Averting Their Eyes from the Abuse

But there is another theory with some plausibility, too—one that is no less offensive to the gay establishment. As repeated studies have confirmed, there is very high prevalence of early childhood trauma among homosexuals, including sexual abuse by older same-sex individuals.

In 2011, Boston University Professor Emily Faith Rothman carried out a meta-analysis of seventy-five studies that involved a total of 139,635 gay or bisexual men and women and found 59.2 percent of the men had suffered childhood sexual abuse. The women had suffered even more attacks, at a 76 percent rate. A 2013 study by psychologist Judith Anderson showed less childhood sexual abuse, but still significantly higher numbers than those for the general population. She found 29.7 percent of gay men and 34.9 percent of bisexual males experienced such abuse in childhood.[54]

Studies also show that gay and bi men and women have suffered many other forms of abuse as children. The Judith Anderson study shows that gays and lesbians have 1.7 times the risk for childhood trauma as heterosexuals—including not just sexual abuse but other forms of physical and emotional abuse as well. Indeed, 47.9 percent reported some form of emotional abuse as kids.[55]

All of this brings us to a scientific truth that gays are loath to admit: how genuinely unhealthy the gay lifestyle is.[56] The CDC reports that men who have sex with men are more likely to abuse drugs and alcohol, and are at increased risk for depression and suicide compared to the general population. They are also more likely to experience and perpetrate partner violence.[57] And it seems as if U.S. government agencies are always reporting alarming statistics on how sexually transmitted diseases are exploding among men who have sex with other men.

Remember the HIV–AIDS scare of the 1980s and 1990s? Everyone was supposed to be at risk. People who weren't remotely in danger of exposure rushed off to get HIV tests. In reality the epidemic was confined to intravenous drug users and men who had sex with men.

Even now, when AIDS is supposedly a manageable chronic disease rather than a certain death sentence, gay sex remains a messy and dangerous business. According to the Centers for Disease Control, "in 2014, gay, bisexual, and other men who have sex with men accounted for 83% of primary and secondary syphilis cases where sex of sex partner was known in the United States."[58] Also, "gay, bisexual, and other men who have sex with men are 17 times more likely to get anal cancer than heterosexual men." This 1.6 percent of the population accounts for 67 percent of all new HIV diagnoses.[59]

In 2014, independent researcher Dale O'Leary[60] published a frightening and frankly disgusting paper in the *Linacre Quarterly* called "The Syndemic of AIDS and Sexually Transmitted Diseases (STD) among MSM"[61] that tells a plethora of uncomfortable truths about men who have sex with men.

Sustaining a Syndemic

O'Leary uses the term "syndemic" to describe something that is beyond either an epidemic or a pandemic. A syndemic is two or more diseases in the same population "in which there is some level of positive biological interaction that exacerbates the negative health effects of any or all of the diseases."

In the homosexual world, it is not just HIV/AIDS that is still rampant and growing. Many other deadly diseases tag along. And contributory pathologies are also rife: promiscuity, alcoholism, drug abuse, and violence.

O'Leary writes, "In the 1970s, physicians were treating the large number of conditions affecting the lower intestinal tract of MSM under the classification 'gay bowel syndrome.' These included viral infections, infectious diarrheal diseases caused by bacteria and parasites, and injuries caused by anal sexual activity."

Before he died of AIDS, journalist Randy Shilts wrote an influential book about the AIDS crisis called *And the Band Played On*: "In San Francisco, incidence of the 'Gay Bowel Syndrome,' as it was called in medical journals, had increased by 8,000 percent after 1973. Infection with these parasites was a likely effect of anal inter-course, which was apt to put a man in contact with his partner's fecal matter, and was virtually a certainty through the then-popular practice of rimming, which medical journals politely called oral-anal intercourse."

According to O'Leary, this practice helps spread other diseases: syphilis; gonorrhea; hepatitis A, B, and C; cytomegalovirus; Epstein-Barr virus; human papillomavirus; cancroid; lymphogranuloma venereum; granuloma inguinale; pubic lice; pinworms; and scabies.

Has this explosion of disease and death changed anyone's behavior? Not much. When the AIDS epidemic first came to the public's attention, there were calls for routine testing and partner tracing, and for the closure of the HIV breeding grounds called bath houses and tea parties. Homosexual advocates resisted any measures that would crimp their lifestyle. Even today on the New York City subways, you can see ads for a drug that is supposed to protect you when you're out having lots of unprotected sex with strangers.

O'Leary reports, "A 1986 study of MSM in New York City found that 49.6% had not changed their behavior (Feldman 1986). A 1987 study found that 67% of MSM admitted engaging in anal intercourse without condoms during the previous year."

It is not like gays don't know about the dangers of their way of life. After all, we are awash in condoms and safe-sex education. As O'Leary says, the problem is not ignorance. Sexual buccaneering is part and parcel of who many homosexuals are. Gabriel Rotello—author of *Sexual Ecology: AIDS and the Destiny of Gay Men* and founder of *OutWeek Magazine*—wrote, "Sexual brotherhood of promiscuity…any abandonment of that promiscuity would amount to a communal betrayal of gargantuan proportions."[62]

Rotello also said, "A stranger to gay culture, unaware of the reality of AIDS, might believe from much of the gay press that HIV infection was a sort of elixir that produced high self-esteem, solved long-standing psychological and substance abuse problems, and enhanced physical appearance…creating the subconscious impression that infection—the 'penalty' of unsafe sex—is really not so bad after all."[63]

One massive problem among homosexuals—something they will deny all day long and call you a hater for pointing out—is promiscuity. As O'Leary writes, "Gay bars, gay bookstores, theaters, certain resort communities, and circuit parties have traditionally provided venues where MSM could engage in various forms of sexual activity with numerous partners."

In the early 1980s, CDC researchers were shocked "by the sheer number of sexual partners reported, typically over 1000." There is no reason to think such behavior has subsided, particularly since who gays are in their own minds is largely defined by what they do. A gay coming-of-age story on the website *Salon* a few years ago told the story of a young man getting his first car and joyfully driving to the first truck stop he could find because he knew there was hot anonymous sex there.[64] This is a long way from the popular image of homosexuality.

While bathhouses were the scene of the gay bacchanals in the 1970s and 1980s, in recent years the scene has shifted to "circuit parties," massive fundraisers for AIDS that became little more than drug- and booze-fueled sex fests attended by thousands or even tens of thousands. There is also "chem-sex," in which the young swain gets jacked up on meth, among the most powerful of disinhibitors, which allows you to go all night long. There have been whole books written about "chem-sex."[65] Does it even need to be pointed out that anyone on meth is likely not concerned about using condoms?

But it's not just meth. There is also widespread use of the animal tranquilizer Ketamine, called "Special K," as well as "poppers," various nitrates that are inhaled to heighten the sexual experience and make anal sex more acceptable. There is an increasing addiction among gays to anabolic muscle-building steroids, which make insecure men more appealing to other men in the hyper-muscularized gay culture.

With the advent of the Internet, men are now able to meet other sex-minded men on a moment's notice "anywhere, anytime," as the website Manhunt.net announces on its homepage, which includes images of two men grappling at a front door, another two getting it on in an office, and six young men in leather cavorting on a couch.

Manhunt.net is only one such site. There is also a truly vile social networking app called Grindr, where men advertise themselves in gruesome detail. Go on these sites and you can arrange a quickie in a bathroom of Starbucks...right now.

The introduction of retroviral drugs, making AIDS a chronic disease, has allowed young homosexuals to maintain that anal sex is their right and due without considering the consequences. As we have seen, this tiny percentage of the population contributes 67 percent of the new HIV cases in the United States.

But it is not just rampant disease that defines the MSM syndemic. There are also psychological disorders and suicidal ideation. O'Leary reports that "well designed studies with large samples done in the US, New Zealand, UK, and the Netherlands have found that MSM were far more likely to have a history of psychological disorders, suicidal ideation, and substance abuse problems."[66]

The Human Rights Campaign, gay blogger Dan Savage, and the *New York Times* all want us to believe that gays are everywhere, that they are just like us, and that gayness is inborn and unchangeable. They want us to believe that homosexuality is all about marriage, white picket fences, and smiling kids. But not even Dan Savage believes that; he invented the term "monogamish" to describe the typical open sexual relationship gay men have—including those gay men who have been together for thirty years that you read so much about.[67]

The truth of the matter is that science does not demonstrate a gay gene. Science and real-world experience show that homosexuality is utterly changeable. Science shows a strong correlation between being gay and abuse in childhood, including sexual abuse. Science shows that active homosexuals are at extreme risk of alcoholism, drug abuse, violence, disease, and death. In short, there is probably no issue where fake science is so at odds with what real science tells us.

CHAPTER 4

Everything They Say about Abortion Is a Lie

When it comes to the defenders of abortion, one is tempted to paraphrase Mary McCarthy's quip about Lillian Hellman: *Everything they say is false including "and" and "the."*[1]

And not just on the subject of abortion. Practically everything they say about human reproduction is a lie. The entire field is fraught with falsehood, and the topics are practically endless.

There is the issue of when life begins—where they flatly deny obvious biological reality. There are the claims they made about legalizing abortion in the first place: that it would reduce crime, poverty, and child abuse. There are the lies they told to win *Roe v. Wade* and *Doe v. Bolton* in the Supreme Court. There is their denial of the established link between abortion and breast cancer, and of the known fact that abortion can harm women psychologically. There is the cover-up of the use of fetal tissue in medical research, including embryo-destructive research. There is the pretense that fetuses who desperately squirm and struggle away from the abortionists' instruments feel no pain. And then there are the myriad false narratives about Planned Parenthood.

Defenders of abortion in the medical and scientific fields use their lofty professional perch to deny any scientific findings that might change people's minds, including changing the abortion-minded woman's decision to have an abortion. There can be nothing that gives either society at large or individual women in a crisis pregnancy any doubt about the goodness of abortion. After all, the science is settled—and abortion is harmless, even good.

Denying When Life Begins

Begin with the determination of when a woman is pregnant. This has been largely noncontroversial, except as we have moved into the abortion age. Even now, a doctor will count a woman's pregnancy as beginning at the time of her last menstrual cycle, before the child is even conceived. But somewhere along the line, the beginning of pregnancy became very debatable.

The Wikipedia entry on this "controversy" states it best: "Generally speaking, ideological and religious commentaries have argued that pregnancy should be stated as beginning at the first, exact moment of conception.... That doctrine has not found acceptance scientifically."[2] Note that word "doctrine." That pregnancy begins at conception is no more than a matter of religious belief. Moreover, this "doctrine" is opposed to "science."

The Alan Guttmacher Institute, founded by Planned Parenthood,[3] says, "The question of when life begins is an eternal one, debated by philosophers and theologians for centuries, and likely destined to forever elude consensus. However, on the separate but closely related question of when a woman is considered pregnant, the medical community has long been clear: Pregnancy is established when a fertilized egg has been implanted in the wall of a woman's uterus."[4] Baloney.

The notion of pregnancy beginning at implantation of the blastocyst in the lining of the uterus was first advocated in 1959 by Dr. Bent Boving at a meeting of Planned Parenthood and the Population Council. Boving openly argued for this unwarranted change in medical vocabulary as a propaganda coup for the pro-abortion cause, saying, "The social advantage of being considered to prevent conception rather than to destroy an established pregnancy could depend on something so simple as a prudent habit of speech."[5] Dr. Christopher Tietze, also connected to the Population Council, argued along the same lines in 1964, "If a medical consensus develops and is maintained that pregnancy, and therefore life, begins at implantation, eventually our brethren from the other faculties will listen."[6]

These propagandists' schemes came to fruition in 1965, when the American College of Obstetricians and Gynecologists (ACOG) defined pregnancy as beginning at implantation. Tietze died in 1984, loaded with honors from the pro-abortion Left.[7]

Moving the start of pregnancy, and thus of a new human life, to the moment of implantation rather than conception enables abortion advocates to classify abortifacient contraception—which prevents the implantation of a conceived and growing human being—as no more than contraception. If a pill or device makes the uterine lining inhospitable to the early stage human and prevents implantation, they say this is not an abortion, merely contraception. This new definition of pregnancy—and the deliberate confusion of it with the definition of conception—came in handy later with in vitro fertilization (IVF). After all, a woman can hardly be said to be pregnant if her fertilized ova are stored in a freezer.

Because of the decision of the professional guild of obstetricians and gynecologists, it is easy for the abortion advocates to assert that "science" has spoken, that the issue is "settled" on their side: pregnancy—and new life—does not start until implantation.

But keep in mind, first, that even pro-abortion obstetricians still count a woman's pregnancy not from implantation, and not from conception, either—neither of which can be seen—but from an even earlier point, the first day of her last menstrual cycle. The redefinition of pregnancy as starting at the time of implantation has had no effect on the actual practice of obstetrics, but it has served as a useful piece of propaganda for abortion.

The time between the moment that male and female gametes join and create a zygote and the time the developing blastocyst adheres to the lining of the uterine wall is roughly a week. But, that week has enormous implications for law and policy.

Abortion advocates are adamant that pregnancy begins at implantation, and they insist that the scientific community agrees. Rachel Gold of the Guttmacher Institute wrote in 2005, "The medical community has long been clear: Pregnancy is established when a fertilized egg has been implanted in the wall of a woman's uterus."[8] But notice her sleight of hand. She refers to a pregnancy being "established." Is "established" the same thing as "beginning"? Abortion advocates want to keep things vague.

What does science really say about when pregnancy begins? Let's look at the medical dictionaries. Dr. Chris Gacek at the Family Research Council (FRC) did just that in 2009.

There are four major medical dictionaries: Dorland's, Stedman's, Taber's, and Mosby's. Dorland's and Stedman's have been published for more than a hundred years. Tabor's came into existence in the Depression era, and Mosby's, founded in the 1980s, is the newest.

Working in the Library of Congress, Gacek and his team from FRC looked at every edition of each dictionary from the beginning down to the most recent editions as of 2009.

His conclusion is that there is no consensus among the four dictionaries that pregnancy begins at implantation.

Take the oldest, Dorland's.

From the first edition in 1900 to the twenty-fifth edition in 1974, Dorland's defined conception as "the fecundation of the ovum." In subsequent editions, up to 1994, the definition changed to "the onset of pregnancy, marked by implantation of the blastocyst in the endometrium; the formation of a visible zygote." Gacek notes the internal tension in the new definition including implantation but also the formation of the zygote, the newly as-yet-to-be implanted human being that comes into existence about a week before implantation. But then in the twenty-ninth edition, published in 2000, this confusion was cleared up. Conception is "the onset of pregnancy, marked by fertilization of an oocyte by a sperm or spermatozoon; formation of a visible zygote." In further editions, "visible" was changed to "viable." Dorland's clearly comes down on the side of pregnancy beginning at conception, not implantation.

Stedman's, the second-oldest medical dictionary, has gone through similar changes over the years. Sometimes its definition has been implantation-based; at other times, it is based on conception. The bottom line is that Stedman's shows no consensus that pregnancy begins at implantation.

From its founding in 1940 to 1997, Tabor's defined pregnancy on the basis of fertilization: "the union of the male sperm and the ovum of the female" or "the union of the male sperm and the ovum of the female; fertilization." In 2001, Tabor's took a sharp turn toward the abortion advocates' deliberate confusion of conception and implantation, defining the former as "the onset of pregnancy marked by implantation of a fertilized ovum in the uterine wall."

Mosby's is the most consistent among the four major medical dictionaries. Through all its editions since its founding in the early 1980s, it has consistently defined pregnancy as "the gestational process, comprising the growth and development within a woman of a new individual from conception through the embryonic and fetal periods to birth."[9]

The tragic phenomenon of ectopic pregnancy sheds an interesting light on this issue. Ectopic pregnancies implant not in the uterine wall but in the fallopian tube or elsewhere. These babies are doomed to die since they cannot find nourishment except in the uterine wall, and their establishment in a part of the mother's body where there's not room for them to grow often threatens her life. Still, even abortion advocates refer to ectopic pregnancies as pregnancies.

Of course, embryology fully supports the fact of life beginning at conception.

The Carnegie stages of human development, which are the scientific standard, begin at "day 1" with "fertilization" and proceed through sixty days of development.[10] With proper nutrition and shelter in the mother's womb, the stage-one human being will flourish without interruption until birth. Human development does not begin at days seven through twelve when implantation occurs.

Putting the start of pregnancy at implantation is one of the great "scientific" frauds of our time. And the important question is when life—not pregnancy—begins. From a medical perspective, pregnancy is a two-patient condition. Babies in freezers or test tubes are not involved in a pregnancy, and the destruction of frozen embryos is not an "abortion," inasmuch as it does not involve the termination of a pregnancy. But destroying them nonetheless kills a live human being. The real, hard science of biology—more specifically embryology—has shown us that *life* begins at sperm-egg fusion. Pregnancy can be can be defined as beginning at the same time, or a week after—or in some cases even years after, in the case of IVF.

Throwing Away the "Unwanted"

But what science cannot tell us is the value of a human life at any stage, and whether it is ever permissible to terminate it.[11] And beginning long before our present lying age, some human beings have declared other human beings' lives unworthy.

Take this gem from Supreme Court Justice Oliver Wendell Holmes in *Buck v. Bell*: "We have seen more than once that the public welfare may call upon the best citizens for their lives. It would be strange if it could not call upon those who already sap the strength of the state for these lesser sacrifices, often not felt to be such by those concerned, in order to prevent our being swamped with incompetence. It is better for all the world, if instead of waiting to execute degenerate offspring for crime, or let them starve for imbecility, society can prevent those who are manifestly unfit from continuing their kind. The principle that sustains compulsory vaccination is broad enough to cover cutting the Fallopian tubes.... Three generations of imbeciles are enough."[12]

The *Buck v. Bell* case involved a young woman named Carrie Bell, who was involuntarily sterilized and deprived of the children she desired. Justice Holmes was a proponent of limiting births to rid society of children deemed undesirable on account of the detrimental traits that they would presumably inherit from their parents: disability, poverty, criminal tendencies, poor health, or low intelligence. The abortion advocates have expanded this logic, in two different directions. They justify the killing of already-conceived human beings. And while Holmes's defense of eugenics depended on the judgment that some human beings were objectively undesirable to society, "pro-choicers" justify killing unborn babies on the completely subjective ground of unwantedness, as defined solely by the feelings of the child's mother.

Planned Parenthood founder Margaret Sanger, who was an influence on Justice Holmes, had already argued that the state of being "unwanted" by one's parents—particularly one's mother—doomed one to a life of misery.[13]

And in 1943, the prominent psychiatrist Karl Menninger published *Psychiatric Aspects of Contraception*, in which he proposed a causal relationship between what he called "unwantedness" and all sorts of pathological behavior—up to and including genocide: "Nothing is more tragic, more fateful in its ultimate consequences, than the realization by a child that he was unwanted. Where one child reacts to this in later life with an acute mental illness, dozens of children (as I have said elsewhere) react to it in more subtle ways."[14] Menninger mentions "offensive behavior" and "criminal acts" as consequences of being unwanted and claims that the unwanted child may live in "constant fear" with "bitter prejudice" against both individuals and "groups." He refers to Southern whites and their "hatred" of blacks, and even invokes what would become known as the Holocaust: "The unwanted child becomes the undesirable citizen, the unwilling canon-fodder for wars of hate and prejudice."[15] Menninger claims to be arguing all this from a purely scientific point of view.

In 1966, Hans Forssman and Inga Thuwe published a study in Sweden tracking 120 children whose mothers had requested abortions but were denied: these were not merely unplanned children but thoroughly unwanted ones. Forssman and Thuwe concluded, "The unwanted children were worse off in every respect, the only exception being due to the one case of a government pension which came from the control series. The differences were often significant, and when they were not, they pointed in the same direction (except for the case just mentioned)—to a worse lot for the unwanted children." Largely overlooked was the fact that "not as many unwanted children were brought up by both their real parents as were control subjects."[16] As we now know from copious research, being raised by anyone besides your two married biological parents comes with a host of negative outcomes.[17] But Forssman and Thuwe blamed all these pathologies on "unwantedness."

The Forssman study was enthusiastically embraced by the 1972 Rockefeller Commission on Population and the American Future: "There was one study in Sweden in which a sample of children born to women whose applications for abortion were denied, was compared over a 20-year period with a control group of other children born at the same time in the same hospital. They turned out to have been registered more often with psychiatric services, engaged in more antisocial and criminal behavior, and have been more dependent on public assistance."[18]

As Rebecca Oas, a colleague of mine at the New York-based Center for Family and Human Rights, explains, "The Swedish study was pounced on by advocates for abortion such as Garret Hardin and James W. Prescott, who published an incredible screed titled *Abortion or the Unwanted Child: A Choice for a Humanistic Society*. This was published post-*Roe*, but it relied on data collected previously, including Forssman and Thuwe. He summarized their findings thusly, 'Unwanted children appear to present certain costs to society: increased delinquency, a higher number of welfare recipients, a more poorly educated citizenry, and a greater number of psychiatric problems.'"[19] James W. Prescott was a developmental neuropsychologist with the National Institute of Child Health and Human Development and served as a member of the Maryland House of Delegates Judiciary Committee's Subcommittee on Abortion Reform from 1967 to 1968.[20]

The same flawed Swedish study was later cited in the abortion chapter of the popular book *Freakonomics*, which argued that the rise of abortion contributed to a national reduction in violent crime (more on this debate below).

Other studies along the same lines followed, including most famously a longitudinal study beginning in the early 1960s conducted in Prague by Henry P. David and colleagues. In David's study, which did correct for some of the flaws of the Swedish study by controlling for family structure and socioeconomic class, each mother of an "unwanted" child had been denied an abortion by the Czech authorities not once but twice. The study found that the control subjects did better than the "unwanted" ones.[21] But the differences were far more subtle than you would ever have guessed from the impact the study has had on the public debate over abortion. In an oral history he gave to Smith College, David would refer to the Prague experiment as a "propaganda coup" and "the most successful and far-reaching and most policy-influencing study I've done, because it's been cited everywhere where people want to legalize abortions."[22]

Selling Abortion with Lies

The early arguments in favor of abortion were that out-of-wedlock births would greatly decline, every child would be a wanted child, and child abuse would decline. Crime rates would also decline, since crime is largely committed by young people who are unwanted. Nascent criminals and sociopaths would simply be eliminated before they began their crime sprees. Finally, poverty would decline because these excess children would no longer burden their families and society.

Well, abortion was made legal in 1973, so we've had plenty of time to measure these claims. And the data demonstrate them to have been utterly false.

Before we look at the data, it is important to understand what *Roe v. Wade* actually did. Most people don't know, and abortion advocates like it that way.

Most people think that *Roe* banned abortion through the first trimester—the "trimester" system of pregnancy having been invented by the Supreme Court—and that after the first three months of pregnancy, states are free to regulate abortion, even ban it. This is utterly false, and the advocates making these arguments know it.

In fact, *Roe* struck down all abortion laws and made abortion legal through the first two trimesters without restriction. And it did say that abortions in the third trimester could be regulated by the states and that women could only get an abortion in the third trimester for reasons of "health." But what most people don't know is that the ridiculously broad definition of "health" in *Doe v. Bolton*, the companion decision to *Roe*, handed down the same day, made the supposed power of the states to regulate third-trimester abortions meaningless. Where *Roe* cited "health," it did not define it. *Doe* did, and the definition was sufficient to give the United States abortion on demand.

This is the definition of "health" in *Doe*: "The medical judgment [for a late-term abortion] may be exercised in the light of all factors— physical, emotional, psychological, familial, and the woman's age—relevant to the well-being of the patient. All these factors may relate to health."[23]

This is a definition broad enough to drive a thousand trucks through, and it has resulted in up to 1.6 million abortions a year in the United States.[24] To invoke the "health" exception in *Roe v. Wade*, all a woman has to do is appear at Planned Parenthood and say that she is too old to have a baby. The same woman could appear a few years later and say she's too young to have a baby. And no one believes Planned Parenthood would turn her away.

What most people also do not know is that both Supreme Court cases that imposed legal abortion on the United States were based on lies. Norma McCorvey, who brought the *Roe* complaint, later admitted that she had lied about being gang-raped. McCorvey later became pro-life. Sandra Cano, who brought the *Doe* case, said she never wanted an abortion. She only wanted help in getting her other three children out of foster care. She ran away from an abortion appointment set up by her lawyers. Cano, too, later became pro-life.

Roe and *Doe* were decided in 1973, so the claims of the Left that abortion would reduce out-of-wedlock births, cure crime, child abuse, and poverty can now be tested.

We know that abortion has not reduced poverty. In fact, poverty was already dropping like a stone until the mid-1960s, when Lyndon B. Johnson's War on Poverty began. Poverty ceased falling at that time and is roughly the same today as it was then, 14 percent of the total population—and this after spending $22 trillion. Fifty-three million abortions later, legal abortion has not lowered the poverty rate, as the abortion advocates promised it would.[25]

Rather than decline, out-of-wedlock births skyrocketed after *Roe v. Wade*. This result might not seem to make sense; after all, now that women had access to abortion, they could easily avoid childbirth. But those are the inconvenient facts: In 1965, 24 percent of black babies and 3.1 percent of white kids were born to single moms. By 1990, those rates had risen to 64 percent for blacks and 18 percent for whites. In the year 2013, 72 percent of births to black women were out of wedlock, while the rate for whites had grown to 29 percent. Abortion on demand did not cure out-of-wedlock births.[26]

In fact, it may have exacerbated the problem. Nobel Prize–winning economist George Akerlof and his wife, Janet Yellen, current chairman of the Federal Reserve, argued in a groundbreaking paper precisely that "until the early 1970s, shotgun marriage was the norm in premarital sexual relations." From 1964 to 1984, however, the tradition of shotgun weddings dramatically declined. Akerlof and Yellen place the decline of shotgun weddings at the same time as the advent of "reproductive technologies." They say, "Seventy percent in the increase in white out-of-wedlock birth rate, and about 60 percent of the black increase, between 1965 and 1990 is directly attributable to the decline in shotgun marriages."[27]

Prior to the rise of contraception and legal abortion, the stigma of out-of-wedlock births was too much to bear for most women. So they abstained from sex, and if they didn't, they got married, even if it wasn't a love match. In fact, according to Akerlof and Yellen, "the only circumstance that would cause a woman to engage in sexual activity was a promise of marriage in the event of pregnancy. Men were willing to make (and keep) that promise for they knew that in leaving one woman they would be unlikely to find another who would not make the same demand."[28] The rise of contraception and abortion made it easier for men to demand sex and harder for women to resist even without the promise of marriage. What's more, while contraception and abortion made women freer to have sex without the risk of motherhood, they also allowed men the freedom to walk away even if a woman did not use contraception or refused to get an abortion.

So after *Roe* conceptions rose by 30 percent, abortions increased, and out-of-wedlock births climbed. Oh, and adoptions dropped, too. There is now a crisis of adoption in the United States.

What about child abuse? Abortion was supposed to make every child a wanted child and therefore less subject to abuse. Does anyone really think child abuse has declined in recent years, particularly since the advent of abortion on demand?

In 1973, the U.S. Senate held hearings to establish a federal agency on child abuse. In those hearings, it was reported that sixty thousand children were subject to abuse each year, some to the point of death.[29] Note that this was the very same year the Supreme Court made abortion a constitutional right legally protected in all fifty states. So that number is a baseline against which we can measure the claim that abortion would fix this problem. By 1994, the number of abused children had grown to more than one million.[30] By 2014, the number had declined to roughly seven hundred two thousand. Even so, it is markedly higher than the sixty thousand reported to Congress in 1973, when abortion became legal across the country. Even more remarkable, a study by Edward Lenoski of the University of Southern California found that of 674 respondents who had abused their children, 91 percent said they "wanted" the child they abused. In 2005, Priscilla Coleman of Bowling Green University reported that women who had abortions "had a 144 percent higher risk for child physical abuse."[31]

Even though one can assume the reporting of child abuse has increased, it is also clear that child abuse has dramatically increased and that legal abortion has done nothing to alleviate it.

What about crime? Have crime rates fallen because we're killing off the future perps in utero?

This argument was a mainstay of the early abortion movement. As we have seen, unwanted children were supposed to be more likely to live a life of crime—and even genocide. Getting rid of unwanted children would therefore reduce the crime rate (and presumably the genocide rate).

And the rate of violent crimes did fall—by 31 percent from its peak in 1991 to 1999, with the murder rate falling by 42 percent. This would coincide with the post-*Roe* generation.[32] *Freakonomics* authors John Donohue and Steven Levitt argued that "legalized abortion may account for as much as one-half of the overall crime reduction" during those years.[33]

Violent crime rates had climbed steeply from 1960 and by the end of the 1960s were picking up breakneck speed. By the time of *Roe v. Wade* in 1973, the national violent crime rate had grown to 417 per thousand, up from 160 in 1960. With the exception of a few years in the 1980s, it continued its upward trajectory until it peaked in 1991 at 747 violent crimes per thousand and then began to decline.[34]

Donohue and Levitt point to that peak year—1991—and say, *Ah ha! Eighteen years after* Roe, *the age cohort most likely to begin a crime spree is smaller than it would otherwise have been. Legalized abortion must have killed a lot of nascent criminals before they could escape the womb.*

But there is readily available counterevidence to this theory. Look at what happened in New York State and California, early adopters of legal abortion. If the *Freakonomics* model is true, then both of those states would have seen a drop in violent crime before *Roe v. Wade* expanded the legal abortion regime to the rest of the country. In fact, neither state did.

Abortion became legal in California in 1971. The year before, the violent crime rate stood at 474 per thousand. In 1988, the year the cohort culled by legal abortion turned eighteen, the crime rate was 929 per thousand. In 1989, it did not decline but rather grew to 977; in 1990 it went over a thousand; starting in 1992, it followed the national trend downward.[35]

The story was the same in New York. Violent crime was 685 per thousand in 1970. Abortion became legal in 1971. In 1988, the year that according to the *Freakonomics* theory violent crime should have declined, it rose to 1,097; to 1,131 in 1989; and to 1,180 in 1990.[36]

The data show that legal abortion did nothing to improve the violent crime rates in New York and California.

There are many more tenable theories to explain why crime began to drop in 1991, chief among them the subsiding of the crack wars and better policing.[37] I lived in New York in those years and remember vividly the changes wrought by Rudy Giuliani and his chief of police Ray Kerik. They did simple things: Got rid of the squeegee men. Cracked down on panhandling. Vigilantly cleaned up the subway cars. They made it clear in a thousand different ways that even minor infractions would not be tolerated and that the city belonged to the citizens rather than the thugs.

As John Lott and John Whitley point out, "In the debate, many plausible explanations [in addition to "legalizing abortion during the early 1970s"] for this decline have been advanced, such as: increased arrest and conviction rates, longer prison sentences, 'broken windows' or 'problem orientated' police policies, the ending of the crack epidemic, a strong economy, right-to-carry concealed handgun laws.... "[38]

The *Freakonomics* thesis that abortion accounts for half of the drop in violent crime in the United States is not borne out by the example of New York and California, which suggests that other factors were at work reducing violent crime starting in 1991, eighteen years after *Roe v. Wade.*

Skewing the Statistics on Abortion and Breast Cancer

And now we move away from society at large and to the woman herself. The abortion industry, with the backing of the heavily pro-abortion medical and "scientific" community, has made many promises to women about abortion, chief among them that abortion is utterly safe, safer than childbirth. The "experts" deny that abortion has any deleterious effects on women. In particular, there is supposed to be no connection between abortion and breast cancer. This assurance to women is vitally important. The fear of cancer, after all, was been the most important reason society turned against smoking. Any link between abortion and breast cancer could be devastating to the abortion regime.

The Guttmacher Institute insists, "Exhaustive reviews by panels convened by the U.S. and British governments have concluded that there is no association between abortion and breast cancer. There is also no indication that abortion is a risk factor for other cancers."[39]

The American Cancer Society is no less adamant. "At this time, the scientific evidence does not support the notion that abortion of any kind raises the risk of breast cancer or any other type of cancer."[40]

In 2009, the American College of Obstetricians and Gynecologists' Committee on Gynecology said, "Early studies of the relationship between prior induced abortion and breast cancer risk were methodologically flawed. More rigorous recent studies demonstrate no causal relationship between induced abortion and a subsequent increase in breast cancer risk."[41]

In 2004, the Collaborative Group on Hormonal Factors in Breast Cancer said, "The totality of worldwide epidemiological evidence indicates that pregnancies ending as either spontaneous or induced abortions do not have adverse effects on women's subsequent risk of developing breast cancer."[42]

The U.S. National Cancer Institute said, "Induced abortion is not linked to an increase in breast cancer risk."[43]

Case closed, right? Science has spoken? The science is settled? As per usual when dealing with "science" that bolsters the Left's agenda—not so fast.

When a woman becomes pregnant, her breasts' cells grow and divide as they are flooded with hormones like estrogen, progesterone, and prolactin. These hormones and the changing cells are preparing her breasts to produce milk. Up to a certain point, these cells are "undifferentiated," which means that it is not yet determined what they will be.

The problem with "undifferentiated" cells is they may turn cancerous, particularly when they are stopped abruptly from developing, which is precisely what happens in abortion. They do not turn into what they were supposed to be; they can and do turn cancerous, as has been reported by the American College of Pediatricians.[44]

The study most often cited to rebut the abortion–breast cancer link is a 1997 study authored by Mads Melbye and colleagues of the Statens Serum Institut in Copenhagen and published in the *New England Journal of Medicine* based on the medical records of a substantial number of Danish women born between 1935 and 1978. The study's authors examined the records of 1.5 million women, including three hundred thousand abortions and ten thousand cases of breast cancer. The authors of the study concluded there was no link between induced abortion and breast cancer, and the study is supposed to have settled the issue.[45]

But Dr. Joel Brind of Baruch College points out "the flaws in the compilation of the data were breathtaking."

To begin with, though the study examined women dating back to 1935, it included records for induced abortion going back only to 1973. This eliminated any abortions of sixty thousand older women, those most likely to have had breast cancer. In short, the women were counted but not their abortions. Including these women in the study as abortion free improperly skewed the study. While the study looked at abortions from only 1973 onward, it used breast cancer data beginning in 1968.

Nevertheless, Brind and his colleague Vernon Chinchilli of the Pennsylvania State University of Medicine calculate that the Melbye data in fact reveal a 44 percent increase in the likelihood of breast cancer after induced abortion—and a significant increase in breast cancer if an abortion is induced after eighteen weeks of pregnancy. Melbye simply dismisses his own data.[46]

There are studies dating back decades that find evidence of a connection between induced abortion and breast cancer. A 1957 Japanese study reported that women who had breast cancer had three times the frequency of having had an induced abortion.[47] The British *Journal of Cancer* published a study out of the University of Southern California in 1981 that, according to Brind, showed "women who had an abortion before they had any children were at a 2.4-fold (i.e., 140 percent) increased risk for breast cancer."[48]

Denying the Depression (and Other Psychological Risks of Abortion)

Besides denying the abortion–breast cancer link, abortion advocates and the pro-abortion medical community want us to know that there are no medical, emotional, or psychological consequences to aborting what is no more than a blob of tissue. Psychological problems often manifest later in life, but the first wave of women who had legal abortions are now in their sixties, and these claims can be measured.

A 2008 report from a task force of the American Psychological Association claims there is no connection between having an abortion and later psychological disturbances. On the other hand, the report says there may *be* psychological disturbances, but they have nothing to do with "abortion per se" but rather with "stigma" and "secrecy."[49] There are no problems caused by the killing of your unborn child, they say, but only by the stigma attached to it.

But the experiences of thousands of women who've had abortions bely the assurances of the APA. More and more of them are taking to the streets and the airwaves to tell their stories of how abortion has harmed them and their families.

One of the more interesting developments in the pro-life movement in the past decade is the number of women who are willing to tell their personal stories of how getting an abortion has caused problems in their lives. And the evidence is not just anecdotal. There are studies to back up their claims.

According to Dr. Priscilla Coleman of Bowling Green University, writing for the *British Journal of Psychiatry*, "Over the past several decades, hundreds of studies have been published indicating statistically significant associations between induced abortion and adverse psychological outcomes of various forms."

Coleman conducted a meta-analysis of studies published between 1995 and 2009 and found significant connections between induced abortion and depression, substance abuse, and other pathologies. In all, she examined the results of twenty-two studies, fifteen from the United States and seven from other countries, which examined thirty-six measures including alcohol abuse, anxiety, depression, and suicidal behavior. Her results found that women who had an abortion experienced an 81 percent higher risk of mental health problems "when compared with women who had not had an abortion." The data showed that 10 percent of these mental health problems were directly attributable to having had an abortion.[50]

A 2003 paper published by Dr. Jesse Cougle of the Department of Psychology, University of Texas–Austin, and colleagues asked the question whether "abortion of childbirth is associated with greater psychological risks." The authors "compared admission rates of women in time periods from 90 days to 4 years after either abortion of childbirth." Using California Medicaid records, they found "overall, women who had had an abortion had a significantly higher relative risk of psychiatric admission compared with women who had delivered for every time period examined."[51]

Studies are one thing. Stories are quite another. Since we live in a narrative age, the stories of those who've become known as "post-abortive women" have become very important and remarkably effective. You can see them each year at the end of the March for Life on the steps of the U.S. Supreme Court telling their stories of depression, alcoholism, divorce, drug abuse, and much worse. One of the groups working to organize them and their stories is the Silent No More Awareness Project.

Calling No Choice Pro-Choice

Some of the more interesting comments you read in these testimonies and even in the statistics of the Guttmacher Institute involve the reasons women give for seeking an abortion. They do not always put it in these words, but essentially they testify: they had no choice. They had been abandoned by those who in older days could have been counted on to stand by them. Today, if a woman finds herself pregnant, her boyfriend is no longer expected to marry her. The woman is expected to have an abortion. "Supporting" your girlfriend in that situation now means paying for the abortion—maybe driving her to the clinic. Even the woman's own family will pressure her to abort. University medical centers help with abortions but not with child care. Women can lose their jobs. This comes out in the Guttmacher research. The women say they are worried about their relationships. They feel pressure from their boyfriend or their families; they do not feel ready to have a child. The hard cases of rape and incest are barely measured. Women chose abortion because they felt they had no choice.[52] The irony is utterly lost on "pro-choice" abortion advocates.

Covering Up the Traffic in Baby Parts

One of the more monstrous aspects of the abortion business came to light in the summer of 2015, when it was revealed that Planned Parenthood was trafficking in the remains of aborted babies. This is actually nothing new. Scientists have always been keen to use the bodies of aborted fetuses.

Attempts were made to transplant fetal tissue to Addison's disease patients in the United Kingdom in 1921, and Italian cancer patients in 1928, neither of which worked. Fetal tissue was first transplanted in the United States to treat pancreatic cancer in 1939 and again in 1959. Both attempts failed. Hundreds of similar attempts were made around the world.[53]

But because of the undercover videos made by David Daleiden and his Center for Medical Ethics, we have been able to see the grotesque traffic in the organs of recently aborted unborn children up close and personal. Daleiden's videos show Planned Parenthood personnel haggling over the prices of brains, hearts, and especially livers.[54] He uncovered a whole supply chain of middlemen who sell the organs to research institutes located at major universities, where researchers believe the organs are the best "cultures" for developing treatments and cures for a whole range of diseases but also the development of entire human organs that they hope to grow for transplant.[55]

There is no doubt that tissue from aborted fetuses has been used in the development of important vaccines. The WI-38 line was developed at the Wistar Institute in Philadelphia in 1962 by taking lung cells from a healthy female baby aborted at the end of the third month of gestation. The cell line MCR-5 was created in 1966 from the lung tissue of an aborted child, an otherwise healthy fourteen-weeks-gestation boy. These lines have been used to develop vaccines to prevent chickenpox, diphtheria, tetanus, polio, hepatitis A, measles, mumps, rubella, rabies, and other diseases. But vaccines from other sources are now available.

Embryonic Stem Cell Research: Lies and Empty Promises

The human embryo is one of the greatest medical and scientific treasure troves man has ever known, and one of the great debates of our time has been over using this material, most recently over embryonic stem cell research.

Embryonic stem cell research relies on the theory that the undifferentiated cells of an unborn human embryo can be coaxed into becoming any type of cells scientists desire. The hope is for life-saving cures of everything from Parkinson's disease to diabetes to even Alzheimer's disease.

Stem cell treatments in and of themselves are not controversial, though the Left likes to pretend that conservatives are against all stem cell research and treatments. In fact, stem cells have been used since the 1950s in the treatment of leukemia through bone marrow transplants, and conservatives are just fine with that—because such transplants are performed using adult stem cells, which are found in several places including cord blood and the placentas from newly born babies. So those treatments don't involve the destruction of human embryos.

There are limitations to the use of adult stem cells, however. They are only "multipotent" and thus restricted in the number of cell types they can be coaxed into becoming. The prize cells are those that are "pluripotent," that is, are capable of producing any of the cell types in the human body. That's where embryonic stem cells come in.

As Dr. Maureen Condic put it in a 2007 essay in *First Things*, there are three essential scientific problems with using embryonic stem cells as treatments in the human body. First, there is the challenge of the patient's immune system rejecting the cells, a situation that can necessitate lifelong immune suppression. Second, there is the problem of these cells turning into tumors. Because they can turn into anything, they can potentially turn into cancers and other nasty things like hair inside a person's body. Third, she says, "there was the disturbing fact that science had thus far provided essentially no convincing evidence that embryonic stem cells could be reliably differentiated into normal adult cell types.... "

And then there is the moral problem: embryonic stem cells are derived from the destruction of a living human being.[56]

Human embryonic stem cells were first derived in 1998 by biologist James A. Thomson of the University of Wisconsin using embryos created through In Vitro Fertilization (IVF). We do not know how many embryos Thomson had to destroy in his attempt to derive the first embryonic stem cells.

Scientists immediately recognized the amazing possibilities of such a discovery. They also knew the political perils associated with such research. Indeed, four years before Thomson's discovery, a committee of the National Institutes of Health had met to strategize about the inevitable opposition from religious troglodytes in Congress to federal funding of research conducted on human embryos.[57]

At that meeting, they created the playbook we have seen the Left using from that time forward. They determined to personalize the research. They would find members of Congress with relatives who suffered from certain diseases and dangle before them the prospect of treatments and cures, if only we could kill a few embryos.

During debates in the U.S. Congress over embryonic stem cell funding, "a series of Senators, one after another, described illnesses suffered by relatives, constituents, and themselves—a parade of maladies, from cancer to Parkinson's to diabetes to asthma. One Senator, explaining his vote in favor of using taxpayer dollars to fund embryonic stem cell research, recounted his mother's physical and mental decline due to Alzheimer's disease: 'When I look at her empty gaze and shriveled body, I cannot help but wonder, if we had started embryonic stem cell research years ago, would she still be suffering today?'"[58]

Actors Christopher Reeve, a quadriplegic since a riding accident, and Michael J. Fox, suffering from Parkinson's Disease, were regularly trotted out to claim they would be cured if only conservatives would allow embryonic stem cell research. Fox was accused of going off his anti-shaking meds to make a stronger case.[59]

During the 2004 Democratic National Convention, Ron Reagan Jr., whose father had died only a few weeks before after a long struggle with Alzheimer's Disease, appeared after the address by Barack Obama to make a plea for embryonic stem cell research.

During this prime-time speech, Reagan told bald-faced lies about embryonic stem cell research: "I am here tonight to talk about the issue of research into what may be the greatest medical breakthrough in our or any lifetime: the use of embryonic stem cells—cells created using the material of our own bodies—to cure a wide range of fatal and debilitating illnesses: Parkinson's disease, multiple sclerosis, diabetes, lymphoma, spinal cord injuries and much more."

Reagan went on to describe a process of taking one of your own skin cells, putting it into a donor egg, and *Voila*! creating new cells that would miraculously yield cures for a plethora of diseases. He talked about a young woman he knew who suffered from diabetes. He claimed the only reason people oppose embryonic stem cell research is because of their theology.[60]

It should be noted that Reagan was not only talking about embryo-destructive research; he was also talking about "somatic cell nuclear transfer," otherwise known as cloning.

The promises of imminent cures and treatments through embryo-destructive research made to sufferers of Parkinson's, diabetes, Alzheimer's, cancer, and thousands of other diseases have been cruelly misleading. The clear implication of the overheated arguments for experiments with embryonic stem cells was that treatments and cures were just a few years away, if only religious conservatives got out of the way and federal funding was allowed. In fact, federal funding has been allowed all along, on a set number of stem cell lines created before August 2001. And then in 2009 President Obama opened the funding floodgates for research involving the destruction of new embryos. And what has been the result?

According to neurobiologist Maureen Condic at the University of Utah, "There are currently 10 FDA approved clinical trials using cells derived from hESC and 5 using direct fetal stem cells (see below), but all are in early phase trials—so no approved treatments yet."[61] And there has not been a single treatment or cure derived from the use of embryonic stem cells. Not even one.

No wonder many of the for-profit corporations that jumped into the field are just as quickly getting out.

In 2011, Geron, the latest company that had invested in embryonic stem cell research, announced it was getting out of the business altogether. Geron cited financial reasons and the wishes of their stockholders. The thing about publicly held companies is that they only have limited room to make claims based on phony science. Soon, the stockholders want an accounting. If the experiments were actually delivering the promised treatments and cures, there is little doubt stockholders would have cared about moral and ethical concerns. As it is, embryonic stem cells have been a disaster, running wild in human bodies, creating teratomas (cancers), and growing skin and hair inside one poor man's brain.[62]

In November 2016, it was announced that a stem cell transplant start-up founded by Harvard Tech and Magenta Therapeutics got $48 million from a gaggle of Silicon Valley venture capital firms. The project has nothing to do with the controversial embryonic stem cells—but rather with the far more successful adult stem cells, the ones that can be used without killing a tiny human being.[63]

As a coda to this remarkable debate, it should be noted that while some scientists continue working unethically on embryo-destructive research, many others are working within the confines of what is morally allowed. The prize is not necessarily embryonic stem cells—it's pluripotent stem cells, which certainly are found in embryos but may also be found or generated in other ways.

The restrictions that President George W. Bush had placed (and that Obama lifted) on embryo-killing research were eminently reasonable, despite the Left's attempt to portray them as benighted, theocratic anti-science.

In August 2001, President Bush made his first prime-time speech, his much-anticipated announcement about federal funding for embryonic stem cell research. His decision pleased pretty much no one. He determined that federal funding would cease for any embryonic stem cell lines that had not already been created. The United States would fund the killing of no more human embryos, but it would fund experimentation on stem cell lines that had been created from embryos already killed. This left a limited number of stem cells lines for scientific experimentation. Not nearly enough, said some; plenty, said others.

It was said that President Bush had banned federal funding of embryonic stem cell research.[64] This was utterly false, part of the massive spin by the Left to try to make stem cell research a wedge issue in national politics. Bush and the Republicans were presented as standing in the way of scientific advances, as being "anti-science." Democrats lived in the "evidence-based" world.

A few months later, Bush announced the creation of the President's Council on Bioethics, which became the venue of some of the most interesting debates the federal government has ever sponsored. Among their most important work was a 2005 report on "Alternative Sources of Pluripotent Stem Cells," looking into "specific proposals for obtaining pluripotent, genetically stable, and long-lived human stem cells by methods that would meet the moral standard of not destroying or endangering human embryos in the process."[65]

Donald Landry and Howard Zucker of Columbia University proposed using embryos that had been determined to have died, in the same way that we use adult cadavers in medical experimentation.[66] Determining the time of death in a four-to-eight-cell organism could be difficult, though.

A second proposal was to derive pluripotent stem cells from living early stage embryos without killing them. Similar procedures are currently carried out in the IVF process for purposes of genetic testing. The primary ethical consideration would be any harm done to the embryo through such a biopsy. Even in IVF the procedure is considered unethical, because it is usually done to find a genetic match for a living child for purposes of medical treatment, or for sex selection.

Yet a third proposal was developed by William Hurlbut, himself a member of the President's Council on Bioethics. He proposed something called "altered nuclear transfer" that would use somatic cell nuclear transfer technology (cloning) but would alter the skin or fat cell transferred to the egg cell so that it would grow not into a human embryo but into what Hurlbut called a "biological artifact" that produces pluripotent stem cells. But would this artifact really just be a damaged human embryo?

Lastly, the Council considered a proposal to reprogram somatic cells back into pluripotent cells, that is, cells at the embryonic stage. The Council found no ethical problem with such a procedure, only purely scientific obstacles. One year later, a Japanese lab was able to overcome those obstacles, and in 2012, that lab received the Nobel Prize for doing so.[67]

Fudging Fetal Pain

Researchers working on cures and treatments and to spare embryonic lives are really the ones living in the "evidence-based" world because they understand that "can" does not necessarily equal "should"—and they do not ignore, as the Left often does, the "Ph" part of Ph.D. It's the Left and its "scientific" allies who deny the evidence when it doesn't fit their agenda. Take the issue of fetal pain. Not only has science shown that the unborn child is more than a blob of tissue, it has shown that she has fingers and toes and a heart within days of conception, and that she can actually feel pain. The implications are obvious. Americans don't want puppies to feel pain, so if they can be convinced the unborn child feels pain, then enthusiasm for abortion may wane. Therefore, abortion advocates are keen to deny fetal pain.

Some states have considered legislation requiring abortionists to inform women seeking abortions that the unborn child might feel pain.[68] And legislation at both state and federal level has been proposed to make it illegal to abort after the twentieth week of gestation, the time at which it can be demonstrated that the unborn child feels pain.[69] There's a very real possibility that this kind of legislation could provide the opportunity for the Supreme Court to limit abortion itself for the first time since *Roe v. Wade*. The threat to our current regime of abortion on demand is obvious.

Naturally, the abortion lobby and their friends in the ideologically driven professional guilds have gone ballistic.

The paper they most often cite to deny that fetuses feel pain is one published in 2005 in the *Journal of the American Medical Association*.[70] And even in that study, the authors admit the unborn child has pain receptors throughout her entire body by the sixteenth week of gestation, and that they are linked to key parts of the brain no later than the twentieth week. Nonetheless the authors deny that the unborn child can feel pain until it has a functioning cerebral cortex. In fact, scientific evidence discovered since that time has demonstrated that having the hypothalamus alone is sufficient for an unborn child to feel pain.[71]

Other claims of the pain-deniers include the suggestion that the unborn child lies in a kind of coma and cannot feel pain—though in fact the unborn child moves, sucks her thumb, and—in cases of fetal surgery—must be sedated to prevent her from thrashing around.[72]

The most revealing fact about the pain-deniers, especially those who produced the report published by the *Journal of the American Medical Association*, is who they were. The *New York Times* reported at the time that two of the five authors had failed to tell the *Journal of the American Medical Association* about their professional affiliations.[73] It turns out they were not objective medical and scientific professionals, but in fact advocates. The lead author, Susan Lee, had been an attorney with the pro-abortion group NARAL. One of the other authors was the medical director of an abortion clinic. In other words, they had a vested interest in denying fetal pain.

Dodgy Data on Planned Parenthood's Abortion Business

I will close with a final note about Planned Parenthood and one of the most deceptive messages they have promulgated in the media in recent years: that they are not really in the abortion business at all. Abortion has fallen into such disrepute in recent years that even Planned Parenthood has had to resort to denying they have much to do with it. They now claim that only 3 percent of their work is abortions.

In the winter of 2016, rap star Nick Cannon came under fire when he said Planned Parenthood was in the business of eugenics and wiping out the black race. He was excoriated by his black sisters, who said he did not know what he was talking about. *Everyone* knows Planned Parenthood's business is only 3 percent abortion. That is how far the pro-aborts' talking points have traveled, all the way to a pop news show called TMZ.[74]

Planned Parenthood has annual revenues of $1 billion, so 3 percent would still be $30 million, which is plenty. But they want you to think what a smidgen of $1 billion that is. In reality, that 3 percent is of their total *transactions*, not their total *revenue*.

This is how they make abortion look like a much smaller part of their business than it really is. Let's say a young woman walks into a

Planned Parenthood seeking an abortion. She gets a pregnancy test. Gets a blood test. Has her blood pressure measured. On her way out the door she's given a brochure, a prescription for contraceptive pills, a prescription for emergency contraception, and maybe a packet of condoms. A few days later she comes back for the abortion. She gets her blood pressure taken once more. Another blood test. She is given anesthesia. She gets an abortion. And more birth control pills. Planned Parenthood counts every single one of these "services" as a *separate transaction*. The abortion is reimbursed by the state at the rate of $500 or more and everything else is pennies, but the $500 abortion is counted the same as the essentially free blood-pressure test. See how that works? In fact, no matter what Planned Parenthood says, at least a third of their billion-dollar revenue is generated from their abortion business.[75] And that's not just conservatives talking. Leftwing *Slate* agrees.[76]

Planned Parenthood is desperate to separate itself from its abortion business in the mind of the public because the pro-life movement has been quite successful in changing America's mind about abortion. According to the Gallup organization, in 1995 only 33 percent of Americans self-identified as pro-life. In recent years, that number has topped 50 percent.[77]

And then David Daleiden began releasing his remarkable undercover videos in the summer of 2015. Keep in mind that the sale of fetal tissue, which is documented in the videos, is against federal law, and the penalties can be severe: massive fines and jail time.[78] Daleiden's videos, released every Wednesday that summer, were played on television news coast to coast. For the first time ever, it appeared that Planned Parenthood was on the defensive.

Planned Parenthood had long counted on the public perception that it was in the business of family planning, cancer screenings, and the like. And now, the public was seeing that not only was Planned Parenthood in the abortion business, it was also in the abortion after-market, selling what were all too clearly actual baby parts.

Public support for Planned Parenthood began to plummet. Bills in state legislatures called for defunding the group. Some passed, though some of them were overturned by federal courts. And here is how Planned Parenthood employees defended what was obviously negotiation for the sale of fetal body parts: they were only negotiating the *remuneration of expenses*, which is allowed under federal law. But why would that have to be negotiated? Wouldn't these Planned Parenthood personnel know the cost of cutting out a baby's liver and putting it in an iced cooler for transport?

But no lie is too big for an organization that was founded as a eugenics project of Margaret Sanger, an out-and-out racist who wanted to cull the less-than-desirables from society. Today, Planned Parenthood's abortion clinics are largely located in poor black and Latino communities. But then, they lie about that, too.[79]

One of the most shameful things about legal abortion is the complicity of the scientific and medical profession in all the lies. Scientists deny the abortion–breast cancer link. Scientists deny the psychological trauma women go through after abortion. Scientists deny the humanity of the unborn child; they deny when human life begins; and they deny fetal pain. One is reminded of the shame of the medical and scientific community during the Third Reich.

CHAPTER 5

Never Mind the Herpes, Full Speed Ahead

Healthy, Happy and Hot is a brochure Planned Parenthood made available to a closed-door meeting of teen and younger Girl Scouts at the United Nations during the UN's annual Commission on the Status of Women in March 2010.

The brochure, which is still widely distributed by Planned Parenthood, explains how kids can have great sex even if they are infected with the HIV virus: "Sex can feel great and can be really fun! Many people think sex is just about vaginal or anal intercourse...But, there are lots of different ways to have sex and lots of different types of sex. Sex can include kissing, touching, licking, tickling, sucking, and cuddling. Some people like to have aggressive sex, while others like to have soft and slow sex with their partners. There is no right or wrong way to have sex. Just have fun, explore and be yourself!"[1]

Also, "Some people have sex when they have been drinking alcohol or using drugs. This is your choice.... If you want to have sex and think you might get drunk or high, plan ahead by bringing condoms and lube or putting them close to where you usually have sex."

It's not like there are no rules in Healthy-Happy-and-Hot-Sex Land. Your target—that is, partner—has to at least be conscious: "It is not okay to have sex with someone who is so drunk or high that they are staggering, incoherent or have passed out." They can be rippingly high or drunk, but they can't be incoherent.

In 2015, the Centers for Disease Control (CDC) reported that the United States is experiencing an epidemic of sexually transmitted diseases (STDs).[2] The CDC estimates that there are twenty million new cases of STDs every single year and that half of them are among those fifteen to twenty-four years old. There are a total of 110 million new and existing cases of STDs in the United States. That is a third of our total population.

Syphilis ran rampant through the middle of the twentieth century, but with the discovery of antibiotics it was slowly being eliminated. It is now making a comeback. According to the CDC, there is also a strain of something called *Neisseria gonorrhoeae* that doctors are running out of options to treat. They estimate that the U.S. healthcare system is burdened each year by $16 billion in treatments related to STDs.[3]

Doubling Down on Disaster

Welcome to the Sexual Revolution. And if you ask a sexual revolutionary—that is, almost anyone on the Left—they will say the solution is just a little bit more—more condoms, more injectable contraceptives, more "comprehensive" sex education, more sex toys, more "sex positivity," and less judgment, man.

The Sexual Revolution was launched two hundred years ago with the promise that mankind would finally be happy once sexuality could be freely expressed outside the shackles of the family and traditional religion. But we can all see the misery it created—rampant divorce, sexual addiction, hard-core pornography, epidemics of STDs, HIV–AIDs deaths by the hundreds of thousands, even abortions can be placed in their column of success—and they say all they need is a little bit more to show how happy we can be if we are sexually free.

In 2010, the United Nations sponsored a World Youth Conference in Leon, Mexico, where youth delegates released a statement calling for access to contraceptives and abortion and an end to discrimination based on sexual preference, sexual identity, and sexual orientation. Conference displays included one from Planned Parenthood that featured the *Healthy, Happy and Hot* brochure. A booth sponsored by Fundacion Collectivo de Mujeres Jovenes "consisted almost entirely of thongs," reported one of my C-Fam colleagues. Yet another booth presented demonstrations of how to put a condom on a phallus; another had postcards that can only be described as pornographic.[4]

All they want is a little bit more sexual liberation, and then we can all finally be happy. And it has to start with the youth, to catch them as early as possible so they won't get away into the traditional morality that has been proven to be harmful to pleasure and happiness.

But their campaign is all built on phony science, wacky theory, and fraud.

Making the Marquis de Sade Their Model

Keep in mind, from its beginning two centuries ago, those who have advanced the Sexual Revolution have been considered the most advanced thinkers of their times. The most important figure in the nascent Sexual Revolution was the Marquis de Sade (d. 1814), whose pornographic and sadomasochistic activities not only caused a sensation and landed him in jail or asylum for thirty-three of his seventy-four years; they also launched a movement that reverberates to this day.

The marquis was a notorious rapist and sadist, charged with drugging, kidnapping, torturing, and raping women. His victims were prostitutes and even women he happened to meet along the street. It was while serving what turned out to be a fourteen-year prison sentence—at the urging of his mother-in-law, no less—that he read all of Voltaire, along with other Enlightenment authors. And it was while he was imprisoned in the Bastille that de Sade wrote his most famous work, *Justine, or The Misfortunes of Virtue*, the story of a young girl from her twelfth to her twenty-sixth year who finds her way alone in a sexually rapacious society. She is set upon and corrupted by the abbess of a convent, and later held as a sex slave in a monastery. Oddly, the marquis projected his own sexual proclivities upon the Church, which he sought to undermine and destroy.

The marquis is also said to have played a role in instigating the French Revolution, for he shouted from the Bastille to the mobs below on July 2, 1789, that prisoners were having their throats slashed. Twelve days later the Bastille was stormed and the Revolution was on. The mobs did not find the marquis there. He was already gone, moved to an insane asylum. What they found was his quite comfortable apartment with six hundred books, sheaves of his own writings, and pornographic tapestries on the walls.

The work of the Marquis de Sade became required reading for sexual revolutionaries throughout the ages. Byron and Swinburne both owned copies. His work was praised by Aldous Huxley in his book *Ends and Means*. Francine du Plessix Gray actually wrote a book called *At Home with the Marquis de Sade*. Filmmaker Pier Paolo Pasolini made a movie supposedly based on de Sade's lost manuscript *120 Days of Sodomy*, which shows the four-month-long sexual torture and murder of eighteen teenagers. The French surrealists called de Sade "the Divine Marquis."

To realize how complete has been the victory of the Marquis de Sade, consider that the sadomasochistic novel *50 Shades of Grey* has become a global sensation, selling 125 million copies and having been translated into fifty-two languages. The movie—made for a paltry $40 million—grossed half a billion worldwide.

One could go step by step through the two centuries since the Divine Marquis and the French Revolution to the present-day holocaust of disease and death that must be laid at the altar of the Sexual Revolution.

There was Alexandra Kollontai of the Russian Revolution, who championed "legalized divorce and abortion, established communal houses, and promoted free love to liberate women from the 'choice between marriage and prostitution.'" According to Kollontai, "The home fire is going out in all classes and strata of the population, and of course no artificial measures will fan its fading flame." She sounds remarkably like present-day academics calling for the end of man-woman marriage.[5]

There is Margaret Sanger, who led a riotous private life and publicly championed the causes of contraception, abortion, and a culling of the races. And there is Margaret Mead, who went to Samoa and lied to Americans, saying that the natives showed her that a state of nature includes free and unashamed sex. Lesser names would include behaviorist John Watson and public relations guru Edward Bernays.

In 1913, Bernays—the nephew of Sigmund Freud—was living in Greenwich Village and editing the *Medical Review of Reviews*. Note the veneer of science. It was a time ripe for the Sexual Revolution. One New York editor called it "sex-o'clock in America."[6]

When Bernays received a manuscript from French playwright Eugène Brieux called *Damaged Goods*, about a syphilitic man who fathers a syphilitic child, Bernays decided to produce the play as a way to "fight sex pruriency in the United States."[7] Bernays also created one of the first front groups in America, called the Sociological Fund Committee. He received financial support from hundreds of the wealthy enlightened, including John D. Rockefeller Jr. and Franklin and Eleanor Roosevelt. Bernays went on to an illustrative career and is now known as the "father of public relations." As he said, "It all started with sex."[8]

Following the Frankfurt School over a Cliff

The Cultural Marxists of the Frankfurt School were vitally important to the development of the Sexual Revolution, and they were a direct link between the old Left of the Bolshevik Revolution and what came to be known as the New Left of the 1960s.[9] Chief among them was sex-mad

Wilhelm Reich, the man credited with coining the term "Sexual Revolution" in 1936—a revolution that, he said, "no power on earth can stop."

Reich, who had worked for Sigmund Freud in Vienna—some have called him Freud's most brilliant student—used to massage his nude patients. In 1920s Vienna, he advocated contraceptives, abortion, and divorce. Though a Marxist, he believed that economic Marxism was held back by the sexual repression of the proletariat. In *The Function of the Orgasm*, first published in 1927, he said, "There is only one thing wrong with neurotic patients: the lack of full and repeated sexual satisfaction."[10]

Before World War II, Reich came to the United States, where he discovered a mysterious force, a biological energy he called "orgone," what others called "God." He eventually built the "Orgone Energy Accumulator." Even the novelist Saul Bellow got one and sat in it every day. So did Norman Mailer, J. D. Salinger, Jack Kerouac, Dwight MacDonald, and William S. Burroughs.[11] Under the influence of Reich, Dwight MacDonald hosted nude cocktail parties and orgies at his Cape Cod retreat. Mailer even built several Orgone Energy Accumulators. So influential was this machine that Woody Allen spoofed it as the "Orgasmatron" in his futuristic 1973 comedy *Sleeper*. Publisher James Atlas has said, "Reich's *Function of the Orgasm* was as widely read in progressive circles as Trotsky's *Art and Revolution* had been a decade before." In 1947, *Harper's* magazine identified Reich as the leader of a "new cult of sex and anarchy."

Reich died of a heart attack in prison in 1957. He had been jailed for selling his machine, which authorities rightly saw as a fraud. But that didn't stop the 1960s zeitgeist from becoming thoroughly enamored of Reich. In 1964, *Time* magazine said, "Dr. William Reich may have been a prophet. For now, it sometimes seems that all American is one big orgone box."[12] And this was before the Pill and the real onset of the Sexual Revolution.

During the student riots of 1968 in Paris and Berlin, students threw copies of his *The Mass Psychology of Fascism* at the cops. They scrawled the author's name on walls. "Read Reich and act accordingly," it was said.[13]

Someone who was plowing the same furrow at roughly the same time, but who had even more impact than Reich, was Dr. Alfred Kinsey.

Making "Science" by Molesting Infants

We have already met Dr. Kinsey as the "scientist" who published data about the sexual abuse of infants. The man was a criminal. His "scientific research" included the work of a mysterious Mr. X who oversaw the sexual abuse of babies in the crib, measuring their sexual responses to their abuse.[14]

And his "research" became the "scientific" justification for the sexual explosion that started in earnest in the 1960s and continues unabated to this day. Wilhelm Reich said it was a revolution that could not be stopped. It appears that he was right.

Kinsey was a sexual freak. From an early age, he was known to insert objects into his penis, starting with drinking straws and working his way up to toothbrushes, a practice he continued his whole life.[15]

Like *Population Bomb* author Paul Ehrlich, Kinsey was trained in entomology, that is, the study of insects. There's nothing quite like seeing your human subjects as not all that different from bugs.

He wasn't the first sexologist—that field of study had started in Austria in the early twentieth century—but he was certainly the most important. In 1947, Kinsey founded the Institute for Sex Research at Indiana University and a year later published the first of two books that would utterly change America: *Sexual Behavior in the Human Male*.[16] He followed this five years later with *Sexual Behavior in the Human Female*.[17]

Among his most important "discoveries," one you hear repeated endlessly even today in debates about human sexuality, is the so-called Kinsey scale, which places human sexual responses on a scale: zero meaning exclusively heterosexual and six meaning exclusively homosexual, with gradations between. The idea is that human sexuality is a continuum, and that no point along the continuum is any better or worse than any other.

Take number two on the scale. It is labeled as *predominantly* heterosexual, which is a tick above *incidentally* homosexual. But how do you measure only "incidental" homosexuality? Well, you can't. But this is supposed to be science, then and now.

Kinsey wrote, "Males do not represent two discrete populations, heterosexual and homosexual. The world is not to be divided into sheep and goats. It is a fundamental of taxonomy that nature rarely deals with discrete categories.... The living world is a continuum in each and every one of its aspects. While emphasizing the continuity of the gradations between exclusively heterosexual and exclusively homosexual histories, it has seemed desirable to develop some sort of classification which could be based on the relative amounts of heterosexual and homosexual experience or response in each history.... An individual may be assigned a position on this scale, for each period in his life."[18]

After Kinsey's first book came out, kids could never look at their fathers or grandfathers in quite the same way again. Where they may have thought their fathers were pillars of rectitude, they now "discovered" that all men were sexually rapacious perverts.

As Kinsey's "research" supposedly showed,

- A whopping 10–37 percent committed homosexual acts
- Fourteen percent performed and 30 percent received homosexual oral sex with climax at least once
- Ninety-four percent had committed adultery
- Eleven percent of married men had participated in anal sodomy at least once
- Fifty percent responded sexually to being—wait for it— bitten!
- Fifty percent of farm boys had sex with animals, 17 percent to orgasm

As Judith Reisman, who did extensive research into Kinsey's phony research and horrifying life, writes, "Although bestiality is not natural behavior, Kinsey argued that even this was normal for human beings."[19] Kinsey wrote, "With most males, animal contacts represent a passing Chapter in the sexual history." Note that "with most males." He said, "such activities are biologically and psychologically part of the normal mammalian picture."[20]

Kinsey is perhaps most famous for creating the notion that a significant percentage of the population is homosexual. The percentage most associated with him is 10 percent, though this is not a claim that he ever made directly, but it's a number pieced together from his work. And as we have seen, that number has actually increased in the public's imagination. According to recent Gallup polling, Americans now believe that 25 to 30 percent of us are homosexual.[21]

The 10 percent claim was created by an early homosexual activist named Bruce Voeller, who founded the National Gay Task Force and led the first delegation of homosexuals to the White House in 1977 to meet with representatives of President Jimmy Carter.[22] Voeller took Kinsey's already shaky social science and arrived at that utterly phony number.

According to Kinsey's research, 7 percent of men and 13 percent of women were predominantly homosexual. So Voeller split the difference. Voila, 10 percent of Americans were homosexual. Voeller knew this number was phony. In 1990, four years before he died of AIDS, he said, "The concept that 10% of the population is gay has become a generally accepted 'fact.' As with so many pieces of knowledge (and myths), repeated telling made it so."[23]

As we have seen, subsequent more robust—you might say authentic—research from the CDC shows the true number of homosexuals is much smaller. In fact, it is vanishingly small, at no more than 1.6 percent of the adult population, which translates into a few million in the whole country.[24]

The importance of the phony 10 percent number is that it fed into the myth, also created by Voeller, that homosexuals "are everywhere."

Would same-sex marriage be the law of the land today if Americans had known that gays aren't in fact "everywhere"?

Among many underlying problems with Kinsey's work is his methodology. Kinsey was researching in a largely closeted society, so it was nearly impossible for him to find a body of homosexuals large enough to do truly scientific research. We have also seen how it is nearly impossible to determine who exactly would qualify as a homosexual. Moreover, his studies were not longitudinal; they did not follow subjects over a course of years. At best, his studies were furtive snapshots of men who were not even remotely representative of the larger population. He was reduced to interviewing such shadowy figures he was able to scrounge up, including men who were in prison for sexual assault, and homosexual prostitutes. It was impossible to make any kind of reliable social science projections for all of society based on such a sample.

And then there were the clinical observations for which he and his researchers should have gone to jail. As Dr. John Bancroft, emeritus director of the Kinsey Institute, has said, Kinsey was "particularly interested in the observation of adults who had been sexually involved with children."[25] The notorious Table 34 in Kinsey's book on male sexuality cites the sexual responses of children—the horrific sexual abuse of infants was the "scientific data" used to show that children are "sexual" from birth.

The impact of Kinsey's work is immeasurable. He has been lionized in popular culture—his work landed him on the front page of *Time* magazine back when that really meant something, with a drawing of him next to a bee pollinating a flower—and his phony, criminal "research" was used as the "scientific evidence" justifying changing hundreds of laws regulating sexual behavior.

According to Westlaw, the most widely used legal database, between 1980 and 2000 there were 650 citations of Kinsey's work. Major law journals have cited him dozens of times. The Supreme Court relied on his work when it imposed abortion on all fifty states. His work was cited in amicus briefs when the Supreme Court made homosexual sodomy a constitutional right in *Lawrence v. Texas*, the case that opened the door to homosexual marriage.

Attacking Innocence

Among Kinsey's most pernicious ideas—one that has taken firm root among scientific advocates—is that children are sexual from the earliest age. Kinsey acolyte Dr. Mary Calderone, who founded something called SIECUS (Sexuality Information and Education Council of the United States) teaches that children are sexual beings from birth and even before birth—she talks about boys being sexually aroused in utero.[26] The group she founded is highly influential, promoting what they call "comprehensive sexuality education," which is now promoted in UN documents and reports. These pernicious ideas are expressed in a UNESCO document called *International Technical Guidelines on Sexuality Education: An Evidence-Informed Approach for Schools, Teachers and Health Educators.*[27] Note how the Left's ideas are always "evidence-based," even if the evidence is tainted by criminality or phony science.

Note that UNESCO is the UN's *scientific* body. This leftist sexual ideology is considered "science" by UNESCO.

The document gives the following advice—for children zero to four years of age:

- Give information about enjoyment and pleasure when touching one's body...masturbation
- Enable children to gain an awareness of gender identity
- Give the right to explore gender identity

Four- to six-year-olds should receive "information about early childhood masturbation, same-sex relationships, different concepts of family, respect for different norms regarding sexuality."

By nine years old, kids should be learning about "different types of contraception, masturbation and orgasm, and sexual rights," according to the document.

By age twelve, kids are taught about "coming out as homosexual," and by fifteen they are taught about gestational surrogacy and how to fight homophobia in themselves and others (that means you and me and certainly their mothers and fathers).

(Re)Defining Discrimination to Further the Sexual Revolution

In 2006, a gaggle of leftwing lawyers—the International Commission of Jurists—and "human rights activists" met on Java to develop and publish a document called the Yogyakarta Principles, calling for the incorporation of "sexual orientation and gender identity" (SOGI) into every aspect of the Universal Declaration of Human Rights and all other UN human rights instruments.[28]

The activists wrote the document as a blueprint for including SOGI in binding international law—on par with other widely accepted categories against which discrimination is illegal, such as race, religion, and national origin.

While the Principles are no more than an activists' document, they have been cited dozens of times by legal authorities, including UN treaty-monitoring bodies. In fact, the UN Secretary General Ban Ki-moon insisted that SOGI is now a part of international law, even though member states have never even voted on it.[29]

This is the full-blown Sexual Revolution as envisioned by everyone from Voltaire to the Marquis de Sade to Soviet theoreticians to Hugh Hefner, Margaret Sanger, Alfred Kinsey, and on down to the present day to entertainers like Miley Cyrus and Katy Perry. In fact, the original progenitors of the Sexual Revolution likely never dreamed this big.

Letting the Liberation Take Its Toll

And what are the fruits of all this marvelous sexual liberation? It is estimated—it is impossible to know since several states, including abortion-mad California, refuse to release their statistics—that there are more than one million abortions a year, though they reached a high of 1.6 million in 1994. So in the United States alone there have been more than sixty million abortions since abortion-on-demand was imposed by the Supreme Court.

And the massive numbers of abortions can be attributed to the Sexual Revolution. Before the attacks on marriage and family began, before the revolution of widespread contraception and abortion, before the divorce culture of the 1960s and beyond, these women would not have been having so much sex outside of marriage. And if they did get pregnant, they likely would have married the baby's father.

And then consider pornography. Porn is the most searched topic on the Internet. It is utterly mainstream, accessible everywhere, even at the playground and on public library computers, where the librarians refuse to do anything about it on First Amendment grounds. So ubiquitous has pornography become that a 2007 survey by the American Management Association and the ePolicy Journal reported that "65% of corporations use porn-detecting software, up from 40 percent in 2001."[30] According to the same survey, of the 30 percent of bosses who fired someone for misuse of the Internet, 84 percent fired someone for use of porn.[31] According to the proceedings of the 2002 meeting of the American Academy of Matrimonial Lawyers, 62 percent said Internet porn played a significant role in the divorce cases they handled that year. And that was fifteen years ago. The number must be even higher now as more and more pornography, and of a harder-core variety, has come onto the Internet.

This is the Sexual Revolution. If you do not think so, suggest to a liberal friend that pornography is a problem and that it harms the people who use it. They will likely accuse you of wanting to violate the First Amendment—or just laugh at the idea that porn harms the people who use it. In fact, though not many people know this, most pornography produced today, with its images of penetration and ejaculation, is a violation of federal law against obscenity.[32] But though that law has been repeatedly upheld by the Supreme Court, it is rarely enforced.

Divorce rates are not as high as they were in the 1970s, but they are still high by historical standards. That is more fallout of the Sexual Revolution, which told married couples they could find true happiness right around that sexual corner in someone else's bed.

Most black kids are now born into a family without a father. And white kids are now closing in on this level of pathology, which no child would choose.

Enabling Epidemic STDs

And then there is the epidemic of STDs that opened this chapter. According to the CDC, we have never seen anything like what is happening now. Old diseases that we thought we had controlled are making a huge comeback. And nobody ever heard of cancer-causing *Human papillomavirus* thirty years ago; now it is so rampant among young people that public schools are pushing an immunization program on kids as young as nine.[33]

New strains of gonorrhea are coming, with no means to cure them. HIV–AIDS has also made a huge comeback in the gay community, mostly among young men who see their lifestyle as a sexual banquet just like their long-dead elders. According to the most recent report from the CDC, homosexual men account for 83 percent of the estimated new HIV diagnoses among all males aged thirteen and older and 67 percent of the total new diagnoses in the United States.[34]

It is impossible to know the total body count of the Sexual Revolution, just as it is impossible to know exactly how many were killed by Stalin, Hitler, and Mao Tse-tung. Taken together, however, it is estimated that the deaths these tyrants were responsible for is somewhere north of a hundred million. The Sexual Revolution dwarfs that. Counting more than a hundred million abortions worldwide, deaths from AIDs, and deaths from other STDs, the Sexual Revolution boasts—if you can call it that—the highest body count of any tyrant or revolution the world has ever known. And it was all—supposedly—based on science, social science, and statistics, and all to set men free.

So at this point what do the revolutionaries want? They want more, of course. They deny any responsibility for all the carnage. The disease and death can all be fixed with more sex ed and increased access to contraception. They insist that people simply do not have access to contraception, and if they do, they do not know how to use it. They say that pornography is healthy and good for relationships. They've invented a new term called "sex positive," and they hold "sex weeks" on the campuses of Ivy League schools. Against all evidence, they suggest the hookup culture is just fine for college boys and girls.

The sexual revolutionary's argument is a lot like the one that Western fellow travelers of the Soviet Union used to make. There was failure and misery throughout the Marxist world: starvation, corruption, human rights abuses, shortages, and misery. But all they needed was a *little bit more* Marxism, and then the world would see that Marxism was the answer. It hadn't *really* been tried. In precisely the same way, the Sexual Revolution may not be working out all that well, but it really hasn't been tried because of all those bluenoses holding us back. All we need is a little bit more. And less judgment, man.

CHAPTER 6

The Grand Experiment on the Children

I n his book *32 Yolks*, Eric Ripert, head chef and owner of Michelin-three-starred Le Bernardin in New York City, tells the story of his parents' divorce when he was five years old: "I went from being a happy kid to a kind of pint-sized depressive. From the time I was five until I went away to cooking school and for many years after, I was rarely truly happy—just different degrees of sad."[1]

Ripert says that from the moment his parents split up, when he was with his mother, he missed his father; when he was with his father, he missed his mother; when he was with his grandparents, he missed them both. His parents' divorce has haunted him his whole life. This is a man who runs one of the most celebrated restaurants in the world. He has his own television show, a wife, and a family; yet his memoir is largely a cry of the heart about his parents' divorce.

Ask almost any child of divorce and you will hear the same story. Or ask any donor-conceived child—who wonders *Who is my father? What is he like? Am I like him? Is he like me? Will I ever know him?*

Every child raised without one parent—whether a child of divorce, a donor baby, or someone growing up in a gay or lesbian family—asks, *Where is my father? Will he ever come back for me?* Or *Where is my mother? Didn't she ever love me?*

Gay men and lesbians want you to believe that the children they raise do not have these questions. They do not long for their mother or their father—whichever is missing from their lives. Gay men and lesbians want you to know that the children they raise are just as happy, just as well adjusted, exactly the same as children raised by their biological mothers and fathers.

Pretending It's All Pretty

The cynical defense of gay parenting has taken center stage in the national debate about marriage and family. Essential to the argument is the pretense that all lesbians and gays want are cute little houses with white picket fences, little league games, PTA meetings, and yard sales. Of course they can be parents—and just as good parents as anyone else! And they have tons of social "science" to show that there is no difference in outcomes between kids raised by two men and kids raised by their biological moms and dads.

The whole discussion is really a sideshow because there simply are not that many gays in America to begin with—as we have seen, there are more Methodists. Stable gay couples are even more rare, and vanishingly small—in fact, practically nonexistent—is the number of gay couples who raise a child together from babyhood through college. There is hardly a large enough sample to measure. But that has not stopped the gay advocates, the academy, and the mainstream media from insisting that the science is settled. They maintain there is no difference in outcomes between children raised in gay households and those raised in homes with their own moms and dads.

In fact, the science actually shows that anything less than the gold standard for children—being raised by their married biological mother and father—is detrimental to the child. But that doesn't stop the advocates from claiming that science is on their side.

An influential 2005 brief produced by the American Psychological Association cited no less than fifty-nine studies in support of the thesis that children raised by gays and lesbians turn out just as well as children raised by their biological mothers and fathers. In fact, some of the studies claimed lesbian moms are even better. The brief concluded: "In summary, there is no evidence to suggest that lesbian women or gay men are unfit to be parents or that psychosocial development among children of lesbian women or gay men is compromised relative to that among offspring of heterosexual parents. Not a single study has found children of lesbian or gay parents to be disadvantaged in any significant respect relative to children of heterosexual parents. Indeed, the evidence to date suggests that home environments provided by lesbian and gay parents are as likely as those provided by heterosexual parents to support and enable children's psychosocial growth."[2]

In 2015, the Columbia Law School published a paper examining "78 scholarly papers" published since 1985. Among those that met the law school's criteria of "adding to knowledge about the wellbeing of children with gay or lesbian parents," only four of seventy-eight concluded that children raised by gays or lesbians faced any special difficulties. All the rest concluded that same-sex parenting was fine. And the Columbia paper criticized the four outliers because the children in those studies all came from "broken homes."[3] Apparently, the science is settled.

There was even a study out of Australia that concluded children raised by same-sex couples are happier and heathier than their peers.[4] It showed that children of same-sex couples scored higher "on general health and family cohesion." On other health issues, such as "emotional behavior and physical functioning, there was no difference compared with children from the general population."[5]

And of course, the message percolated into the popular press. In 2009, the *New York Times Magazine* ran a short piece called "What's Good for the Kids" that—while it bemoaned the lack of good data to prove it—reiterated what everyone already knows: gay parenting is just fine. The writer cited Clark University's Abbie Goldberg, who assured us in so many words, "These children do just fine."[6] Goldberg had just published her own analysis of one hundred studies purportedly showing that children raised by lesbians and gays are not markedly different—except in a good way. They are "less conventional and more flexible when it comes to gender roles and assumptions than those raised in more traditional families."[7] Little girls raised by lesbians, for instance, are more likely to want to be doctors and lawyers than little girls raised by moms and dads.

In June 2015, two days before the Supreme Court handed down its gay marriage edict, the *Washington Post* ran a story with the headline, "How Kids Became the Strongest Argument for Same-Sex Marriage."[8]

Built on Bias

But while in any conversation about gay parenting, you will hear that science shows us there is no difference—the science is settled—as a matter of fact, none of the studies that purport to show that there is no difference between the two groups of children meets the basic requirements for robust social science research. The "scientific" findings that advocates and the pro-gay media cite tend to come from convenience samples.[9] That is, these are "studies" on subjects that have not been gathered randomly. Instead, they're done on decidedly unrepresentative samples that have been collected from places like bulletin boards at gay parenting support groups, where everyone has an interest in proving that gay parenting is a success. Moreover, even if the samples were not put together for the convenience of the campaign to normalize homosexual parenting, the numbers are inevitably tiny, so that the findings cannot be projected accurately to larger populations.[10]

Even worse, these "no differences" studies tend to interview the parents rather than the kids. It is inevitable that gay parents are going to say their kids are doing just fine—particularly if they know that it is their own gay parenting that is being measured.

Finally, most important, each of these no-differences studies tends to compare gay parenting not to the intact biological two-parent household—

the gold standard for positive outcomes—but rather to other damaged households: single parents, divorced and stepparents, and cohabiting parents.[11] Even liberal social scientists, including those friendly to gay marriage, agree that anything less than intact biological families tends to work to the detriment of children.[12]

Setting the Record Straight

Two social scientists—Mark Regnerus of the University of Texas and Paul Sullins of Catholic University of America—have done the most robust work in examining the "no differences" thesis and the "scientific" studies that purport to back it up.

Among the many valuable aspects of Mark Regnerus's work is the fact that he actually interviewed young adults—2,988 of them—rather than the parents who raised them. This allowed the children to speak for themselves. What's more, the study compares lesbian-raised and gay-male-raised children to children raised in intact biological families, not just to children from other non-standard and broken homes. Finally, the Regnerus study drew from a large random sample—insofar as that is even possible when studying the vanishingly rare phenomenon of stable gay couples raising children from birth to maturity.[13]

Regnerus has come under vicious attack for his New Family Structures Study. He has been accused of using small samples—when the real problem is that there are hardly any children raised for any length of time in intact gay relationships for him to study. The dearth of gay couples raising children in a stable situation is a factor of how gay relationships tend to be formed and how they (don't) last. As Ana Samuel put it in *Public Discourse*, "The study found that the children who were raised by a gay or lesbian parent as little as 15 years ago were usually conceived within a heterosexual marriage, which then underwent divorce or separation, leaving the child with a single parent."[14]

Only 23 percent of respondents said that they had lived for at least three years in the same household with their own mother and their mother's lesbian partner. Only *two* out of *fifteen thousand* persons who were initially screened lived for eighteen years with the same two mothers. And of those who reported their father had a same-sex romantic relationship, only 1.1 percent reported living in the same household with both fathers for at least three years.[15]

Regnerus's study got the blame for these sad but true facts about gay and lesbian relationships, which social science has shown are inherently unstable and not long lasting.[16] But this inherent instability was hardly *his* fault.

In any case, Regnerus reported startling results about same-sex parenting. While there is not a great deal of difference between children raised by lesbians and gays and those raised in single-parent, divorced, and step-parented families, he found significant differences when he compared them to children raised in homes with their own biological mothers and fathers.

Children raised by lesbians were almost four times more likely to be on public assistance and 3.5 times more likely to be unemployed. Children raised by lesbians had a higher propensity for criminal behavior, and the average criminality of children raised by gay men was even higher.

Children raised by gays were three times more likely to have been touched sexually by a parent or other adults—and those raised by lesbians were *eleven* times more likely to have experienced this kind of sexual abuse. Children raised by gay men reported being forced into sex against their will at three times the rate of children raised by their biological parents, and children raised by lesbians were *four times* as likely to have been forced into sex.

Children raised by gays were three times more likely to have a sexually transmitted disease; children raised by lesbians were 2.5 times more likely. Children raised by lesbians reported the lowest level of safety in the home, followed by children raised by gays.

The news was so bad for gay parenting that the only thing to do was to attack the messenger, and that is just what the gay-positive academic world proceeded to do. They pushed for the University of Texas to fire Regnerus, but the university declined to do so. They demanded the revocation of the paper, also to no avail. They pulled out all the stops to sully

Regnerus's reputation, which sadly they achieved. On the Left, in the pro-gay media, and to many in the academy, he is now "the discredited Mark Regnerus."

And yet his work is the best actual science we have on the question of gay parenting. What's more, Regnerus's results have been replicated by Paul Sullins. Sullins, who is both a tenured professor of sociology and a Catholic priest—a juicy avenue of attack for his enemies—has published a study based on the national data set from the *National Longitudinal Study of Adolescent Health*, which experts call "one of the most impressive, thorough, and expensive survey research efforts still ongoing."[17] The study tracks subjects over time—over decades, in fact—asking them the same questions as they age. This approach is critical because some problems only reveal themselves later in life.

The Sullins study, published in the online *Journal of Depression Research and Treatment*, drives the final nail in the no-differences theory of gay parenthood.

Sullins found that children raised by lesbians and gays were less prone to depression than children raised in intact biological families, *but only during adolescence*. By the fourth wave of the survey—that is, when the respondents were between twenty-four and thirty-two years old—*more than 50 percent* of the young adults raised by lesbians or gays were reporting ongoing depression, an increase of 33 percent from their younger years. Depression among the young adults who had been raised in intact biological homes had decreased from 22 percent to 20 percent.[18]

Obesity has become another massive problem for adult children of lesbians and gays. Fully 72 percent of them reported it as a problem, while only 31 percent of adult children of opposite-sex couples did. Seventy-three percent of children raised by lesbians and gays felt "distant from one or both parents." While suicide ideation declined for those raised by lesbians or gays over time, from 43.5 percent to 30.1 percent, these numbers were still far higher than for their counterparts raised by opposite-sex couples (13.6 percent versus 7.1 percent).

Like Regnerus, Sullins came under vicious attack. *Slate* called his work a "dishonest assault on LGBTQ families."[19] *The Atlantic* said the study "revealed more about the researcher than his subject."[20] ThinkProgress called it a "hugely flawed" study.[21] Overnight, Sullins, longtime tenured professor of sociology at Catholic University, saw his reputation trashed by the sexual Left. [22]

Clever headlines for "no differences" stories in the press quoted the The Who song, "The Kids Are Alright." There was even a film by that name—the 2010 box-office dud starring Julianne Moore and Annette Bening. It's a propaganda film about two lesbians and their children conceived by the same sperm donor, who then comes into their lives and almost breaks up this perfect marriage. Of course, the kids were all right.

But in reality, the kids are not all right, not by a long shot.

And why should we have thought they would be? The fact is, adults are experimenting with kids' lives on a massive scale. We have seen this before, in the divorce revolution, and we know the results. The kids were sacrificed for the supposed happiness of adults.

Saving Single Parents from Criticism

For those old enough to remember, one of the more remarkable public debates in American history happened after the horrific 1992 Los Angeles riots, when Vice President Dan Quayle delivered a speech to the Commonwealth Club of California on the subject of those riots. He blamed them in part on the decline of moral values associated with the rise of fatherlessness.[23] After all, thousands of largely fatherless young men had poured into the streets, setting fires and beating strangers. Quayle pointed to the culture's celebration of fatherlessness, exemplified by TV character Murphy Brown (played by Candice Bergen) choosing to have a child out of wedlock. He said the show "mocked the importance of fathers." It should not be forgotten what a cultural watershed the *Murphy Brown* story line was—a deliberate act of social revolution and a stick in the eye to all the pro-family pecksniffs.

Diane English, the producer of the show, called Quayle's speech "political" and "irresponsible." She dared him to debate "anywhere, anytime" but suggested he wouldn't because she "had better writers."

She also vowed to dish out revenge, on an upcoming episode of *Murphy Brown.*[24]

Critics accused Quayle of attacking single mothers. Inevitably any criticism of single parenthood is deplored as an attack on single mothers. Praising the bravery and remarkable accomplishments of "heroic" single mothers becomes necessary before one can even think about suggesting that absent fathers, broken homes, and, yes, single motherhood are problems for families, children, and society as a whole. In fact, social science abundantly demonstrates that single motherhood is akin to a prison sentence—for the kids, but also for the single moms themselves.

In the Quayle debate, the Left pushed the very unscientific notion that moms and dads do not matter to the well-being of children. The same arguments are being made today in the same-sex marriage debate, and they were made back in the 1960s, too, when the divorce revolution began.

Anyone born before the 1960s will remember the whispered shame of divorce. Divorced families were "broken homes." Divorce existed, but it was rare and it came at a cost in terms of social prestige both for the divorced and their children. The question of divorce was always seen through the lens of what was best for the kids. It was understood that children would be better off even in a home where love between spouses was absent than in a home that was altogether broken.

That assumption was reflected in American laws and customs. In her masterful analysis of the divorce culture, which grew from her defense of Dan Quayle published in the *Atlantic Monthly* in 1993, Barbara Dafoe Whitehead followed the evolution of divorce through the work of influential etiquette writer Emily Post: "In editions of *Etiquette* spanning more than twenty-five years, Miss Post compares divorce with both natural disasters and epidemic disease, writing that 'the epidemic of divorce which has been raging in this country for the past forty years must be rated as a catastrophe along with floods, dust bowls, and tornadoes.'"[25]

Post published this in 1960, with the divorce tsunami a scant few years away. But in her subsequent advice, you can read the impending change. Post began to argue for a more welcoming attitude toward those who had been through divorce.[26]

Sociology professor David Popenoe writes that the modern nuclear family, created in the Victorian era, was the first to have been based mainly on romantic love.[27] The family was oriented toward childrearing, of course, but the marriage itself was not formed on the basis of an economic need, with the two spouses banding together and even the children pitching in to create a family economy, as in centuries past. Instead it was formed on the basis of romantic love between a man and a woman.

Remaking Marriage with Romantic Love

One can see how later arguments for gay marriage were possible only because of this earlier evolution in marriage. It was during the development of the Victorian-era nuclear family that the family also became privatized. Not only was the family now behind closed doors, fathers lost the power of the father as mothers took on a larger role in running the household—something that, ironically, latter-day feminists would rebel against. The Victorian father was not the iron-fisted tyrant he is in the popular imagination. In fact, compared to his predecessors, he was a largely absent softie.

As David Popenoe points out, "Fatherhood in the Victorian era became a part-time activity. From once having had a wife as the assistant in the running of the home, a man increasingly was considered a part-time assistant to his wife."[28] The father's chief role became that of breadwinner, with his time spent largely outside the home. Mothers became the primary parent of the children. Parenting literature changed its focus from fathers to mothers. In an even more powerful change, legal rights began to shift as well. Up until the nineteenth century, although men did not "own" their children as in Roman times, fathers, not mothers, had the presumption of custody in case of divorce. But eventually the presumptive custodian—particularly of young children—became the mother.

It was this version of the family—the nuclear unit grounded in romantic love, established as the norm in Victorian times—that the feminists rebelled against. They called it a patriarchy, a prison, a domestic tyranny. It was an institution that repressed women sexually and damaged children for life. That feminist revolt against the nuclear family was helped along by the confluence in the 1960s of a number of social trends that conspired against marriage, family, and certainly children.

Consider that before the mid-twentieth century, men and women had plenty of pressing matters to attend to besides their own happiness. They had other things to examine closely, other than their own feelings, other than their own navels, other than their own self-actualization. World wars and global depressions have a way of taking the mind beyond one's inner thoughts and feelings.

With the Great Depression and World War II receding in memory, the booming 1960s economy allowed men and especially women the leisure to examine these inner feelings and to decide they weren't truly happy. Egging them on in their novel search for happiness was the explosion of the therapeutic business, specifically of marriage and couples counseling. Measuring personal happiness against markers put down by therapists, popular writers, and trendy political and sociological gurus was never going to turn out well.

Making Marriage the Problem

The feminist movement was bent on persuading women that they were desperately unhappy. Betty Friedan's *The Feminine Mystique* convinced women—over-educated, bored, stuck in the suburbs without a car, the high point of their day hubby traipsing through the door at 6:00 demanding his dinner—that they were missing something. There had to be more than this.

Social scientists began to argue that marriage was bad for women—very good for men but very bad for women's health and well-being. Jessie Bernard's seminal 1972 *The Future of Marriage* was especially important.[29] Though it is unlikely that much of anyone outside a small coterie of aging feminists have heard of Bernard today, at the time she was considered a pioneer in sociological research on marriage.

Bernard was widely respected throughout her long career in higher education, but it is hard to read her book today without laughing out loud. It is almost a satire of feminist thinking. Bernard argued that marriage literally made women sick, and also that the women who were likely to enter into marriage were a tad crazy to begin with.

The importance of her work is that it was taken so seriously at the time. It was the academic theory underpinning the great feminist attack on the institution of marriage. It has been cited at least twenty-five hundred times in the academic literature.[30]

Bernard describes two different marriages, one for men and one for women. For men, marriage is wonderful. It makes them healthy, wealthy, and wise. Married men live longer and have sex whenever they want it. And they are happier than their single peers. But Bernard's interest in men is slight, to say the least. Her chapter on men is a mere nine and one-half pages. And, except for men's bellyaching, every bit of it is good news. No matter how much men may complain and have complained down through the ages, marriage was literally made for them—at the expense of women.

Bernard's interest is in women, and here she goes to town. It is best to let Bernard speak for herself:

> A study by R. R. Willoughby a generation ago found that married more than unmarried women were troubled by ideas that people were watching them on the street, were fearful of falling when on high places, had their feelings easily hurt, were happy and sad by turns without apparent reason, regretted impulsive statements, cried easily, felt hurt by criticism, sometimes felt miserable, found it hard to make up their minds, sometimes felt grouchy, were burdened by a sense of remorse, worried over possible misfortune, changed interest quickly, were bothered when people watched them perform a task, would cross the street to avoid meeting people, were upset when people

crowded ahead of them in line, would rather stand than take a front seat when late, were self-conscious about their appearance, and felt prevented from giving help at the scene of an accident. [31]

Bernard was only getting started on the dangers of marriage to women.

She cited a study from one Genevieve Knupfer, who found that married women more than unmarried women "tend to be bothered by feelings of depression, unhappy most of the time, disliking their present jobs, sometimes feeling they were about to go to pieces, afraid of death, terrified by windstorms, worried about catching diseases, sometimes thinking of things too bad to talk about, and bothered by pains and ailments in different parts of the body."[32]

But there was even more. Bernard cited a study showing that "at least in the culture of Western civilization, the amount of crime committed by married women—independent of age—seems to be higher than the amount of crime committed by single women."[33]

Crime. Fear of windstorms. Marriage is rough on women. Obviously, they needed help. Bernard thought that work outside the home could be good for them: "They may still be neurotic but they are less likely…to be psychotic."[34]

In short, to be happily married, a woman must be mentally ill.

But here is the truly laugh-out-loud part: Bernard recognizes that married women, as crazy as she is sure they are, still say they are happier—far happier—than their unmarried sisters. Yes, she admits it. But she claims that happy married women are merely conforming to a societal ideal that marriage is better than spinsterhood—and it isn't really, when you drill down deep. Married women say they're happier, but they are just brainwashed by society.

Bernard says the problem starts with which women are attracted to marriage in the first place: they are the dim, slightly crazy, weak-willed ones in high school, the ones that the men want, in the first place. So of course, they end up even crazier in marriage—committing crimes and fearing windstorms, and so forth.

Bernard holds out hope for marriage—of a different sort. Swinging could help. She also likes the ménage à trois, and the sexual commune. She also makes a pitch for reproductive technologies: some would breed for others, or maybe there would be robot-like creatures with wombs to host growing babies.[35]

It is highly unlikely that the average unhappy housewife ever even heard the name of Professor Jessie Bernard, but we know how these things work. She published her book, and her ideas sifted down into the zeitgeist via academic studies, magazines, newspapers, TV chat shows—and before too long everyone knew—just knew—that marriage was unhealthy for women. Good for men, bad for women. Science says so; haven't you heard? College girls probably looked at their moms and saw them as trapped. Married women having a bad day thought they needed to get out of their marriages for their mental health.

The pace of marital dissolution was exacerbated by the Sexual Revolution, which the Kinsey Reports had jump started in the fifties. Then it really got going in the sixties and seventies, with the promulgation of the Playboy philosophy, which even housewives began to buy into. When I was in grade school, our next-door neighbor was bored while home sick, so his wife offered to trade some of his *Playboys* for some of my father's Western paperbacks—Zane Grey and the like. That was a sign of the times. My mother, God bless her, nixed the deal.

Around the same time, *Everything You Ever Wanted to Know about Sex but Were Afraid to Ask* became a best seller in fifty-one countries and left its mark on the American sexual psyche. (After selling a hundred million copies, it would fall out of favor for its retrograde but accurate assessment that homosexuality is little more than furtive grappling in public restrooms and that trans "women" are simply surgically altered homosexuals. But for a time it was hot stuff for husbands and wives everywhere. I vividly remember one of my friends swiping his parents' copy and reading it to us wide-eyed teens in the basement.)

And there was the contraceptive pill, which made its debut in 1965. Many will recall that condoms, then called "rubbers," were only for sailors and truck drivers. The Pill brought the sailor-and-truck-driver ethos into every bedroom. It was whispered in my respectable neighborhood that the wife of a lawyer had been caught in bed with someone other than her husband. Thank you for the new and improved suburban lifestyle, Mrs. Friedan.

Given this toxic Sexual Revolution stew, did marriage have a chance? It is a tribute to the durability of the institution that marriage has survived at all. It took a real drubbing, one that it has not yet recovered from. And neither have the children.

All this divorce-for-the-sake-of-adult-happiness was supposed to be good for kids. Losing a parent from the home was going to be great. Having two daddies and two mommies was going to be wonderful.

Different Kinds of Divorce

It's not like divorce was unknown before the 1970s. It was always a fact of life, even in colonial times. But before the second half of the twentieth century, divorce was always frowned upon. As Barbara Dafoe Whitehead reports, there had been a spike in divorce—though not to the atmospheric peak of twenty-two per thousand that it would hit in 1980[36]—early in the twentieth century, when what was known as "vulgar divorce" became an avenue for financial and social advancement.[37] Eminent novelist Edith Wharton wrote several novels on the topic, dramatizing the terrible cost paid by the children.

Whitehead explains how almost overnight in the 1960s, "vulgar divorce" morphed into what she calls "expressive divorce," whereby "divorce became a subjective experience, governed by the individual's needs, desires and feelings." The rise of the therapeutic culture changed the concept of divorce: "Leaving a marriage offered opportunities to build a stronger identity and to achieve a more coherent and fully realized self."[38] Whitehead describes the explosion of divorce literature, which described divorce as an experience of personal growth: in ending their marriage, both spouses were walking away from a lie and coming to know their true selves. And screw the kids.

Well, not exactly screw the kids, but the kids would understand. They would have maybe two moms and two dads, and lots more brothers and sisters, and the happy divorce would be wonderful for them. They would have twice as many Christmas presents!

In the long history of divorce in America, whenever there was uptick in the divorce rate—after World War I, for instance—the nation eventually became concerned about the havoc that would follow. Society knew. Emily Post knew. Because the powers that be were concerned about not replicating what had happened after World War I after World War II, programs were instituted to ensure that returning soldiers and their recently liberated Riveting Rosies would get back together. They were remarkably successful. The divorce rate dropped like a stone.[39] And yet just a couple of decades later, when the divorce revolution kicked in, hardly anyone was concerned. Everyone seemed to buy into the divorce culture.

The most important and most damaging change in our views on divorce was with respect to the children. Before the 1960s, both couples and society thought of the children first. Doing what was best for the kids often meant staying together for their sake. How quaint that now sounds. How laughable. Whitehead writes, "Before the 1960s, divorce was viewed as a legal, family, and social event with multiple stakeholders; after that time, divorce became an individual event defined by and responsive to the interests of the individual."[40]

For the convenience of the adults, divorce was made easier. Back in the day there had to be a good reason to split up a marriage. Often one party had to be at fault—of adultery or abuse, for example. There were long waiting periods. Roadblocks had been set up to caution the couple that down this road lay danger. But soon "irreconcilable differences" was all you needed to break up a family. And as something called "no-fault" divorce swept the nation, all the roadblocks came down. One party could unilaterally dissolve the marriage—changing forever the other party's relationship with his or her children. The no-fault divorce "reform" swept the nation with the widespread support of both Left and Right. The first state to permit it was California in 1969—under Governor Ronald Reagan. Fifteen years later, all fifty states had some form of no fault divorce.[41] The floodgates for divorce were now wide open. The experiment could really take off.

Consider that according to the U.S. Census Bureau, there was roughly one divorce per thousand marriages in 1860. There was a spike after World War I to almost eight per thousand married women, another spike up to eighteen per thousand after World War II, and then a rapid decline to less than ten per thousand in 1960. And then the explosion. Starting in the mid-1960s, the divorce rate went almost straight up: twelve per thousand; fourteen per thousand; sixteen, eighteen, twenty, and twenty-two, until it peaked at twenty-two per thousand in 1980 and finally began to decline. The divorce rate now stands at roughly sixteen per thousand married women, about what it was in 1970.[42]

Nineteen-seventy-four was the year that more marriages ended in divorce than in death—for the first time in history.[43] Before that, most kids living in single-parent households were there because a parent had died.

Before 1960, the increase in single-parent families was so slight that hardly anyone paid attention. In 1900, it was 8.5 percent. Sixty years later it had increased to 9.1 percent. David Popenoe points out that no one in 1960 was writing about family breakdown. It was not an issue. Though the divorce rate was rising for the first six decades of the twentieth century, the death rate was dropping faster. So, "By 1960 more children were living with both of their natural parents than at any other time in world history"[44]—for those born between the late 1940s and early 1950s, an astounding 80 percent.

And then, Popenoe says, "The nuclear family cracked." Princeton family historian Lawrence Stone reports, "The scale of marital breakdowns in the West since 1960 has no historical precedent that I know of, and seems unique. There has been nothing like it for the last 2,000 years, and probably longer."[45]

Consider the baby bust period: 1970–1984. The percentage of children born in those years who lived with both parents at age seventeen dropped from 80 percent to 50 percent. It simply fell off a cliff. White children born between 1950 and 1954 spent only 8 percent of their childhood with one parent; black kids, 22 percent. Of children born in 1980, a third of whites spent their childhood without a father; nearly 60 percent of blacks lived without a father.

But there is another trend that may be even more ominous—the decline of marriage itself. According to Popenoe, in 1990, 94 percent of men and 95 percent of women aged forty-five to fifty-four either were or had been married. Between 1970 and 1993, the percentage of never-married young men aged thirty to thirty-four increased from 9 to 30 percent. Marriage seemed to be withering away.[46]

Wholesale Flight from the Family

In a 2015 column for the *Wall Street Journal*, demographer Nicholas Eberstadt called this "the world flight from the family": "All around the world, pre-existing family patterns are being upended by a revolutionary new force: the seemingly unstoppable quest for convenience by adults demanding ever-greater autonomy. We can think of this as another triumph of consumer sovereignty, which has at last brought rational choice and elective affinities into a bastion heretofore governed by traditions and duties—many of them onerous. Thanks to this revolution, it is perhaps easier than ever before to free oneself from the burdens that would otherwise be imposed by spouses, children, relatives or significant others with whom one shares a hearth."

According to 2013 Centers for Disease Control and Prevention data, over 40 percent of babies in the United States were born outside marriage. For 2014, the Census Bureau estimates that 27 percent of all children (and 22 percent of white children) lived in a fatherless home. But the data show something even more remarkable, says Eberstadt: "A 2011 study by two Census researchers reckoned that just 59% of all American children (and 65% of 'Anglo' or non-Hispanic white children) lived with married and biological parents as of 2009." Because this "revealed preference," as he calls it, for raising children in nonmarital unions, Eberstadt sees a future where "American children who reside with their married birthparents will be in the minority." [47]

He and others have documented an increasingly "child-free" society. The proportion of childless forty-something women is one in five in Sweden and Switzerland, and one in four in Italy. The birth dearth has even hit the Muslim world. According to the UN, the "proportion of never-married women in the late 30s was higher in Morocco in 2004 than in the U.S. in 2009. The percentage of single women in their early 40s was higher in Lebanon in 2007 than in Italy in 2010. The percentage of unmarried Libyan women in their 30s in 2006 stood at 32%, 20 times the percentage two decades before, and higher even than Denmark."[48]

Writing in the influential journal *Foreign Policy*, University of Virginia sociologist W. Brad Wilcox punctures the notion that cohabitation, which is sweeping the world, is just the same as marriage either for adults or children. He and his Georgetown University colleague Laurie DeRose examined data from the United States, Europe, Latin America, and even the Scandinavian countries and found that children raised in cohabiting families are much more likely to experience parental breakup by age twelve—and therefore more likely to experience a range of problems and pathologies.[49]

It was in 1965 that Daniel Patrick Moynihan wrote his report raising the alarm about the high illegitimacy rate in the black community, and was excoriated for it. But in 1965, only 25 percent of black babies, and 5 percent of white babies, were born to single moms. By the early 1980s, these figures had risen to 50 percent for blacks and 15 percent for whites. By 2010, a whopping 72 percent of black children and 36 percent of whites were born to single mothers.[50]

Now consider the extremely high correlation between single motherhood and poverty. Forty percent of single mothers with kids under eighteen live below the poverty line. For blacks that percentage is 47 percent.[51] Single motherhood is a near guarantee that you and your children will live in straitened circumstances, if not outright poverty.

But it's worse than mere poverty. Kids raised by single moms face all sorts of serious obstacles in life. And it's not just conservatives saying so. Professor Sara McLanahan of Princeton University has found that boys raised by single moms have a much greater likelihood of landing in jail by age thirty than those raised by their married biological mothers and fathers.[52] Even after controlling for race, income, education, and ethnicity, boys raised by single moms are twice as likely to be incarcerated than those raised in a marriage between their own mothers and fathers. As Brad Wilcox has written at *Slate*, "Research on young men suggests they are less likely to engage in delinquent or illegal behavior when they have the affection, attention, and monitoring of their own mother and father."[53]

Wilcox points to a study by Bruce Ellis of the University of Arizona that "found about one-third of girls whose fathers left home before they turned 6 ended up pregnant as teenagers, compared with just 5 percent of girls whose fathers were there throughout their childhood." The research suggests that girls are less likely to be supervised and therefore are more likely to engage in early sex.[54]

And the kids of divorce are screamingly unhappy. They will tell you so. Having two dads and two moms and two houses to visit at Christmas is not wonderful. It is awful. Social commentator Mary Eberstadt's remarkable book *Home-Alone America* devotes a chapter to listening to teenage music, which she calls their "primal scream."[55] Eberstadt urges us to "enter into the roiling emotional waters in which that music is created and consumed—in other words, actually to read and listen to some of it." Eberstadt says, "The odd truth about contemporary [circa 2004] teenage music is its compulsive insistence on the damage wrought by broken homes, family dysfunction, checked-out parents, and (especially) absent father."[56] She cites musicians now largely off the scene: Tupac Shakur, Eddie Vedder, Kurt Cobain, Snoop Dogg, Papa Roach, Everclear.

Papa Roach sang a song called "Broken Home" with the lyrics, "I know my mother loves me / But does my father even care?" In "Father of Mine," Everclear sang, "Take me back to the day / When I was still your golden boy."

Blink-182 actually had a top-40 hit in 2001 called "Stay Together for the Kids."

Tupac Shakur, one of the most influential rappers in history, recorded a song called "Papa'z Song Lyrics," which Eberstadt describes as a "lacerating description of growing up fatherless that might help to explain why Shakur is an icon not only to many worse off teenagers from the ghetto, but also to many better off suburban ones. Here is a boy who 'had to play catch by myself,' who prays: 'Please send me a pops before puberty.'"

Then there is Pink's 2002 megahit album "Missundaztood," including this very revealing plea to her father not to leave: "I won't spill the milk at dinner." Pretty much every child of divorce thinks at least at one point—and some of them for all their lives—that the divorce was their fault. An old friend of mine from New York told me that he had thought for years that his folks split up because he ate the chocolate cake.

Eberstadt should be given a medal for listening to so much awful music and sussing out anecdotal evidence that most of us would simply have missed.[57] Divorce damages kids, and pretty much all kids hate it. They miss their dads.

Even the *New York Times* has gotten into the act. A July 2014 report tells the story of a single mom who looks with envy at her married friends and the extra hands and money that can be devoted to raising their children.[58] The piece cites the work of Princeton sociologist Sara McLanahan and others who point out that higher income and better-educated individuals are now largely getting and staying married. "It is the privileged Americans who are marrying, and marrying helps them stay privileged," said Andrew Cherlin, a sociologist at Johns Hopkins University.[59] McLanahan calls it "diverging destinies."[60] One of the most remarkable books of the 2016 campaign season was J. D. Vance's *Hillbilly Elegy*, about the author's growing up in a West Virginia home utterly devastated by drugs, ennui, state dependency, anger, poverty, sexual incontinence, and all of the hideousness of the Sexual Revolution pathologies that Vance left behind as he fought his way into Yale, Silicon Valley, and a stable marriage.[61]

The notion that marriage is hard and maybe not worth it is deeply ingrained in our society. One of the first things a newly engaged couple will hear from friends and family is, *Congratulations, that is so wonderful. But keep in mind, marriage is hard work. It is compromise. But, more than anything, it is hard work. You have to work at it.* No one— and I mean no one—will tell you that marriage is actually fun and that it is good for you, even though the social science abundantly says this is so.

Marriage Matters

In 1998, Steven Stack and J. Ross Eshleman of Wayne State University published a seventeen-nation study on marital status and happiness.[62] Note this was only twenty years after the days when we were told that marriage did not matter—even that it made people, especially women, utterly miserable. There are dozens of studies that thoroughly disprove that notion. But the zeitgeist wants what the zeitgeist wants, and the zeitgeist really wants to believe that marriage does not matter.

But it does, as the real science establishes beyond a shadow of a doubt. Stack and Eshleman looked at married, cohabiting, divorced, and widowed persons and measured whether they were "not very happy, quite happy, or very happy." They found that married persons were the happiest of all, by any measurement and in every country of the seventeen they studied.

Married persons have a higher level of financial satisfaction and report higher levels of health. Cohabitation, in contrast, was not related to either financial satisfaction or greater health. Marriage increases the reported happiness for both men and women as opposed to single men and women and protects both men and women from unhappiness.[63]

There is a myth, perpetrated mostly by late-night comedians, that marriage is the death of sex. Far from it, according to a 2004 study published by David G. Blanchflower and Andrew J. Oswald in the *Scandinavian Journal of Economics*. In fact, Blanchflower and Oswald show that it is singles who are sex-deprived.

Their paper looked at data from sixteen thousand Americans interviewed for the General Social Survey between 1988 and 2002 and found that "married people have more sex than those who are single, divorced, widowed, or separated."[64] Maggie Gallagher and Linda Waite go into great detail on why this is so in their 2001 book, *The Case for Marriage*. It is quite simple. Married men and women have a ready, willing, and able sex partner right there next to them. Singles have to go out on the hunt, spend a lot of time, and spend a fair amount of money to find a willing partner. Not everyone they meet wants to be with them.[65] Compare those complications to the ease of a simple "Honey, do you feel like it tonight?"

And then there is the 2015 study by Tim Wadsworth of the University of Colorado at Boulder, comparing the overall happiness of married and unmarried persons. He reports, "Controlling for all of the other factors married respondents are 89% more likely to report being very satisfied than non-married respondents.... Separated and divorced individuals report being the least happy or satisfied, and the mean happiness/satisfaction levels of the never married and widowed respondents fall in between the married and divorced/separated categories."[66]

One of the more remarkable findings of social science, one that is highly significant not only for the lives of individuals but also for society and certainly public policy, is that the best way out of poverty is for a mother to marry the father of her children, and for a father to marry the mother of his children. In fact, the poverty rate for married couples with children under the age of eighteen is less than 10 percent. If you toss in a high school education and weekly church attendance, it is practically guaranteed that you and your family will not fall into poverty but will in fact flourish. A burgeoning library of social science supports this assertion.[67]

Sadly, the battle for the family has gotten even crazier. Public policy experts urge us never to refer to "the family," but rather to "families." At the UN, we battle over the phrase "various forms of the family." At this point, a child born of gestational surrogacy can now have up to five individuals with a plausible case for a slice of parenthood: There is the sperm donor, if you can call a man who ejaculates into a cup for money a donor. There is also the egg donor, who is paid to hyper-ovulate so doctors can harvest her eggs. There is the "surrogate mother," the woman who rents out her womb. And there is the couple who pays upwards of $100,000 for the designer child who is never allowed to know his DNA parents. In the United Kingdom, they have recently allowed the use of mitochondrial DNA so that a child can have three *biological* parents—could be three men, three women, or any combo package.[68]

It's all one great big experiment about maximizing the fulfillment, pleasure, and convenience of adults—at the expense of children. No matter how much social science data confirms the failure of the experiment for all concerned, the Left will continue to promote sexual "liberation" from traditional morality and the traditional family—which is precisely what science tells us children need to thrive. No substitute will do.

CHAPTER 7

One Hundred Eighty-Two Pounds of French Fries

C alifornia law requires the labeling of any food that contains a minuscule amount of even a single one of eight hundred chemicals—including acrylamide, a naturally formed compound that can be found in bread, cereals, cookies, potato chips, and French fries. But it's "known to the state of California to cause cancer or reproductive toxicity"! The thing is, a kid would have to eat 182 pounds of French fries every single day to hit the cancer danger zone. Not even a teenager could do that—not even on a dare.

Welcome to the "science"-driven world of food scares.

Frightening Us about Our Food

Remember Alar? It's a chemical sprayed on apples to regulate their growth, making harvesting easier and preventing them from falling off the tree too soon. In the 1980s, the Left started a panic about Alar.

The U.S. Environmental Protection Agency (EPA) had run tests on mice, concluded Alar was carcinogenic, and proposed banning it for use on crops. A year later, the EPA backtracked, instead requiring farmers to reduce their usage of the chemical by 50 percent. Then the National Resources Defense Council issued a report—supposedly a two-year peer-reviewed study—that said children were at "intolerable risk" from a plethora of chemicals, including Alar. Their risk of cancer was supposed to be 240 times greater than what the EPA considered acceptable.

CBS's *60 Minutes* followed with its own scary exposé, and a national panic was underway. Alar in apples dominated the national news, and the EPA decided to ban Alar altogether.

The problem with the "science" was typical. The lab tests in the study that had started the scare predicted the cancer risk of the consumption from *five thousand gallons of apple juice every single day*, something not even the thirstiest toddler could do.

Around the time of the Alar panic, California voters passed Proposition 65, which was supposed to protect people from exposure to toxic chemicals that could cancer. It is the law to this day—and has transmogrified like a cancer.

More than eight hundred chemicals—twenty-five pages of them in the Prop 65 Wikipedia page—are listed, and businesses have to slap a warning on any product that may contain any trace of any of them.[1] The state of California can go after any business for not warning consumers. What's more, private citizens backed by rapacious law firms are legally allowed to bring civil suits. Proposition 65 has spawned an entire industry: since 2000, lawyers bringing suits under Prop 65 have brought in a haul totaling $150 million.[2]

Chemicals are listed if they can cause "one excess case of cancer in 100,000 individuals exposed to the chemical over a 70-year lifetime." That is a high bar and remarkably hard to measure unless you jigger the science. Consider the French-fry eating teen and the apple-juice guzzling toddler.

Going All Out against Golden Rice

The anti-food Left uses the same arguments against genetically modified foods (GMOs), one of the great miracles coming from the mind of man.

Take beta-carotene. Beta-carotene is a natural part of plants that, when digested, produces vitamin A, vital to every diet. Vitamin A deficiency, in fact, can lead to blindness. Sadly, in many parts of the world, regular diets do not produce enough beta-carotene, and 250 million kids around the world suffer from a vitamin A deficiency. Every year two hundred fifty to five hundred thousand of them go blind. Half of that number will die from the vitamin deficiency.[3]

Enter GMOs. Only not yet. The solution to the deadly vitamin A deficiency epidemic has been tied up in testing and litigation for going on two decades now.

Vitamin A deficiency hits hardest in locales where rice is a dietary staple because rice does not contain nearly enough beta-carotene to supply our need for vitamin A. So, way back in 1990, scientists in Switzerland set out to engineer a new kind of rice, one that makes increased levels of beta-carotene. This required genetic engineering. Their goal was to develop a strain of rice that would deliver the equivalent of two high-dose vitamin A pills per person per year, something governments had been trying to do for years. And getting vitamin A through food is far superior to getting it through pills, and far less expensive.

Ingo Potrykus and his team at the Swiss Federal Institute of Technology transplanted genes from daffodils and bacteria and created the world's very first beta-carotene rice. They called it Golden Rice. Problem solved? Nope. Golden Rice has never been taken to market. It has been tied up by the anti-food Left every step of the way.

The principal enemy of Golden Rice is the radical environmental group Greenpeace, which originally claimed that Golden Rice does not deliver *enough* beta-carotene.[4] And besides, poor people should *be* encouraged to grow home gardens instead—never mind that hundreds of millions of them do not own land to plant on. Researchers eventually created a new Golden Rice that had eight times as much beta-carotene as the original. A few years later, they came out with one that had twenty times the beta-carotene.[5] Problem solved? No. The arguments shifted.

Critics charged that Golden Rice was a financial scheme to make corporations rich—until the inventors said it would be provided for free to farmers. Then they said that Golden Rice would "contaminate" nearby crops. And then the critics began to argue that Golden Rice now had *too much* beta-carotene and it was therefore dangerous—it would cause birth defects.[6]

Did the alarmists produce any proof for their claims? Of a kind. David Schubert, a neurobiologist at the Salk Institute, produced a paper that the *Journal of Medicinal Food* published in 2008 claiming beta-carotene could produce "retinoids" that are "likely to be teratogenic" and could cause birth defects.[7]

But as leftwing journalist Will Saletan, writing at *Slate*, has pointed out, "Schubert systematically distorted the evidence."[8] Schubert cited a 1994 study from the *New England Journal of Medicine* that found "smokers who supplemented their diet with beta-carotene had an increased risk of lung cancer." But, as Saletan explains, Schubert "neglected to mention that the daily beta-carotene dose administered in the study was the equivalent of roughly 10 to 20 bowls of Golden Rice [per day]. He also failed to quote the rest of the paper that in general, beta-carotene was actually associated with lower risk of lung cancer."[9]

But Schubert's less-than-scientific conclusions became the "scientific" cover the anti-GMO people needed. They have been cited endlessly. A group called Ban GM Food, for example, wrote, "Golden Rice is engineered to overproduce beta-carotene, and studies show that some retinoids derived from beta-carotene are toxic and cause birth defects."[10]

In his lengthy defense of GMOs, Saletan explains the shell game of opponents. *Every* plant—naturally bred or GMO—creates the now-dreaded carotenoids. When the opponents of Golden Rice argued that poor people should grow their own food, they were essentially arguing for them to produce carotenoids—that would be just as toxic as the carotenoids in Golden Rice. Saletan writes, "GMO critics didn't seem to care how much beta-carotene people ate, as long as the food wasn't genetically engineered."[11] In fact, Golden Rice opponents have argued in favor of massive doses administered orally. They just don't like GMOs.

Anti-GMO zealots have been shameless in coming up with any argument against the rice. Greenpeace has argued Golden Rice is a violation of "religious beliefs, cultural heritage and sense of identity."[12] Greenpeace also worries that this life-saving product might violate freedom of choice—but is fine with government programs that require consumption of beta-carotene in other forms.[13]

In 2008, clinical trials were undertaken in China to measure how much vitamin A can be delivered through various means, including Golden Rice, vitamin capsules, and spinach. In tests with both children and adults as subjects, the results showed that Golden Rice delivers 60 percent of the daily recommended allowance of vitamin A—more than spinach and just as much as capsules, and enough to make a serious dent in the epidemic blindness and death caused by vitamin A.

Greenpeace was incensed. They and others said the kids were guinea pigs, and the families had not been properly warned of the risks in the study. Horrors! In these irresponsible experiments on children, the kids were given less than two ounces of rice per day.

Salk neurobiologist David Schubert was also outraged by the study. He complained that the rice overproduces beta-carotene and has "never been tested in animals," citing a supposed "extensive medical literature showing that retinoids that can be derived from beta-carotene are both toxic and cause birth defects"—including his own phony study.[14]

Tufts University scientists reviewed the China study and endorsed the results.

But the enemies of Golden Rice will never throw in the towel. As *Slate*'s Saletan points out, "There's no end to the arguments and demands of the anti-GMO watchdogs. They want more studies—'systematic trials with different cooking processes'—to see how much vitamin A the rice delivers."[15]

Twenty-five years after its invention, Golden Rice has still not come to market—and millions more children are dead.[16]

You may have noticed that I am quoting liberally from liberal Will Saletan. Among the more honest writers on the Left, Saletan is not alone in supporting genetically modified food from that side of the ideological spectrum. The Rockefeller Foundation and UNICEF, for instance, have supported Golden Rice. Even the World Health Organization has given GMOs a clean bill of health. Moreover, the U.S. government—whose bureaucrats can usually be counted on to support the leftist position— gives its imprimatur to genetically modified foods. Still the opposition to GMOs comes largely from the Left and, as usual, they lie about scientific evidence to make their case.

Breeding for Better Nutrition and Pest Control

Genetically modified foods are those that have been manipulated at the genetic level to produce new traits. Man has been manipulating the animal and plant gene pool since ten thousand years before Christ, ever since catching on to the benefits of breeding certain fine specimens together. For thousands of years, plants have been bred for better taste and nutritional value. For instance, the ubiquitous wheat we all know today—the one that virtually all our baked goods are made of—did not happen by accident. It was bred from wild grasses by human beings who repeatedly planted and harvested them over millennia. And now it is a staple food across the world. Seven hundred *million* tons were produced in 2013, the third largest crop on the face of the earth, after corn and rice—which were also deliberately improved by breeding.

What's new is changing the genetic structure of food directly in the laboratory. It is this that for some reason has horrified the Left and even some on the Right.

Genetically engineered organisms are created in the laboratory by adding one or more genes to an organism's genome. Genes can also be removed, or their expression altered or silenced. In 1985, the U.S. Department of Agriculture approved four genetically modified organisms for field tests. That number has grown to roughly eight hundred a year today.

More than seventeen thousand genetically engineered organisms had been approved as of the end of 2013.

The first genetically modified crop that came to market was a tomato called Flavr Savr. Maybe what freaks out the anti-food Left is that Flavr Savr also goes by the name CGN-89564-2. Scary! Also, that CGN-89564-2 was created using aminoglycoside 3'-phosphotransferase II. Hmmmm. Sounds tasty. Aminoglycoside 3'-phosphotransferase II delayed ripening and therefore gave the tomato a longer shelf-life. The tomato never took off, and the company with the original patent ceased production a few years later and was then acquired by Monsanto.

The genetically modified papaya was more successful. Papayas are an important crop in the developing world. In the 1990s the papaya industry in Hawaii faced disaster because of a deadly ringspot virus. To battle the virus, Hawaiian farmers tried crop rotation, selective breeding, and quarantine. Nothing worked. A scientist at Cornell University proposed transferring a gene from the virus to the DNA of the papaya itself as a kind of inoculation. It worked. No more ringspot virus. The Hawaiian crop was saved.

Three federal agencies, including the EPA, approved the process. The anti-food Left said the altered papaya DNA might create even more dangerous diseases. Radical environmentalists attacked experimental fields at the University of Hawaii. Greenpeace destroyed a genetically modified papaya orchard in Thailand.[17]

The U.S. Public Interest Research Group called for a national moratorium on such genetic testing. A Dutch study argued that a protein in the new papaya DNA now matched a protein in worms that creates allergies. The supposed "match" involved only six amino acids out of 280. By the same standard, Will Saletan points out, ordinary corn would have to be labeled allergenic.

The U.S. government kept testing the genetically modified papaya, and the papaya kept getting a clean bill of health. At this point, by the way, papaya consumers had been eating ringspot-infected papayas for years with no deleterious effects, and researchers found that the offending allergen appeared at a rate eight times higher in the infected papayas than in the GMO ones.

The Chinese fed the papayas to rats for weeks; the rats were just fine. The new DNA dissolved quickly in the rats' digestive systems, leaving no traces internally.

Still, the anti-food Left kept coming. When an anti-food leftist named Jeffrey Smith testified before the Hawaiian County Council, which the leftists have forced to consider this issue over and over, he said that the new DNA could interfere with human immunity and lead to HIV and hepatitis. The 2013 study he cited didn't even mention papayas. Echoing Schubert's line about Golden Rice, Smith made the patently false claim that no animal tests had been done on the GMO papaya. Genetically modified food, he argued, needed to be tested—for fifty to a hundred and fifty years![18]

Meanwhile, the Hawaii papaya industry thrives on the genetically modified papayas. People have been happily eating them for fifteen years. And no one has gotten sick.[19]

The hundred-year-old story of Japanese silkworms and a bacterium called *Bacillus thuringiensis* (Bt) shows the miraculous interplay between man and nature.

Bt was killing the Japanese silkworms. And then it occurred to the Japanese that this bacterium could be deliberately used to kill insects that harm plants. By the 1920s, scientists found a way that it could be used by farmers in crystalline or spray form. The natural pesticide was highly effective—and considered environmentally safe.

But then, in the early 1980s, scientists used GMO technology to figure out how to create plants with Bt *in them*—no need to spray, just plant the seeds. Pests that eat the plant die. By 1995, the U.S. government had approved Bt potatoes, corn, and cotton. The EPA said the toxin produced by these new plants was "identical to that produced naturally in the bacterium...and affects insects when ingested, but not mammals."[20]

Environmentalists had had no problem with the Bt spray, but they came unglued when GMO Bt crops came to market. They said the plants would create insecticide-resistant insects—even though the spray never had. Greenpeace claimed the Bt plants had a thousand times the bacterial concentration of the spray. That was a lie, and they knew it. Their own private study found the toxin level was severely "limited." So what did Greenpeace do? Simply did a one-eighty pivot and argued instead that the problem with Bt plants is they have *too little* toxin. Will Saletan points out the pretzels Greenpeace and the other critics of GMOs twist themselves into. Greenpeace "argued, in essence, that the Bt in transgenic crops was unsafe for humans but insufficient to kill bugs."[21] Critics said Bt plants in India weren't working effectively because the level of toxin was too low: insects were flourishing, crops were failing, and Indian farmers were killing themselves. It was an utterly false story.[22] Classic fake news.

Even though numerous studies have shown that Bt is among "the safest bio-insecticide available at present,"[23] claims of harm to humans keep coming from the anti-food Left. No "scientific" argument is too silly for the Left to make. It doesn't matter if people die. The only thing that seems to count is stopping the miracle of GMOs.

The harm from phony leftwing "science" is very real.

Following the Fads

But not all food panics are deadly. Some are merely faddish—even simply ridiculous.

Have you ever gone to a restaurant with someone who insists she is "gluten intolerant"? It can be torture. Long and detailed conversations follow about each of the ingredients in every single bite. Your companion might settle on a burger but without the bun. The burger arrives; a bite is taken. "Are there breadcrumbs in this?" Back to the kitchen. Back to the menu and an even longer disquisition on what she can eat. Dollars to donuts—gluten-free donuts!—most of those who are "gluten intolerant" are merely food-fashion forward.

There really is such a thing as celiac disease. And it can have serious repercussions including anemia, osteoporosis, and increased risk of lymphoma. In children, it can slow growth and weaken bones. But it does certainly not affect the millions of people queuing up in the gluten-free aisle at Whole Foods or the increasing number opting for the wine instead of the bread at church.

And then there are the "lactose intolerant." Lactose intolerance, like celiac disease, is a real thing, though not such a dangerous one. It does cause digestive problems in some people. But for many it is no more than a fad.

Lactose intolerance comes about when your body does not produce sufficient amounts of the lactase that the small intestine uses to break down milk sugar (lactose). Thus the undigested milk sugar passes from the small intestine to the large intestine, where bacteria break it down and cause gas, bloating, cramping, and diarrhea.

Ironically, real lactose intolerance occurs most frequently in Africans and Asians and is relatively rare among those of European descent, but it is precisely among affluent whites in Europe and the United States that it has become a fad. Researchers ran a study in which participants were given an eight-ounce glass of milk to drink every day for two weeks and asked to rate their abdominal discomfort after drinking it. What the subjects of the study did not know is that for one of those weeks their milk was laced with lactase, the enzyme that breaks down milk sugar in the small intestine and therefore prevents lactose intolerance. The volunteers rated their discomfort exactly the same for both types of milk. In other words, their lactose intolerance was not in their guts but in their heads.[24]

There is no end to the food scares, fads, and scams. Some are harmless, if a bit silly. Go ahead and order your gluten-free pizza; just make mine with extra-yummy gluten.

As we have seen, other fads are much more dangerous, and even deadly.

The fact is, the campaign against genetically modified crops that could save millions from blindness and death is just one battle in the war the "progressives" are perpetually waging against scientific progress—at phenomenal cost to human health and happiness.

The banning of DDT is the classic case. This may seem like an old and rusty debate, but it's not. Today malaria is rampant in Africa and elsewhere—though DDT very nearly wiped it out decades ago.[25] The whole of this book's argument is summed up in this tragedy.

DDT was one of the great heroes of World War II, a story now almost completely unknown. In 1943, American soldiers advanced upon Naples to relieve that city from the Nazis. Before their retreat, the Nazis blew up the city's water supply system, its reservoirs, and even its sewer system. The city was liberated on October 1, but within a few weeks horrible epidemics broke out that threatened the lives of the city's million inhabitants. Typhus, transmitted by lice, was among the deadliest, killing 25 percent of those infected. In *The New Atlantis*, Robert Zubrin says it was like the Black Death; the dead were brought by the hundreds to the streets and carted away.

DDT was first synthesized in 1874, but its use in killing pests was not discovered until 1939 by a Swiss chemist who later won a Nobel Prize for his discovery. This use for it came to the attention of the U.S. military for whom malaria was a serious problem in the South Pacific: according to Zubrin, the entire First Marine Division on Guadalcanal had been "rendered unfit for combat" because of malaria infections.

Three months after liberation, Italy began receiving DDT—eventually sixty tons of it. The streets of Naples were sprayed, buildings were sprayed, people and clothing were sprayed. Within a month, the epidemic was over.

DDT was used when the Germans blew up the dikes of the Pontine Marshes near Rome. Drained by Mussolini, they had become a veritable factory for mosquitos and therefore malaria. DDT fixed it.

DDT went with American GIs as they marched across Europe. DDT was used in the death camps as they were liberated, no doubt saving many of those devastated and delicate people who had somehow survived to that point.

When the war ended, DDT became available for civilian use and was particularly effective in Africa, where 80 percent of all infectious diseases—including malaria, which has killed hundreds of millions—are carried by insects. With DDT, malaria began to disappear. In South Africa, malaria cases dropped by 80 percent. In Sri Lanka, cases went from roughly a million a year to—get this—eighteen cases in 1963. It should be noted that when DDT use was halted in Sri Lanka on account of the cost, malaria cases shot up to six hundred thousand in 1968. Malaria was virtually wiped out in Europe shortly after the war.

It came to widespread use in the United States, and people of a certain age, including me, fondly remember those summer nights when the DDT truck came rumbling down the street shooting out an enormous cloud of mist. We would gleefully run behind it. Moms would say, "Maybe that isn't good for you. Oh, go ahead."

But then, the phony science of the Left reared its ugly head. In 1957, there was an effort to limit DDT's use in Nassau County, New York, something that came to the attention of Wallace Shawn, editor of the *New Yorker,* and writer Rachel Carson. Carson wrote a series of articles that later appeared in book form. Like Paul Ehrlich's *Population Bomb,* another phony book of science, *Silent Spring,*[26] simply exploded in popularity. With its 1962 publication, Carson's book single-handedly created the modern environmental movement and led eventually to Richard Nixon founding the noxious EPA.

Silent Spring made many dubious claims. The title is a reference to her main argument, that DDT and other pesticides were killing birds, who soon would sing no more. Many species would become extinct, she said. She claimed DDT would cause cancer in humans.

None of this was true.

Part of her evidence that birds would become extinct—indeed, what brought DDT to her attention—was a letter to the *Boston Globe* that claimed birds had died after DDT had been sprayed in suburban Boston. As Zubrin points out, pretty much all Carson's evidence about birds was no stronger than this, anecdotal at best.

She claimed the bird population in the United States had declined precipitously since the introduction of DDT after World War II. In fact, according to the Audubon Society, which had nonetheless bought into her thesis, the U.S. bird population had quadrupled between 1941, before

DDT, and 1960, the height of DDT use. Carson raised particular alarm about the threatened extinction of the robin—which she called "the tragic symbol of the fate of birds." During that period, the robin population actually increased twelvefold. Zubrin points to bird counters over Hawk Mountain, Pennsylvania, who have been reporting bird sightings since 1930. Osprey sightings increased from 200 in 1945 to 600 in 1970. Migrating raptors increased from 9,291 in 1946 to almost 30,000 in 1968. There is voluminous data that Carson's claims about birds are unscientific and utterly phony.[27]

What about cancer in humans? Scientists don't agree with Carson's claim.[28]

In 1971, the newly formed EPA initiated an investigation into the arguments for and against DDT. After 125 witnesses and 365 exhibits, the panel concluded that Carson was wrong on all counts.[29]

The report pointed out that DDT had been the most tested and most widely used pesticide for the previous twenty years, and that not a single case of toxicity had been reported anywhere in the world, not even among industrial workers who produced the stuff and had thus been exposed to it for two decades at significantly higher levels than civilians in the field. The only evidence presented about human harm was a few experimental tests on mice. The most powerful claim made in the hearings was by a Dr. Samuel Epstein, who essentially argued there was no evidence that DDT *didn't* cause cancer. The report concluded, "There is no serious testimony which would support any theory that DDT has been shown to have teratogenic effects."[30]

The ruling of the panel was almost immediately overturned by liberal Republican William Ruckelshaus, the EPA's very first administrator. Ruckelshaus, who had not attended any of the hearings and did not read the report himself, declared that DDT was carcinogenic and banned it in the United States. The U.S. Agency for International Development tied foreign aid to banning DDT.[31]

Some say banning DDT has led directly to a hundred million deaths.[32] Anti-DDT advocates get tetchy when anyone compares this to the millions Hitler killed. In fact, it is obviously far greater. One could throw in Stalin and Pol Pot to boot and begin to approach the deaths due to Rachel Carson and William Ruckelshaus and their hooey about DDT.

This may be an old debate with hardly any chance of being revisited, not even with the 2016 outbreak of the Zika virus, also mosquito-borne, that became the cause du jour for those promoting abortion and other liberal desiderata. Zika could be wiped out by DDT, as could malaria, which has once more reached epidemic proportions in Africa.

The World Health Organization, which still says DDT is not carcinogenic, reports there were 214 million cases of malaria in 2015 that resulted in 438,000 deaths. Almost all of them occurred in Africa. It is reported that economic losses in Africa—due to healthcare costs, lost work, and declines in tourism—amount to $12 billion a year.

Imagine lying in a hut all day, sweating, feverish, unable to move or work, with a chance (25 percent in adults, 40 percent in kids) of developing severe respiratory problems and a great likelihood of dying. That is malaria. Is it any wonder that Africa is a basket case?

All of this could be fixed by DDT and likely many other pesticides scientists would develop if not for the tremendous cost in time and treasure fighting the leftwing liars of science. To this day, administrators at USAID insist the DDT restrictions were a good idea.

Anne Peterson, USAID assistant administrator for global health, told ABC's John Stossel, "I believe that the strategies we are using are as effective as spraying with DDT.... So, politically correct or not, I am very confident that what we are doing is the right strategy."[33]

In 2005, USAID chief Kent Hill said his agency does not "ban" the use of DDT: "USAID strongly supports spraying as a preventative measure for malaria and will support the use of DDT when it is scientifically sound and warranted."[34] This is slippery at best. Perhaps USAID does not have an absolute ban on DDT, but it allows it only in limited circumstances and only inside of buildings. See that malarial swamp over there? It's not getting sprayed. USAID's priorities are pesticide-treated sleeping nets for women and children, anti-malarial pills for twenty-four hours after the onset of fever, and "intermittent preventative treatment" for pregnant women.[35]

USAID thinks this is effective. And the death toll grows ever higher. At this point, millions of deaths can be directly attributed to the Left's war on scientific progress. Phony science literally kills.

CHAPTER 8

Poverty Could Make You Rich

You could get rich peddling hunger in America. Some already have: the CEO of Feeding America makes $650,000 a year. With annual revenue of more than $2 billion and $109 million in assets, the charity is ranked the third largest in the country by *Forbes*.[1]

A more apt name might be "Fleecing America," because the spoils all come from the hunger grifters conning the rubes—in this case, the taxpayers, as well as the elites who are eager to believe the worst about America: that we are willing to let millions of kids go to bed hungry and that millions of adults go without meals for whole days so their kids can have a few scraps. But it's all a lie, a sleight of hand, and, tragically, a distraction from what really drives hunger. Not that we talk about "hunger" any more. It's now "food insecurity." Just like "global warming," which became "climate change," "hunger" has had to be re-branded.

Profiting from Poverty

Tragically, a few poor children in America do go to bed hungry—
because their parents prioritize drugs or smoking over food and splurg-
ing at McDonalds over keeping a steady supply of ingredients for healthy
meals in the fridge at home. In fact, research shows that "food insecurity" in America could be quickly solved if poor people would just smoke
fewer cigarettes, cut out their daily Coke habit, and replace all those Big
Macs with rice and beans and a few fresh vegetables. But the anti-hunger
advocates are not addressing this very real problem of behavior. And so
it's the anti-hunger professionals, not the hungry children in poor and
often dysfunctional families, who benefit handsomely from the supposed
campaign against hunger.

The hunger con goes like this. The activists claim that one in eight
Americans struggles with "food insecurity." This statistic is supposed to
make us think that 12.5 percent of Americans, 40 million people, sometimes go hungry. That would make the hypothetical State of Hunger
larger than any state in the Union, larger than California, twice the size
of both Florida and New York. For these millions of poor hungry fellow
citizens, you are supposed to dip into your pocket and send Feeding
America money. You are supposed to call your representative in Congress
and demand that he or she support billions more for Feeding America
and all the other hunger grifters.

Don't I care about millions of hungry kids in America? I would care
about them—if they existed. Like catastrophic climate change, hunger
in America is largely a hoax, a massive money-sucking hoax.

Listen to what the hunger hustlers say. Robert Egger, founder of
the DC Central Kitchen, says, "hunger threatens our economic future
and our national security." He claims that our national security is
threatened because poor kids are not physically fit enough to be soldiers. True, but they're not too skinny—they're too fat. So Egger is
reduced to arguing, "Even those who eat three meals a day may be
malnourished."[2]

The U.S. Department of Agriculture (USDA) enables the hunger
con. It defines hunger as "the uneasy or painful sensation caused by a

lack of food."[3] This temporary feeling is unpleasant, but it is something regularly experienced by millions of Weight Watchers® members—and even just people who skip lunch to work on an urgent project at the office, or realize too late that they should have made reservations for their date at that popular restaurant. It is not the same thing as malnutrition, or true hunger.[4]

Surveying "Security" instead of Hunger

Starting in 1995, the USDA has conducted a regular survey of food security that measures food choices, intakes, shortages, and budgetary constraints. The 1995 report ties the lack of "food security" to lack of funds—an important fact to remember, in light of how the "food insecure" spend their money.

Between 1995 and 2006, the USDA defined four broad categories of food security: "food secure," "food insecure without hunger," "food insecure with moderate hunger," and "food insecure with severe hunger." In 2006, they changed their categories to persons with "low food security" and those with "very low food security." They dropped "food insecurity with hunger" because not enough respondents reported that they felt hunger at any point during the reporting year. This ought to be a tip-off that something is fishy with government hunger numbers.

The USDA reports that the "eating patterns of one or more household members were disrupted and their food intake reduced at least some time during the year because they couldn't afford enough food."[5] Those households reported cutting back on intake—but also eating unbalanced meals or relying on cheaper food. Wait a minute. Is this really "hunger"? Who hasn't had an unbalanced meal from time to time, or decided to go with the cheaper option on the menu?

Other stats from the survey do seem alarming at first. One in thirty adults in the United States is said to have experienced very low food security. One in thirty-five was hungry for at least one day because there was not enough money for food in the household. One adult in a hundred did not eat for a whole day because of a lack of money for food.[6] But keep that "lack of money for food" in the back of your mind—more on it later.

According to the government, one child in 165 experienced very low food security. One child in 125 went hungry for at least one day because of a lack of money for food. One child in 250 skipped at least one meal because of a lack of food resources. One child in a thousand did not eat for an entire day because there was not enough money for food.[7] Feeding America claims that thirteen million children are food insecure. But in fact the one-in-165 USDA statistic yields a total less than one tenth of that number. And the one child in a thousand who spent a whole day without eating equals about seventy-four thousand kids in the whole country. Even one hungry child is a tragedy. But the "anti-hunger" lobby is grossly exaggerating the scope of the problem—and proposing the wrong solutions.

It should be clear that though children are usually trotted out as at most risk of hunger, it is really adults who are most exposed to food insecurity. Only 4 percent of the food insecure are kids. About 7 percent are elderly, and a whopping 89 percent are non-elderly adults.

In congressional testimony in the summer of 2015, Heritage Foundation hunger and poverty expert Robert Rector said, "For Americans to go without food for an entire day represents a social problem, but it is a problem that is limited in scope, and it requires a well-informed policy response."[8]

How is it possible for Americans not to be able to feed themselves? Rector pointed out, "In fact, filling a stomach is quite cheap; 1,000 calories of rice, purchased in bulk, costs only 30 cents. In a pinch, an adult can fill his stomach and meet all his daily calorie needs with healthful but inexpensive foods for a dollar a day."[9]

The culprit is adults' bad choices. "Cigarette smoking is a major cause of very low food security," Rector told Congress. He is not a no-smoking scold; he is concerned about the cost of the habit. "Very low food security adults are much more likely to smoke than are food-secure adults, and money that is spent on cigarettes cannot be spent on food."

According to Rector, "45% of adults with very low food security during the year smoked cigarettes during the 30 days before the survey."[10]

Using data from the National Health and Nutrition Evaluation Survey, Rector pointed out that 62 percent of adults "who reported they 'did not eat' for at least one whole day during the last 30 days before the survey because 'there was not enough money for food,' had smoked cigarettes during the month."[11] Lesson: stop smoking, eat, and feed your family. Rector figured that very low food security smokers consumed nineteen packs of cigarettes per month, at an average cost of $112 per month. That's 63 percent of the cost of food for a single adult under the USDA's "Thrifty Food Plan."

Besides money wasted on cigarettes, there is the belief, particularly harmful to the poor, that fast food is a cheap way to eat. But fast food is not the poor man's friend. Nothing could be further from the truth. A regular diet of fast food not only makes you fat and can kill you, but it's also far more expensive per calorie than cooking and eating at home.

Rector pointed out that "a nutritious meal of rice and beans cooked at home provides around 2,200 calories for each dollar of food spending; by contrast, a Big Mac provides 138 calories for each dollar spent, as well as a lot of unhealthy fat."[12] Traditional food stuffs are far cheaper per calorie than fast food. All-purpose flour provides 4,717 calories per dollar; rice provides 3,599; rice and beans, 2,178; peanut butter, 1,750.

Sadly, low food security households spend 25 percent of their food budget at fast food restaurants or at vending machines.

And then there are the sugary soft drinks that make you fat and also cost a lot. Very low food security adults drink an average of two sodas per day. Presumably they buy them at $1.00 or $1.25 per can out of vending machines. This can run north of $70 per month.

Eliminating smokes and Cokes would put almost $200 more in the family food budget every month—just from cutting one person's wasteful habits. Double that for a couple.

"Food insecurity" is a question of money. Folks spend unwisely, run out of money by the end of the month, and end up skipping a meal, eating less, or being worried about food. The vast majority of food insecurity—even very high food insecurity—could be alleviated by simple changes in behavior.

But the answer the massive food lobby favors is quite different: more and more money. They lobby for ever-more government spending, and they work feverishly to convince Americans to kick in yet more private donations as well. Lobbying and fundraising is where they spend a sizable chunk of their vast fortune. They also spend some of their lucre on food pantries and food banks, of which there are something like thirty thousand in this country. Rector, though, calculates that only a third of "very low food secure" families avail themselves of food banks or pantries. Two-thirds say they don't have access to them.[13]

And the "anti-hunger" lobby is only one part of the vast complex of "charitable" professionals and federal bureaucrats making a comfortable living off poverty in America.

Waging War, but Never Winning

The War on Poverty has been by far the most expensive and least successful "unconditional war" the United States has ever fought. When he declared that war in January 1964, President Lyndon Johnson said he meant to strike "at the causes of, not just the consequences of poverty." He claimed that he wanted to "cure" and "prevent" poverty—to make "taxpayers out of taxeaters."[14] Can you imagine even the most conservative Republican speaking like that today, let alone a Democrat? Sounds a lot like the "makers versus takers" rhetoric that the Republicans abandoned a few years ago.

Johnson didn't set out to create a permanent underclass utterly dependent on the government—or at least that's not how he sold welfare to the American people. He was proposing temporary assistance that would lead the poor to self-sufficiency. Maybe he believed it. Maybe he didn't. But his Democratic heirs certainly saw the permanent benefit to having a sizable electoral constituency relying on them to keep the money flowing.

In fact, the War on Poverty was not needed, even at the time. In fact, it was counterproductive from the start. Poverty in America was decreasing rapidly at the time Johnson declared war on it in his 1965 State of the Union speech—right up until he got the government into the business of subsidizing it. The percentage of individuals who were poor by the official poverty standard was plummeting consistently, year after year, from shortly after World War II until the institution of the War on Poverty in the mid-1960s. Poverty had reached a peak of almost 35 percent in 1950—and then it fell off a cliff. At the time of Johnson's announcement, the poverty rate stood at less than 20 percent, and continued to decline for a few years to roughly 14 percent. But under the War on Poverty regime, the eradication of poverty ground to a halt. With a few ups and downs since the mid-1960s, the poverty rate today stands at roughly 14 percent. That's right: the poverty rate is the same as it was when the War on Poverty kicked in. It should be understood, though, that the poverty threshold has changed over time.[15] What counts as poverty today may not have qualified in 1965—something that makes sense because standards of living do change over time.

But the War on Poverty has, if anything, had a counterproductive effect—slowing to a virtual halt the eradication of poverty that was well under way when it was announced. And we've paid an almost incredibly high price for these dismal results. During all these years that the poverty rate has remained basically unchanged, the United States has spent a breathtaking $22 trillion (in constant 2012 dollars) in poverty relief. We have created a permanent dependent class and destroyed the main engine of poverty relief to boot—the family.

As Robert Rector pointed out, "Adjusted for inflation, this spending (which does not include Social Security or Medicare) is three times the cost of all military wars in U.S. history since the American revolution."

Today the U.S. government runs more than eighty means-tested welfare programs—including cash, food, housing, medical care, and other social services. A whopping hundred million people get some kind of aid. That is a third of the total population.

Moving the Metrics

How can it be that we spend so much on helping people out of poverty, yet the poverty rate is the same as when we started? For one thing, there is a bit of a shell game going on with the statistics.

When determining if a person or a family qualifies as "poor," the government excludes almost all government benefits from the calculation. As Robert Rector pointed out, "this neat bureaucratic ploy ensured that welfare programs could grow infinitely while 'poverty' remained unchanged."[16]

A 2014 story in the *New York Times*, for example, described the situation of Anthony Goytia, a Southern California Walmart night-shift worker who says he's reliant on payday loans to pay his bills. He is a father of four, making "about $16,000 a year." What the *New York Times* did not report was the cash value of federal and California benefits that Mr. Goytia and his family likely receive. He certainly qualifies for assistance, but it is not mentioned. It never is.[17]

Robert Rector extrapolated from Department of Labor statistics that "poor families spend $2.40 for every $1.00 of their reported income. If public housing benefits are added to the tally, the ratio of consumption to income rises to $2.60 for every $1.00. In other words, the 'income' figures that the Census bureau uses to calculate poverty dramatically undercount the economic resources available to lower-income households."[18]

So, how poor are America's poor? We have seen how the hunger mafia jiggers the numbers to inflate their customer count. The poverty mavens pull the same stunt by not including welfare benefits in the poverty calculation.

But the real eye-opener is that America's poor live lives that the middle class of just a few years ago would envy.

When the War on Poverty began, 12 percent of *all Americans* owned an air conditioner. Today, 80 percent of poor households own one. According to the Census Bureau, almost 75 percent of poor households own a car or truck. Thirty percent own more than one. Nearly two-thirds have cable or satellite television. Keep in mind how expensive cable is: upward of $150 per month. Forty percent have wide-screen plasma or LCD TVs. Fifty percent own a personal computer. Twenty-five percent own a digital video recorder. Ninety-two percent own a microwave.

The Left routinely mocks these statistics. Technology always drops in price, and big-box stores like Walmart always drive prices down to a manageable number. A fifty-five-inch TV set, however, stills costs more than $1,000, even at Costco.

Jordan Weissmann writes in *Slate*, "How punishing is poverty in 2014? That depends. When it comes to consumer goods, low-income families might have it better than ever. The poor can now buy cheap cellphones and televisions that would have seemed like fantastical luxuries to yesteryear's rich. Microwaves and air conditioners are standard. Food is relatively inexpensive, as is clothing."[19] Weissmann does not mention the one and often two cars and trucks owned by the poor, or that the caloric intake of the poor closely matches that of those in higher income brackets.[20]

Want to know what else the poor own? Houses. The poverty industry wants you to believe that the poor live in dire circumstances: ramshackle homes, cold-water flats crammed ten to a room, rundown trailers at the end of Tobacco Road. Nothing could be further from the truth. Forty-two percent of poor families own their own homes, and the average home owned by a poor family has three bedrooms, one and a half baths, a garage, and a patio or porch. Only 9.5 percent live in mobile homes.

The typical poor person in America has more living space than the typical person living in every European country except Luxembourg. The square footage of the typical *poor household* in the United States was fourteen hundred in 2005. The non-poor in Austria had 1,060 square feet; Denmark, 1,231 square feet, Germany, 968 square feet, and so on and on throughout Europe. Luxembourgers lived in households averaging 1,437 square feet, only 37 square feet more. Keep in mind that these statistics compare America's poor with Europe's non-poor.

How are poor Americans doing in other areas? Surprisingly well, though you won't hear this from the Left.

There is no evidence of malnutrition in America. In fact, "nutrient density (amount of vitamins, minerals, and protein per kilocalorie of food) does not vary by income class," according to Robert Rector.[21] Low-income and middle-income people have the same high fat intake. Nutrient intake for well-off preschoolers is the same as that among poor preschoolers. The typical poor person consumes roughly the same amount of nutriment as someone from the middle class. Children below the poverty line actually eat more meat than children from the upper middle class. Poor kids consume protein well above the amount recommended by the government.

Poor kids are hale. Stuntedness and thinness due to nutritional deficiencies are virtually unknown in the United States. Only 2.6 percent of children in the United States are either stunted or thin, and this 2.6 percent falls within the range that is expected in any normal prosperous population. Compare that to Africa, 38 percent; Asia, 22 percent; Latin America, 22 percent; and Oceana, 41 percent.

Poor boys today between the ages of eighteen and nineteen are actually taller and heavier than boys of similar age in the general population in the 1950s. They are also an inch taller and ten pounds heavier than GIs in World War II. They are twenty pounds heavier than the doughboys in World War I.[22]

Wailing about Welfare Reform

In 2016, we celebrated the twentieth anniversary of President Bill Clinton's Personal Responsibility and Work Opportunity Act, otherwise known as welfare reform. That 1996 legislation replaced Aid to Families with Dependent Children with Temporary Assistance for Needy Families. The new reform required, for the first time, that some recipients work or train for jobs as a condition of receiving aid.

At the time welfare reform was passed, you would have thought the world was coming to the end. The Left went nuts. Even someone as sober as the revered Daniel Patrick Moynihan predicted that children would be "sleeping on grates, picked up frozen in the morning."[23]

What happened? Robert Rector reports, "Reform cut welfare case-loads by over 50 percent, employment of the least-skilled single mothers surged, and the poverty rates of black children and single-parent families dropped rapidly to historic lows."[24]

This resounding success hasn't stopped the Left from continuing their fearmongering. In 2015, Kathryn J. Edin and H. Luke Shaefer claimed that welfare reform had forced 3.55 million children to live on less than two dollars per day.[25] *Bloomberg News* reported that America's poorest poor now had incomes lower than "disabled beggars of Addis Ababa in Ethiopia."[26] Edin and Shaefer claim that the typical extremely poor family must sell their blood and collect aluminum cans to survive.[27]

All of this is bosh. Most of these folks who are supposedly living on the streets actually have air conditioning, and almost all have cell phones, VCRs, or DVD players. Only 1 percent frequently did not have enough food to eat sometime over the last four months; 8 percent sometimes didn't have enough to eat; the remaining 91 percent reported always having enough to eat.[28]

The horror stories are largely sleight of hand by the Left. That two dollars a day the poor supposedly have to live on excludes just about all of the substantial welfare benefits these families receive. As we have seen, based on Department of Labor statistics, the typical poor household spends $2.40 for every dollar of income. The same Department of Labor Consure Expenditure survey shows the extreme poor spend $25 for every $1 of income.[29]

Using government data, Robert Rector and his team report that from 1984 through 2015 there were only *sixty-one* instances of any families actually living on less than two dollars per day in the United States. Further, two-thirds of those sixty-one families lived in public housing. Edin and Shaefer claim that one family in every twenty-five lives on less than two dollars per day.[30] In fact, based on self-reporting, it is one in 4,469.[31]

But there is a *conservative* caricature of the typical welfare recipient that also does not comport with the truth. Remember Linda Taylor, named the "welfare queen" by Ronald Reagan? Taylor was a welfare cheat who used multiple aliases to bilk the system.

The modern "welfare queen" has a very different profile. He's a surfer dude named Jason Greenslate who was outed three years ago during the September 2013 U.S. House of Representatives debate on reducing the food stamp budget by a measly $40 million over—get this—ten years (out of a total $74 *billion*).[32]

Fox News found Greenslate, a "blissfully jobless California surfer," living the "rat" life and using food stamps while trying to launch his career as a rock musician. Greenslate was first spotted by a Fox reporter buying sushi and lobster with his food stamp card. "All paid for by our wonderful tax dollars," he said. "This is the way I want to live and I don't really see anything changing. It's free food; it's awesome."[33] By his own account, Greenslate is not interested in any paid work; he considers his band practice his job.

Both Taylor and Greenslate are outliers, without a doubt. There are truly poor people in America, even some who are desperately poor.

Promoting Permanent Underclass Status

But the true picture of poverty in America is far from the Left's dystopian nightmare. They simply lie about the numbers to milk ever more cash from the U.S. taxpayer. And to what effect? The War on Poverty has not only failed on its own terms. It has actually exacerbated the problem, so that there is now a permanent underclass relying not on marriage, family, education, and work to advance themselves but instead on spirit-sapping government largesse.

Poverty has almost everything to do with family formation, a topic the Left considers racist or misogynist even to bring up. Daniel Patrick Moynihan, then at the Department of Labor, reported in 1965 that black poverty was intractably tied to a lack of family formation. Lyndon Johnson believed him and called the issue "the next and more profound stage of the battle for civil rights." The Democrat president specifically mentioned "the breakdown of the Negro family structure." He blamed black poverty on past injustice but also mentioned the family formation problem in what he later called his "greatest civil rights speech."[34]

The Left went crazy. They condemned Moynihan and came down hard on Johnson, who never mentioned the issue again. Whitney Young of the National Urban League claimed that family formation was no more than a "peripheral issue." He said, "The problem is discrimination." William Ryan, writing in *The Nation*, called Moynihan's report a "highly sophomoric treatment of illegitimacy" and said that whites might have the same problem except they had access to abortion and contraception.[35]

As Kay S. Hymowitz has written in *City Journal*, "For white liberals and the black establishment, poverty became a zero-sum game: either you believed, as they did, that there was a defect in the system, or you believed that there was a defect in the individual."[36]

Not only did the Left push back against family instability as an explanation for poverty, they went all in celebrating single mothers. The matriarchal family became all the rage. What's more, the two-parent family came under attack as dangerous for children and women. Robert Hill of the Urban League claimed, "Research studies have revealed that many one-parent families are more intact or cohesive than many two-parent families: data on child abuse, battered wives and runaway children indicate higher rates among two-parent families in suburban areas than one-parent families in inner city communities."[37] But as Kay Hymowitz would point out, "That science, needless to say, was as reliable as a deadbeat dad."[38]

But the attack on the two-parent family fed right into the feminist narrative that the nuclear family is an oppressive patriarchy. In the Sexual Revolution, as we have seen, marriage and family became a prison where women's happiness went to die.

And as for all those women and, increasingly, girls who fell for this leftwing propaganda and had babies out of wedlock and lapsed into poverty, the ever-burgeoning welfare state often required them to stay single. Their benefits would be cut if they married. It became a vicious cycle.

Consider that when Moynihan raised the alarm about illegitimacy in the black community, it stood at 25 percent. This was significantly up from previous decades. In 1940, it had been just 14 percent. It would grow to 56 percent in 1980. Today the number is 72 percent. Nearly three-quarters of black babies are born into a family without a father present. It should be noted that the white illegitimacy rate today stands at 32 percent, higher than the black rate that so alarmed Moynihan long ago.

At long last, even lefties have begrudgingly started to agree that family formation is the solution to poverty. Originally, Princeton social scientist Sara McLanahan largely bought into the criticism of the Moynihan report, that its critique of inner-city families was tinged with racism. But she is an honest scholar, and she went to work. In her research, she discovered that it is in fact true that single-parent families do not do as well as two-parent families on a whole host of measurements. She determined the two-parent married family is the gold standard. Other honest social scientists followed in her footsteps.

Even one *New York Times* columnist has gotten on board with the real, hard social science. Writing in 2014, economics reporter Annie Lowrey wrote a column "Can Marriage Cure Poverty?" Marco Rubio had been arguing just that on the campaign trail. And Lowrey actually agreed. Marriage *can* solve poverty. She pointed out, "Almost no marriages in which both partners work full time fall below the poverty line; about one-third of households headed by a single mother are poor. One in eight children with two married parents lives below the poverty line; five in 10 living with a single mother do."[39]

But these facts are certainly not common currency on the Left, and the hunger and poverty grift continues largely unabated. Under the Trump administration, you can be sure that the poor and the hungry—who went largely unnoticed during Obama's eight years in office—will be miraculously rediscovered. Just know that pretty much everything the Left says about this is a lie.

CHAPTER 9

Flaming Water, Flaming Lies

I t was the most serious of matters so, of course, it called for Yoko Ono to sing about it. On Jimmy Fallon she sang, sort of, in that unmistakable warble, "Don't frack your mother." Singing right along was her son Sean, who looked every bit the Asian version of his dad—her husband. Dr. Freud, call your office.[1]

Celebrities, noted for their Algonquin-like wit, took to the word "frack" with gusto and glee. Google will quickly take you to thirty-second videos with Hayden Panettiere, Wilmer Valderrama, and Marisa Tomei mugging for the camera and shouting kind of tongue-in-cheek at their buddies President Obama and Governors Brown and Cuomo, "What the frack? Are you fracking kidding me? Ban fracking now." Clever, right?

Fear-Mongering about Fracking

The celebrities string together a series of "scientific" claims: "Fracking pollutes our oceans." "Fracking poisons our water." "Fracking makes climate change worse." "Fracking relies on toxic chemicals that cause cancer." "Fracking pollutes our drinking water." "Fracking is making people sick across the country."[2]

Hydraulic fracking is a most remarkable technology, a miracle, a gift from God for a United States that had become dependent on $100 per barrel oil from Arab sheiks. The United States is sitting on an ocean of natural gas that lies a few miles below the country's surface. There are actually several oceans of natural gas under the United States—and other countries, too, but while most countries are busy banning fracking technology, we are making use of it.

A few miles below the surface of the earth, natural gas is trapped in sandstone, limestone, and shale formed by the decomposition of dead organisms. It had long been known that the gas could be used if it could somehow be released and brought to the surface—an exceedingly difficult proposition. Early drillers used explosions. Later they began pumping pressurized water to break up the rock and therefore release the gas. This is hydraulic fracturing, popularly known as fracking.

It is estimated that one million wells have been fracked since the 1940s, but for decades these were limited to the more porous sandstone or limestone. The prize has been the gas trapped in the harder strata of shale below that.

A major breakthrough came with the development of sideways drilling in the 1990s. Think of those bent straws you drink from in the hospital. Suddenly it was possible to drill down a mile or two, sideways a mile or more, and then shoot in highly pressurized water mixed with sand and a small amount of chemicals to fracture the shale and release the gas. "Chemicals added to the water dissolve minerals, kill bacteria that might plug up the well, and inset sand to prop open the fractures," as Susan Brantley and Anna Meyendorff explained in the *New York Times*.[3]

The world's largest shale field, by both oil and gas output, is the Marcellus Shale, which stretches from the western edge of New York State, covers the western half of Pennsylvania, and includes all of West Virginia. It produces roughly forty thousand barrels of oil and fourteen billion cubic feet of natural gas every day.[4]

Next is the Eagle Ford Shale in Texas, which produces a total of 2.45 million barrels of fuel a day, with a gas-to-oil ratio of 45 to 55.[5] The third largest shale field is the Permian Basin, also in Texas, producing 2.33 million barrels a day (nearly all oil), followed by the Bakken Shale in North Dakota with an oil and gas combination of 1.28 million barrels a day. Shale deposits in North Dakota have also gotten a lot of ink in recent years because of the how the Bakken Shale has utterly rejuvenated that region's economy.

In November 2016, news of yet another shale reserve in Texas broke. The U.S. Geological Survey announced discovery of the Wolfcamp Shale near Midland, Texas, "one of the largest reserves of recoverable oil in the agency's history," with 20 billion barrels of oil, 16 trillion cubic feet of natural gas, and 1.6 billion barrels of natural gas liquids.[6]

There are also shale fields throughout the western United States, which you can see if you peer out your window on your flight to Los Angeles.

There are abundant reasons to be thrilled about what fracking brings us. For the greens among us, it "produces fewer harmful particles in the air." It's not me saying this, it's the environmentalists at the Yale Climate Connection.[7]

They point out that natural gas is replacing dirty coal. As recently as 2008 coal made up 50 percent of U.S. electricity generation, but it was down to 37 percent in 2012. Natural gas went from generating 20 percent of our electricity to fueling 30 percent. During that time frame, nitrogen oxide and sulfur dioxide emissions dropped dramatically.

The Yale greens point out that "natural gas produces somewhere between 44 and 50 percent of the greenhouse gas emissions compared with burning coal." They say that while methane, one of the bugaboos of anti-frackers, has a twenty-year time horizon, in the hundred-year time horizon used for measuring global warming, methane is "negligible."

As with GMOs, the criticism of fracking comes largely, though not exclusively, from leftwing activist groups rather than scientists. In fact, it seems the opposition to fracking really got going when a gadfly off-Broadway hipster from New York made a documentary film called *Gasland* that got picked up by HBO, turning him into a star and putting the issue of fracking on the front page of the *New York Times*. Josh Fox is his name, and he is a fabulist.

This is Josh Fox, from a 2001 script called Hyper Real America:

> You know, I met a genius on the train today. He was only six years old. He sat beside me and as the train ran down along the coast we came to the ocean, and he looked at me and he said, It's not pretty. That was the first time I had realized that. Don't be ashamed of anything. I guess God meant it all, like locks on doors. You may not believe it, but there are people who go through life with very little friction or distress. They dress well, eat well, sleep well. They are contented with their family life. They have moments of grief but all in all they are undisturbed and often feel very good. And when they die it is an easy death, usually in their sleep. Your IQ may be one-six-fiver, but you still got to know these things. You hungry?[8]

Deep, right?

Before Josh Fox made *Gasland*, with its iconic poster of Fox wearing a gasmask and whimsically playing a banjo in front of a fracking well, the *New York Times* had published no more than three stories that mentioned fracking. The first was in a letter to the editor in 2007.[9]

Gasland received critical raves even though it is ponderous and repetitive, thanks to Fox's monotone, mumbly-mouth narrative. It was in release for only four weeks at a single theater, and it brought in a measly $30,000, but that wasn't the point. The point was to qualify for the following year's Academy Awards. And it succeeded. *Gasland* won a boatload of awards, including an Oscar nomination for best documentary. It also won three Primetime Emmys.

And, as intended, it all created a huge buzz and gave dim-bulb young Hollywood and the zombie environmentalists a new cause—opposition to fracking, which up to that point wasn't getting any traction to speak of.

Misrepresenting with Methane

Gasland created a movement, a huge movement, built almost totally on lies, lies that Josh Fox has repeated over and over in interviews and in a documentary sequel, too.

The most iconic, arresting image from *Gasland* is one in which a grizzled fellow from Weld County, Colorado, turns on his tap water and lights it on fire. The flame shoots up and burns the hair off his arm. It's pretty amazing. Josh Fox does his best aw-shucks grin for the camera, slumps his shoulders, and collapses in utter amazement against the counter.

Fox fooled his gullible viewers into believing that methane gas released from nearby fracking fields had invaded the poor guy's water supply and made his drinking water flammable. Bang. Proof positive that fracking was nothing short of a heinous heartless plot of the greedy energy companies.

But here's the thing. In 2008, two years before *Gasland* came out—in fact before Fox even began production of the film—Colorado State environmental watchdogs had investigated the gentleman's water and concluded that the methane was not coming from fracking: "Dissolved methane in well-water appears to be biogenic in origin. Tests were positive for iron related bacteria and sulfate reducing bacteria. There are no indications of oil and gas related impacts to water well."[10]

In *Gasland II*, Fox's even longer and more ponderous sequel, there was a still more dramatic demonstration of flaming tap water. A rich guy named Steve Lipsky is shown by Fox lighting up a garden hose like a flame thrower. Again, Josh Fox is simply amazed. Again he wants his gullible viewers to think that hydraulic fracking has turned Lipsky's home into a potential bomb. What Fox does not tell you is that roughly at the same time he was filming the flaming hose, a judge was handing down a judgment that Lipsky had conspired with an attorney to "attach a garden hose to a gas vent—not to a water line— and then light and burn the gas from the end of the hose." It seems Lipsky was embroiled in a lawsuit with the oil and gas company and was using phony evidence in his case.[11] Fox never let his viewers know about any of this.

Freelance Irish journalists Phelim McAleer and Ann McElhinney made a counter-documentary called *FrackNation*.[12] In one memorable scene McAleer confronts Fox at one of his public lectures and questions him about flaming water.

It turns out that flaming water is not uncommon. In fact, George Washington and Tom Paine lit New Jersey's Millstone River on fire as a scientific experiment.[13] Imagine Washington and Paine in a little boat poking the mud and lighting the bubbles that came up. "By God, Paine. You were right. The river burns." In those days, it was called swamp gas.

Stories of flaming tap water are part of American lore. In *FrackNation*, McAleer shows an old clip of a fountain lit on fire in a small American town. It was so fascinating, especially at night, that the city fathers left it that way and let children swim in it.

Flaming water was common in the region Josh Fox was most concerned about, the Delaware River Basin, near his parents' weekend house.

When questioned in *FrackNation* about why he didn't point this out in *Gasland*, a clearly uncomfortable Fox didn't want to answer. Finally, he admitted that there were stories about flaming tap water as far back as "1936, so what?" The answer to that "so what" is pretty obvious. The water that his documentary showed on fire was apparently flammable for generations—not just all of a sudden when the frackers and Josh Fox showed up.

Cancer-Causing Contamination?

But these are the searing images that make good TV. Much of Fox's arguments center on a tiny town in Pennsylvania called Dimock and have less to do with flaming water than with drinking water that has supposedly been contaminated with cancerous agents pumped into the ground and then is bubbling back up into the aquifer, making people and animals sick.

There are images of horses losing their hair, and cats, too. Kids with bloody noses. Moms who say they have constant headaches.

But are these claims any more true than the flaming water?

The main focus of these claims made in *Gasland* were a few families in Dimock located smack on top of the Marcellus Shale and near those pesky fracking wells. One couple was particularly insistent and particularly entertaining. They had the brownest water, too. It was murky, very murky, oh-so-murky.

According to documentary film *FrackNation*, Craig and Julie Sautner made claims that "weapons-grade uranium" was in their well and that Cabot Oil was at fault. They made other wild claims as well. Put on the spot by filmmaker Phelim McAleer, Craig Sautner hemmed and hawed and seemed like an all-around con artist, but he was damn sure his water was tainted. McAleer asked him to draw some water from his tap, something Sautner did not want to do. He explained that on some days it was clear and some days murky, and you never knew just what would come out. Sure enough, the water that day came out crystal clear.

Eventually, the state environmental protection agency tested all the wells in the town, and all of them came up clean.[14] The Sautners demanded that the federal EPA test the wells, and it did. When those tests also came back clean, McAleer went to Dimock to interview the Sautners, and Julie Sautner threatened him with arrest, with a lawsuit, and with a gun—though she never brandished one, only her permit to carry.[15]

These were the folks Josh Fox and the other anti-fracking campaigners rely upon to make the case against fracking. Thin reeds.

Not all the people in Dimock were grifters. Some little old ladies talked about how their daddy's well way back when had methane in it, and methane "don't hurt you." There were a whole bunch of farmers, too, who just wanted to maintain their way of life. They needed the licensing money from the gas companies for the upkeep of their farms, but Josh Fox and his allies were blocking what was a remarkably good deal for their mineral rights.

Josh Fox and the anti-frackers make many other unsubstantiated claims that bona fide scientists easily swat away. For instance, the anti-frackers say that fracking causes breast cancer, that wherever fracking occurs there is a concomitant spike in that dreaded disease.

Josh Fox even produced an "emergency film" called *The Sky is Pink* in which he made the ridiculous claim, "In Texas, as throughout the United States, cancer rates fell. Except in one place: in the Barnett Shale. The five counties where there was the most drilling saw a rise in breast cancer throughout the counties."[16]

The claim by Fox was quickly and easily rebutted not only by scientists connected to Duke University and the University of Texas Southwestern Medical Center but also by Susan G. Komen for the Cure, the well-respected cancer research philanthropy.[17]

"The debate is becoming very emotional. And basically not using science," said Avner Vengosh of Duke.[18]

David Risser, an epidemiologist with the Texas Cancer Registry, said in an email to the Associated Press, "researchers checked state health data and found no evidence of an increase in the counties where the spike supposedly occurred."[19]

Simon Craddock Lee of the University of Texas called Fox's claim an "ecological fallacy."[20]

Spooking Us with Scary Chemicals

We're supposed to be spooked by the use of chemicals in fracking, including such scary-sounding compounds as "Benzene, Acrylamide, Ethylene Oxide, Bisphenol A, and formaldehyde," and some seven hundred others—all listed in a report from U.S. House Democrats.[21]

Keep in mind that fracking—the busting up of shale rock with high-pressure water and chemicals—happens between one and two miles below the surface of the earth. The aquifer from which drinking water is drawn is no more than a few hundred feet below the surface. Between the two are five to ten thousand feet of rock so hard that the early drillers had to blast it with explosions to get gas out and modern-day frackers have to blast water at a rate of fifteen thousand pounds per square inch. It is simply impossible for the water and the chemicals sent down the pipe to seep back up through the rock and settle into the aquifer.

As *Yale Climate Connections* reports, "It is highly unlikely that well-run drilling operations, which involve extracting oil and gas from thousands of feet down in the ground, are creating cracks that allow chemicals to reach relatively shallow aquifers and surface water supplies. Drinking water and oil and gas deposits are at very different levels in the ground."[22]

It is possible for the pipes, made of high-grade steel and cement, to rupture. But, as the Yale climate group says, preventing this is just a matter of "making sure the steel tubing, the casing, is not leaking and that the cement around it doesn't have cracks."

Note that 99 percent of the liquid sent down the pipe under furious pressure is water. The remaining 1 percent is sand and those nasty-sounding chemicals. Keep in mind also that there are chemicals in cabbage that will give you cancer if you eat enough cabbage—but you won't.

According to the definitive study by the EPA, there has never been a single instance of drinking-water contamination from the fracking process—the actual blasting of 99 percent highly pressurized water and 1 percent chemicals underground to fracture shale rock. There have been instances of minor contamination due to spillage of waste water, but not from the fracking itself.

The EPA, no friend to business, finally issued its definitive study in June 2015, the long-awaited report that anti-frackers had hoped would be a broad-based condemnation of fracking on grounds of water contamination.[23] It was far from it.

First, the EPA reported that there is a staggering amount of fracking—all the more opportunities to find the supposed widespread water contamination. Somewhere between twenty-five and thirty thousand new wells were drilled and fractured every year between 2011 and 2014. Fracking took place in twenty-five states, with half of the wells in Texas. Colorado had the second highest number of wells, followed by Pennsylvania and North Dakota. The EPA found 9.4 million people living within a mile of a fracking well and sixty-eight hundred sources of drinking water located within one mile of a well.

If drinking water contamination was a problem, you'd think there would be plenty of it to issue thunderous warnings about. But the EPA's findings are milquetoast: "We conclude there were above and below ground mechanisms by which hydraulic fracturing *have the potential* [the italics are mine] to impact drinking water resources." "Have the potential…" No better than that.

The report further found "no evidence that these mechanisms led to widespread, systematic impacts on drinking water resources in the United States." As we have seen, there were a few cases of contamination, a very few, and these were all due to spillage of waste water, not from the fracking itself.

Back in Dimock, the Sautners naturally refused to show filmmaker McAleer the EPA report giving their water a clean bill of health. McAleer submitted a Freedom of Information Act request for the film of the Sautners' meeting with the EPA that took place in their kitchen when they got the bad news about their clean water. It shows Craig Sautner and his wife going utterly ballistic, yelling and screaming and slamming things around. Poof went a major payday for the greedy, lying couple. They later sold their property for a mere $4,000 and moved out of state. Fracking continues largely unmolested in Pennsylvania.

But Governor Andrew Cuomo bought Josh Fox's argument, agreed with his Hollywood buddies, and banned fracking in New York State in the summer of 2015. Jobs-starved New Yorkers take note. He is largely and foolishly alone. Vermont is the only other state to join New York in the ban. As a measure of how rich we are in this natural wonder, there are now eighteen U.S. ports approved for construction for the export of the abundance of American gas.[24]

For the most part, the dumb Europeans are banning fracking, and it is reported that the Russians are behind the ban. The Russians are quite happy to have the Europeans sucking on the Russia-owned Gazprom teat until hell freezes over.[25]

The Fracking Scare Fades

In 2010, the year Josh Fox's movie came out, the *New York Times* ran thirty-seven stories about fracking—up from the three total in previous years. The *Times* ran 205 stories in 2011, and the anti-fracking fad peaked in 2012, with 315 stories in the *Times*. It was all downhill from there. Not even Josh's 2013 sequel *Gasland II* could stop the slide. By December 2016, the number of stories was down to 164. Poor Josh. Poor silly celebrities.

Sometimes the Luddites lose.

CHAPTER 10

Global Warming Is Real—and It's a Good Thing

There's global warming—and then there's the global warming scam. They're two different things. Global warming is real. The Earth did in fact start to get warmer at the end of Little Ice Age in 1870. And that has been a boon to mankind! Just like the Medieval Warm Period from AD 950 to 1250, which was a remarkable time for man's development. The global warming scam, on the other hand, is an unjustified panic over the claim that temperatures are rising dangerously because of industrialization. All manner of global catastrophe is upon us—disaster awaits if we don't stop using fossil fuels right now.

Creating a Climate Crisis

There are many variables that go into the world's climate. But the global warming alarmists are sure there's a single "culprit": our prosperous, developed industrial economy, powered by man's use of fossil fuels.

The weakness of the scamsters' arguments is clear from their desperate rebranding of their whole movement: what used to be "global warming" to "catastrophic climate change." Now they can claim that virtually anything that happens in the weather is proof of imminent catastrophe.

The remarkable and satisfying thing about the climate change panic—for skeptics, anyway—is its utter failure as a matter of public policy. The alarm has simply failed to catch on with the public at large, and so not even politicians who have bought into the global warming scam have been able to do much of anything to implement the economy-crippling regulations that the climate change fanatics are pushing.

In 1989, 32 percent of Americans "worried a great deal about global warming." Twenty-five years later, 32 percent of Americans "worry a great deal about global warming."[1] Sure, there have been fluctuations, but according Gallup, public opinion has not changed that much. And this is after what has been the most massive propaganda effort the world has ever seen: Billions of dollars spent to scare school kids. Billions on meetings and conferences and papers. More than 174 million hits come up on Google for "climate change" and the number grows daily.

There have been endless conventions and toothless protocols—the most recent being the Paris Climate Agreement that may never come into effect, and even if it does, it is entirely voluntary. Most likely it will simply fade into oblivion, just like its predecessor, the Kyoto Accords.

The story of global warming is one of scare-mongering, propaganda, mass hysteria, faked hockey sticks, and phony science.

The "scientific" theory behind the scare campaign is quite simple: with the rise of industrialization the levels of so-called "greenhouse gases" (that phrase alone is a stroke of propagandistic genius) have risen alarmingly, so that the sun's rays are more readily absorbed in the lower atmosphere, with the result that temperatures are rising, with increasingly disastrous results.

The primary driver of global warming is supposed to be CO_2—carbon dioxide—coming from the fossil fuels that heat our homes, drive our cars, and move the food and other goods we consume. And so the Left has declared war on oil, gasoline, coal, and natural gas, indeed on the world's modern industrial economy itself. During the negotiations for the 1997 Kyoto Protocols, some delegations wanted to include population reduction in the "basket" of emissions they pledged to reduce. China, already deep into forced abortion with its one-child policy, was happy to put its own people on the chopping block in exchange for authorization to use more coal.

According to the Environmental Protection Agency, "Earth's temperature has risen by 1.5 degrees Fahrenheit over the past century, and is projected to rise another 0.5 to 8.6 degrees Fahrenheit over the next hundred years."[2] The proofs of global warming and its deleterious effects are all around us, they say. The glaciers are melting. The snow on mountains is disappearing. The seasons are changing. The polar ice caps are disappearing. Antarctica is about to collapse. The sea levels are rising—Al Gore says up to twenty feet—and will wipe out the Hamptons and Miami Beach, and plenty of other places, too. There are more hurricanes and they are more violent and cause more damage. More tornadoes. More flooding, but more drought, too. New diseases have arisen, and old ones have come back. Species are disappearing. The ice floes are all melting. The polar bears are going to die![3]

The keystone of the alarmist argument is the theory that more CO_2 has caused the surface temperature of the earth to increase. In his deadly dull documentary *An Inconvenient Truth*, Al Gore tells the story one of his professors, who began to measure CO_2 in the middle of the Pacific Ocean in the 1950s. By the mid-1960s, when Gore was in his class, he had found a marked increase in CO_2.

Gore took the issue to Congress and failed. The Clinton administration attempted to secure a broad-based tax on energy but ended up with only a tax on gasoline, diesel, and special motor fuels.

Hiding Data with a Hockey Stick

Things heated up immeasurably in 1999 when Michael Mann et al. published their famous "hockey stick" graph in *Nature* magazine, purporting to show Northern Hemisphere temperatures from AD 1000 to the end of the twentieth century. The story of the "hockey stick" must be belabored because it demonstrates the mendacity of the climate alarmists.

The graph showed a slow decline in temperature in the Northern Hemisphere from the year 1000 until roughly 1915—coinciding with industrialization, which flooded the atmosphere with CO_2—when the trend line shoots dramatically skyward. It's called the "hockey stick" because the cooling period is shown essentially as a flat line (the handle) with the warming period going straight up (the blade).

The impact of the "hockey stick" was massive. It exploded in the fevered imaginations of environmentalists everywhere. At long last, here was "scientific" evidence of what they all *knew*. The earth had been cooling until wicked man began the wicked use of coal and other fossil fuels, driving up our temperature and ruining our planet in a million different ways. Significantly, the hockey stick was reproduced in the 2001 report of the UN Intergovernmental Panel on Climate Change (IPCC).[4] The IPCC asserted that the 1990s was likely the warmest decade on record, with 1998 to be the warmest year ever.

Besides the hockey stick itself, perhaps the most iconic global warming image is Al Gore in his movie, standing on a motorized ladder going up and up and up, seemingly to the sky, as he shows how high the temperature has gone and is projected to go. The handpicked audience gasps in horror, precisely on cue.

But not everyone was as fooled by the global warming shtick. In fact, warning flags went up almost immediately. Looking at the hockey stick, some wondered, *Where was the Medieval Warm Period, that time between AD 950 and 1250 when experts say the temperature was* warmer *than today?* The Medieval Warm Period should have appeared somewhere along the handle of the hockey stick—except that if it had appeared, the hockey stick would not have been a hockey stick. There would have been an unsightly bump in the stick—and a big bump in the road on the way to convincing anyone of the warmist theory. The global warming scam relies on the notion that ours is the hottest time the earth

has experienced. If there was an earlier hotter one—and the planet survived it just fine—then their little theory would be in deep trouble. So
the Medieval Warm Period, which was actually a time of great population growth and advances in farming, had to go. In fact, as British journalist and climate skeptic Christopher Monckton reports, "In 1995, a
senior researcher into early climate told David Deming, a climate
researcher, that 'we have to abolish the medieval warm period' (Deming,
2005). Not 'we need to re-examine the temperature record of the past
millennium, but 'we have to abolish the medieval warm period.'"[5]

Here's the thing about the Medieval Warm Period, among many
reasons they want to get rid of it. It was very good for the world. That
period of global warming "brought grapes to England, and grain to the
coasts of Greenland; it doubled the population and revived town life all
across Europe."[6]

Among the many scientific errors that the "fabricators," as skeptic
Monckton calls them, perpetuate is their use of tree rings to measure
temperature. Even a UN panel has warned that "wider tree-rings do not
always indicate warmer temperatures. Trees grow faster not only when
it is warmer but also when there is more carbon dioxide in the atmosphere, because carbon dioxide is not a pollutant but a naturally-occur-
ring substance that is plant food."[7]

The "fabricators" gave the unreliable tree ring measurement 390
times the weight of any other measurement because that data gave them
the dramatic "hockey stick" trend line they wanted. But more than that,
they did away altogether with the tree ring data from the Medieval Warm
Period. According to critics, they simply hid it. The most serious charge
made by Monckton (and other critics) is that Mann and his co-authors
claimed in the paper that accompanied the hockey stick graph in *Nature*
that the Medieval Warm Period tree ring data had been included—when
in fact it was not. Instead the data was hidden in a file called "CEN-
SORED_DATA." For the Medieval Warm Period, they substituted the
hidden tree ring data with their own estimates that had the effect of wiping out the Medieval Warm Period altogether in their computer modeling.[8]

Along the most dogged skeptics of the "hockey stick" are researchers Steve McIntyre and Professor Ross McKitrick, who have been carving pieces off it for decades. It was they who discovered the "CENSORED_ DATA": the medieval tree ring measurements that Mann and his colleagues had hidden.[9] When McIntyre and McKitrick reinserted the missing data, voila!, evidence of the Medieval Warm Period reappeared. But *Nature*, the journal that had first published the "hockey stick," refused to publish their findings. Eventually, their paper was published in *Geophysical Research Letters*.[10] According to Monckton, that was the moment when "many honest scientists who had previously accepted the climate scare at face value began to question the methods and the motives of the handful of politicized scientists who, between them, were chiefly responsible for creating and promoting the now-failed scare."[11]

There's a sad sideshow to the "hockey stick" controversy that reveals how eager climate alarmists are to shut down dissent. Mann initiated a civil law suit against two critics—Rand Simberg and Mark Steyn—a suit that has now dragged on for years and cost millions of dollars.[12]

So, has the earth warmed over the past hundred years? You bet. Something on the order of 1.53 degrees Fahrenheit since the late 1800s.[13] But what was happening during that time? The Earth came out of what's called the Little Ice Age, lasting from roughly 1300, around the end of the Medieval Warm Period, to 1850.[14] As scientist and skeptic William Briggs says, "Doesn't it make sense that temperature would tick up after the end of an Ice Age?"[15]

And then there is the pesky problem that most years of the twenty-first century have seen no measurable increase in temperature. There was an uptick in 2015 and 2016 because of a naturally recurring El Nino, which will also naturally recede—as even the UN climate panel concedes.[16] But otherwise temperatures have not increased measurably since the turn of the twenty-first century, as satellite measurements clearly show.[17] The warmists created a new propaganda term to deal with that. They called it "the pause," as if the end of the warming trend is only that, a pause, before the elevator resumes its dangerous climb skyward. And then they began to deny the pause. The warmists have come up with sixty-six different excuses why temperatures have not been increasing since 1996.[18] Among their many excuses—suddenly the satellite data is not the most accurate for judging temperature, though in the past it was considered the gold standard.

As we have seen, the central argument of the warmists is that increased levels of CO_2 have caused the rise in temperature.[19] One warmist blog claims that we are at the highest levels of CO_2 in fifteen million years.[20] But some scientists say we are at the lowest levels in history, going back to the Precambrian period.[21] As writer-philosopher-scientist and skeptic William Briggs told me, "Good grief, we're nowhere near the peak of CO_2. This always used to be known before politics took over."[22]

Creating a Fake "Consensus"

Whatever the actual status of CO_2 levels in the earth's atmosphere, there is a consensus that the temperature of the earth has increased at least slightly in recent times, yet, as scholars at the Heritage Foundation demonstrate, "no consensus exists that man-made emissions are the primary driver of global warming or, more importantly, that global warming is accelerating and dangerous. Climatologists differ on the various causes of climate change, the rate at which the earth is warming, the effect of man-made emissions on warming, the most accurate climate data and temperature sets to use, and the accuracy of climate models projecting decades and centuries into the future."[23]

The notion of scientific "consensus" is something that bedevils many of the issues discussed in this book, but especially the global warming debate. The supposed scientific "consensus" on man-caused and catastrophic climate change is a talking point that any school child can trot out to shut down debate, a cudgel to shout down opposing views on television panel shows. It's the old weak argument from authority—which is exactly the opposite of the truly scientific attitude of free inquiry and demonstration by experiment.

Consider how anti-science is the notion of "consensus" and "settled science." Science, properly understood, is constantly being tested and probed. Our understandings of scientific hypotheses are always being improved. To suggest that something as new as the "global warming" theory is "settled" is laughable political hackery.

Still, we are told unendingly that 97 percent of climate scientists agree that global warming is real, that it is catastrophic, and that it is caused by man. If you dare question the "consensus," you are cast into outer darkness. When my C-Fam colleague Stefano Gennarini questioned Archbishop Marcelo Sanchez Sorondo, Chancellor of the Vatican's Academy of Science, about inviting well-known abortion advocates like Columbia University's Jeffrey Sachs and the UN's Ban Ki-moon to the Vatican for a meeting on "climate change," Sanchez lashed out, saying that anyone who opposed the theory of global warming was in the "Tea Party" and in the employ of the oil companies.[24] Because, after all, there is this 97 percent consensus among the *scientists*. But is there really?

The number and the notion come from very sketchy studies.

In 2004, *Science* published a piece purporting to show that 75 percent of 928 papers published in scientific journals between 1993 and 2003 agreed that humans had caused warming over the previous fifty years, while not even a single paper dissented. But Joseph Bast and Roy Spencer, writing the *Wall Street Journal*, pointed out while the paper did demonstrate a consensus for "man-made" global warming, it failed to demonstrate that scientists agreed that that warming was "dangerous." More damning still, it left out "scores" of dissenting papers by such scholars as Richard Lindzen, John Christy, Sherwood Idso, and Patrick Michaels.[25]

A more recent and similar study conducted by Australian John Cook and published in *Environmental Research Letters* looked at the abstracts of twelve thousand academic papers on climate change and global warming between 1991 and 2011. Most of them were silent on man-made global warming. According to Cook, of the 33 percent that expressed an opinion on whether global warming is man-made, 97.1 percent endorsed that theory (the report says nothing about how dangerous the studies make the problem out to be). But a team led by David R. Legates, former Director of the University of Delaware's Center for Climatic Research, looked at the same papers and concluded that a mere *1 percent*—a far cry from the 97.1 percent Cook had claimed—of the 4,014 papers making a claim about global warming considered that it was man's doing.[26]

In 2009 *EOS, Transactions American Geophysical Union* published the results of a two-question online survey about whether global temperatures have risen and whether humans have been a significant factor. They claimed that 97 percent of respondents agreed.

But author Mark Steyn, scourge of the alarmists—still locked in a lawsuit with Michael Mann over his "hockey-stick"[27]—took a deep look at this "research" and found:

> The online questionnaire was sent to 10,257 earth scientists, of whom [only] 3,146 responded. Of the responding scientists, 96.2 percent came from North America. Only 6.2 percent came from Canada. So, the United States is overrepresented even within that North American sample.
>
> Nine percent of US respondents are from California. So, California is overrepresented within not just the US sample: it has over twice as large a share of the sample as Europe, Asia, Australia, the Pacific, Latin America and Africa combined.
>
> Of the ten percent of non-US respondents, Canada has 62 percent.
>
> Not content with such a distorted sample, the researchers then selected 79 of their sample and declared them "experts."
>
> Of those 79 scientists, two were excluded from a second supplementary question. So, 75 out of 77 made it through to the final round, and 97.4 percent were found to agree with 'the consensus.' That's where the 97 percent comes from.[28]

Despite the fact that this 97 percent consensus figure has been thoroughly discredited, it continues to be cited endlessly, and even now is being drilled into the heads of school kids all over the globe. As I write this, the Trump transition is under way. TV personality Chris Cuomo interviewed a Republican congresswoman about Scott Pruitt, Trump's pick for administrator for the Environmental Protection Agency, who has been a foe of the EPA's mission creep. Cuomo demanded to know "how someone could be for clean air and clean water yet deny global warming, especially given the scientific consensus of 97% of the scientific community that it is real." The phony 97 percent figure simply will not go away.

Getting Greenland
(and the Polar Bears) Wrong

What about the dozens of other alarmist claims made by Al Gore and "climate scientists"? How are those polar bears doing? Well, fine, just fine. In fact, pretty much all the claims made by Al Gore in *An Inconvenient Truth* were false when he made them, and they have certainly not been borne out since, though the same claims keep getting made.

As I write this, the *Huffington Post* reports that Greenland's ice shelf is even in worse shape than we thought. As Christopher Monckton explains, "Greenland...is one of the alarmists' favorite poster-children for climate panic. Headlines talking of unprecedented warming and sudden collapse of the vast Greenland ice sheet are commonplace. Yet the burial-ground in the principal medieval Viking settlement, at Hvalsey in south-western Greenland, is under permafrost to this day. It was certainly not under permafrost when the Vikings buried their dead there during the Middle Ages."[29]

One of the enduring images from Al Gore's movie is the image of polar bears clinging desperately to what appear to be the last ice floes they can find. Once they're gone, those poor bears are dead. The image is deeply dishonest. One of the most dishonest images in a deeply dishonest movie. But highly effective. Google "polar bear decline," and you get hundreds of thousands of hits. It's widely believed that the polar bears are in decline, and they are all going to die. In fact, the global polar bear population stood at twenty to twenty-five thousand in 2013—unchanged from 2001. This according to the Polar Bear Specialist Group.[30] In fact, go practically anywhere in the world where polar bears live and they are doing just fine.[31] At an October 2009 press conference, Irish journalist Phelim McAleer, the scourge of environmentalists everywhere, was able to ask Al Gore about his polar bear claims from *An Inconvenient Truth.* Gore refused to address the fact that the polar bear population is larger now than in the 1960s. Gore's environmental thugs tore the microphone from McAleer's hands.[32]

Typically, the alarmists do not point to an actual decline in bears—because they can't, the numbers have not declined. Instead they point to the supposedly receding ice and then suppose that the bears will inevitably *have to* decline. This language from the National Wildlife Federation is typical: "Remarkably, Hudson Bay polar bears have been able to catch enough seals during the winter to tide them over during this period of on-shore fasting."[33] Remarkably!

But is sea ice in fact retreating? Maybe a bit, but not much. It has only been since satellite measurement began in 1979 that we have been able to see the amount of sea ice at the North and South Poles. At that time, there was roughly twenty-two million square kilometers of sea ice. That number has shrunk to twenty-one million square kilometers in 2015. Between 1979 and 2015, there were periods when the area of ice went both above and below these numbers.[34]

The climate alarmists' efforts to prove their theory sometimes yield amusing results. In the summer of 2016, the Polar Ocean Challenge sent a ship north from Bristol, Alaska, to Norway, on to Russia through the Northwest passage, to Greenland and back to Alaska. The purpose of their journey was to show "that the Arctic sea ice coverage shrinks so far now in the summer months that sea that was permanently locked up can allow passage through." As of July, though, the ship was stuck in the ice in Murmansk.[35]

This was not the first global warming ship to become locked in ice trying to prove there's no longer any ice. In 2014, fifty-two climate alarmists had to be rescued from their frozen ship in the Antarctic. The experts calmly assured us that the fiasco had nothing to do with climate change; it was just "weather."[36]

In 2015, a global warming expedition to the Arctic out of Canada also became locked in sea ice and had to be rescued.[37]

Such comical disasters do not stop the climate alarmists. Even now, there are reports that the Arctic is "hotter than ever," "36 degrees hotter" than normal.[38] The end is nigh. Get your research ship ready to go. Just make sure an ice-cutter is standing by.

But are the seas rising? Is beach-front property about to be inundated? What about the Hamptons? What about Miami Beach? And Vanuatu? What *about* Vanuatu?

The image from Al Gore's movie that frightens children the most—the one that brought a rebuke from a British judge, along with eight other claims said to be false—is the image of the sea level rising to cover most of southern Florida, most of Manhattan, all the Netherlands, and many other places around the world. Gore predicted a twenty-foot rise. It is a truly creepy image. And it is false.

It is true that the sea level has risen—roughly four hundred feet in the *20,000 years* since the end of the last global ice age. But in the last 130 years, since the end of the Little Ice Age, the sea level has risen a paltry eight inches, roughly six inches *per century*.

Hyping Hurricanes

And then there is what the warmists call "extreme weather."

The climate alarmists love "extreme weather." In March 2012, James Hansen of the Space Administration Goddard Institute for Space Studies published a paper purporting to show that global warming was causing "extreme weather."[39] Naturally, the Union of Concerned Scientists agreed.[40] *Scientific American* got on board.[41]

The *New York Times* reported, "The moderate global warming that has already occurred as a result of human emissions has quadrupled the frequency of certain heat extremes since the Industrial Revolution, scientists reported Monday, and they warned that a failure to bring greenhouse gases under control could eventually lead to a 62-fold increase in such heat blasts."

Ahead of the Paris Climate Summit in 2015, the American Meteorological Society reported, "Human activities, such as greenhouse gas emissions and land use, influenced specific extreme weather and climate events in 2014, including tropical cyclones in the central Pacific, heavy rainfall in Europe, drought in East Africa, and stifling heat waves in Australia, Asia, and South America...."[42]

Climate change advocates really loved "Superstorm Sandy" that hit the East Coast of the United States in October 2012, doing an estimated $75 billion in damage. Al Gore told a New York radio station, "This storm *was* related to global warming. Dirty energy causes dirty weather. We're putting 90 million tons of global warming pollution into the atmosphere every single day; spewing it up there as if the atmosphere of the planet is an open sewer, free to use, free of charge, just put as much junk up there are you want to."

Hurricane Katrina, too, was a godsend to them. It featured heavily in Gore's *Inconvenient Truth*—both the original movie, and later the book of the same name. Gore blamed the deadly hurricane on global warming, citing the "emerging consensus linking global warming to the increasing destructive power of hurricanes...based in part on research showing a significant increase in the number of category 4 and 5 hurricanes." He was likely referring to the 2005 Webster study that purported to show an increase in the number, percentage and intensity of hurricanes and cyclones and linked that increase to rising sea surface temperature.[43] Gore made much of the fact that Katrina picked up power as it entered the much warmer Gulf of Mexico.

But is it even true that hurricanes have increased in frequency and intensity in recent years?

The Webster study was rebutted immediately by climatologist Patrick Michaels, who found that the "trends observed by Webster et al. disappeared once data going back to 1940 were included. Roughly the same number and percentage of intense hurricanes occurred during 1940–1970 as occurred during 1970–2004."[44]

More than a decade later, the Competitive Enterprise Institute reported on new science revisiting the 2005 Webster study and vindicating Patrick Michaels' original skepticism. Conducted by scientists at Colorado State University and the National Hurricane Center, the new study looked at ten years of additional data and found that "the global frequency of category 4 and 5 hurricanes has shown a small, insignificant downward trend while the percentage of category 4 and 5 hurricanes has shown a small, insignificant upward trend between 1990 and 2014."

Additionally, they found, "Accumulated cyclone energy globally has experienced a large and significant downward trend during the same period. In other words, there has been a large decrease in the overall destructive power of hurricanes based on an assessment of the number, strength, and duration of all individual hurricanes worldwide."[45]

And then in May of 2016 came the most amazing news—sad for the climate change alarmists but good for everyone else: the United States set a record of 127 months without a major hurricane, defined as a category 3 or above making landfall. The last hurricane to make landfall had been Wilma, which ripped across the southern tip of Florida in 2005.

And the dearth of major hurricanes continued after that. It should be noted that "landfall" is defined as the eye, the most dangerous part of a hurricane, coming across land. You may read that Hurricane Matthew made landfall in October 2016, but while it made impact, it cannot be said that Matthew made landfall because the eye of that hurricane never touched shore. You may also read that Hurricane Hermine came ashore. Hermine did come ashore, but it was not a hurricane, rather a tropical storm, something much less intense than a hurricane. The U.S. record stands now at 134 months without a hurricane making landfall, the longest period since the establishment of the National Oceanic and Atmospheric Administration's (NOAA) Hurricane Research Division, which keeps data on all the hurricanes that have struck the United States since 1851.

But hasn't there been a huge increase in tornadoes? After all, there are all those storm chaser shows. Those would be impossible except for an ungodly increase in the incidence of tornadoes, right? Wrong.

In 2000, the United States experienced 1,072 tornadoes. Five years later, it had jumped to 1,157. In 2010, it was 1,894; 2013, 906; 2014, 886; 2015, 1,177; 2016, 1,046 (estimated).[46] That's the hard data. Still, the climate alarmists have an answer for everything. Since there has not been an increase in tornadoes, they are saying there has been an increase in tornado "clusters."[47]

Manipulating Models

The climate alarmists' computer models predicting future global temperatures have been spectacularly wrong. For decades now, they have failed to predict actual observed temperatures as measured by the unadjusted satellite data. As William Briggs points out, "Every year, the consensus models predict temperatures higher than are observed, and the discrepancy between what is predicted and what happens grows larger." In December 2015, Patrick Michaels and Chip Knappenberger, two climate scientists at the libertarian Cato Institute, released a working paper comparing observed global surface temperature warming rates since 1950 to what 1,087 climate models used by government climate scientists would have predicted for those years. In "a devastating indictment of climate model performance," they found that the government climate scientists' models were wrong, regularly projecting much higher warming rates than actually occurred. So there is good reason for skepticism when climate "scientists" claim that the temperature of earth will be X degrees in a hundred years: their computer models don't work for the temperatures we actually know![48]

Global warming alarmism is not science. Empirical evidence does not support it.

Co-opting the Catholic Church

Global warming is an article of faith. Perhaps that explains why the climate change apologists have worked so hard to co-opt the major religions, most especially the Catholic Church. They have found a very receptive audience in Pope Francis and the men and women around him.

In his much-awaited encyclical *Laudato Si'*, which *The Guardian*, the *Washington Post*, and many other newspapers called the pope's "encyclical on climate change," Francis wrote, "The earth, our home, is beginning to look more and more like an immense pile of filth."

So grave were the pope's concerns about global warming that the Vatican invited Jeffrey Sachs of Columbia University and UN Secretary General Ban Ki-moon—who have long been the Catholic Church's aggressive opponents at the UN on several dogmatic issues including abortion and contraception—to an April 2015 conference on climate change and welcomed them like old friends.

Then, shocking faithful Catholics everywhere, on December 8, 2015, which happens to be one of the most important feast days of the year for the Catholic Church, the Vatican displayed a light show on the façade of St. Peter's Basilica, the first of its kind—but not images of the Virgin Mary and her son Jesus. No, it included images of wildlife: a lion, butterflies, and wolves. Obviously, this was a celebration not of the feast of the Immaculate Conception but of quite another feast, that is, the UN climate change conference then under way.

And in the winter of 2016, the Vatican issued a brand-new document on priestly formation explaining that besides aspects of the faith, like the Virgin Birth and Transubstantiation, the seminaries must catechize nascent priests on environmental issues, all the better to catechize the flock.

In early 2017, it was announced the Vatican Academy of Science had invited population bomb hoaxer Dr. Paul Ehrlich to participate in a conference on the environment. (See chapter eleven below for Ehrlich's dismal record on both scientific facts and human rights.)

Also invited was Dr. John Bongaarts of the Population Council, one of the main proponents of population control for environmental reasons.

Putting the co-optation of the Catholic Church aside, many have noted how belief in global warming has become very much like an old-fashioned fire and brimstone religion. When it comes to the climate, there is original sin and personal sin. Man is responsible for the inevitable disaster being visited upon Mother Earth. There is the need for confession and atonement. We must admit our sinfulness, change our behavior, and make up for past wrongs—by recycling, taking mass transportation, replacing fossil fuels with so-called renewables like wind and solar, and imposing taxes on the use of wicked fossil fuels.

There are also indulgences, of the medieval kind, that is, ones that you can buy: carbon off-sets for the use of private jets, for instance, or for larger homes that guzzle down energy—like Leonardo DiCaprio's and Al Gore's. And China wanted to offer population reduction as part of its Kyoto Protocol commitment: human sacrifice to the gods of global warming.

Global warming even has its own feast days. What is Earth Day after all?

There is also a priesthood. These are the scientists who intone the truths from on high, truths we are not allowed to question. And there is a climate change Vatican: the UN, which regularly holds councils where the climate change bishops meet and issue climate change pronouncements that are infallible.

And finally, there is damnation and burning at the stake for heresy. If you do not believe in climate change, or if you believe in it in a different or slightly heterodox way, you are cast into the outer darkness.

In the Hot Seat for Heresy

That's what happened to a man named Roger Pielke, a climate scientist who believed it all, every bit of it, except one little thing. That one little heresy ended his climate science career forever.

Roger Pielke had been a professor of environmental studies and political science at the University of Colorado for more than twenty years. In the early teens, Pielke ran afoul of the global warming police, even though he believes in man-made global warming and even favors a carbon tax to deal with it.

His story demonstrates how the climate change alarmists are so unsure of their case that they now insist on punishing disagreement and at least running dissenters out of town.

That story begins in 1993, when Pielke started studying extreme weather and climate at the National Center for Atmospheric Research at Boulder, Colorado. Pielke's first sin against the climate change religion was to question the UN's Intergovernmental Climate Change report of 2007, which included "a graph purporting to show that disaster costs were rising due to global temperature increases." The author of the graph himself later recanted, but by then the damage to Pielke's reputation was already done.

When Pielke attempted to fraternally correct the errors of his climate change brothers in the press, Justin Gillis, the lead climate reporter of the *New York Times*, promptly blocked Pielke from his Twitter feed and according to Pielke "other reporters did the same." Andrew Freedman, Mashable's lead science editor, told Pielke that he was on a blacklist. *Foreign Policy Magazine* put Pielke on a list of climate "deniers"—a characterization he vehemently denies, by the way.[49]

Pielke says that Pulitzer-prize winning reporter Paige St. John, who was hassled for even quoting him in a 2015 story in the *Los Angeles Times*, told him, "You should come with a warning label: 'Quoting Roger Pielke will bring a hailstorm down on your work from the *London Guardian*, *Mother Jones*, and *Media Matters*.'"[50]

In March 2014, when Pielke was hired as a blogger for Nate Silver's nascent *FiveThirtyEight* blog, he lasted all of six columns—the first two of which debunked the notion that climate change is causing hurricanes to be more expensive.

That's Pielke's heresy. Here's his pitch for it: We know that hurricanes have not increased in number. Indeed, we know that no hurricane has made landfall since Hurricane Wilma in 2005, without a doubt, the longest such period on record. But we also know that the cost of hurricane damage is higher than ever before. How can this be? Simply because we are richer than ever before. When a hurricane bears down on the East Coast of the United States, it is not bearing down on fishing shacks. It is bearing down on multi-million-dollar mansions. Moreover, the coasts are more built up than ever before. Superstorm Sandy did more damage in two days than the global annual average of natural disasters in the 1980s.

Global-warming-carbon-tax-loving Roger Pielke was cast into the outer darkness simply because he did not believe the extreme weather argument. It got so bad that he was demoted at *FiveThirtyEight* and eventually quit. It got so bad that he was hauled before a U.S. Senate committee to explain himself. He was accused of being on the payroll of Exxon Mobil.

It got so bad that Roger Pielke, who had dedicated his scholarly life to climate issues, got out of that field of study altogether and is now working on sports governance.

Pielke wrote about his ordeal in a *Wall Street Journal* column in December 2016, after it was discovered in the WikiLeaks dump that he had in fact been targeted for his dissent by ThinkProgress, the group set up by White House Chief of Staff John Podesta. The attack was funded by leftwing billionaire Tom Steyer. As Pielke explained, "In a 2014 email, a staffer at the Center for American Progress, founded by John Podesta in 2003, took credit for a campaign to have me eliminated as a writer for Nate Silver's FiveThirtyEight website. In the email, the editor of the think tank's climate blog bragged to one of its billionaire donors, Tom Steyer: 'I think it's fair [to] say that, without Climate Progress, Pielke would still be writing on climate change for 538.'"[51]

This is what happens to you if you cross the high priests of global warming.

Besides lock-step agreement in all their doctrine, what exactly is it that the climate change crowd want?

Climate Cuts That Won't Fix the Warming (But Will Wreck the Economy)

Well, they want mankind to stop using fossil fuels. Or at least they want us to cut our consumption way back. This is what was asked of governments in the failed Kyoto Protocols, and it is what the UN asked and what the governments agreed to at the Paris Climate Summit in December 2015.

Of course it's important to consider what would happen to the U.S. economy if we lived up to those promises. But it's also instructive to ask what would happen to global temperatures if every single country lived up to every single promise made at Paris.

First, we will examine effects on the U.S. economy. A very useful analysis has been provided by the Heritage Foundation.

President Obama's "intended nationally determined contribution" (INDC) at Paris was to reduce U.S. greenhouse gases by 26 to 28 percent below 2005 levels by the year 2025. To meet this goal, Obama proposed carbon dioxide regulations for new and existing power plants, fuel-efficiency and greenhouse gas regulations for light and heavy-duty vehicles, energy-efficiency regulations for commercial and residential buildings as well as appliances, EPA-approved alternatives to hydrochlorofluorocarbons, methane regulations for landfills and the oil and gas sector, and executive orders to reduce greenhouse gas emissions by the federal government.[52]

Essentially President Obama proposed waging war on the carbon dioxide-emitting fuels—coal, oil, and natural gas—that have supplied the overwhelming majority of our energy needs in the past decades, in fact over the past century. According to the Heritage report, the proposed reductions would significantly harm the U.S. economy—directly through higher energy costs, but also by raising the cost of "almost all the goods and services [Americans] buy because energy is a necessary component of production and service." Higher energy pricing would inevitably be passed along to the consumer, hitting the poorest hardest. The effects would ripple through the economy, as consumers bought less, companies had to cut back on jobs, and some of them closed altogether or moved to more energy-friendly countries. As Heritage said, "The result is fewer opportunities for American workers, lower incomes, less economic growth, and higher unemployment."

The Heritage Foundation estimated that if the United States "abided by the provisions of the Paris Agreement, there would be 206,104 fewer manufacturing jobs between 2016 and 2040. But almost all sectors would lose jobs. Overall, Heritage projected a total of 400,000 fewer jobs in the United States and an income loss of $20,000 for a family of four, an aggregate gross domestic product (GDP) loss of over $2.5 trillion, and an increase of household electricity expenditures of between 13 and 20 percent.[53]

But surely it would be worth it! Cutting greenhouse gases back by 28 percent will slow the warming of the planet!

Perhaps the best resource on this question is by Danish scientist Dr. Bjorn Lomborg, who has studied these issues for decades. Lomborg has been something of a climate change skeptic, believing there are more pressing issues than global warming. He has also been an advocate for aggressive research and development for "green" solutions to the slight warming the earth is experiencing. He rejects the so-called "renewables"—solar and wind power—as not cost-effective. Lomborg has come under sustained attack for years but has successfully fought off charges of scientific fraud. Unlike Pielke, Lomborg has not left the field.

In a peer-reviewed paper published in *Global Policy Journal*, Lomborg demonstrated,

> The climate impact of all Paris INDC promises is minuscule: if we measure the impact of every nation fulfilling every promise by 2030, the total temperature reduction will be 0.048°C (0.086°F) by 2100.
>
> Even if we assume that these promises would be extended for another 70 years, there is still little impact: if *every nation* fulfills *every promise* by 2030, and continues to fulfill these promises faithfully until the end of the century, and there is no 'CO_2 leakage' to non-committed nations, the entirety of the Paris promises will reduce temperature rises by just 0.17°C (0.306°F) by 2100.

US climate policies, in the most optimistic circumstances, fully achieved and adhered to throughout the century, will reduce global temperatures by 0.031°C (0.057°F) by 2100.

EU climate policies, in the most optimistic circumstances, fully achieved and adhered to throughout the century, will reduce global temperatures by 0.053°C (0.096°F) by 2100.

China climate policies, in the most optimistic circumstances, fully achieved and adhered to throughout the century, will reduce global temperatures by 0.048°C (0.086°F) by 2100.

The rest of the world's climate policies, in the most optimistic circumstances, fully achieved and adhered to throughout the century, will reduce global temperatures by 0.036°C (0.064°F) by 2100.[54]

Lomborg also pointed out that the assumption that all nations will keep their promises was very optimistic: "Consider the Kyoto Protocol, signed in 1997, never ratified by the US, and eventually abandoned by Canada and Russia and Japan. After several renegotiations, the Kyoto Protocol had been weakened to the point that the hot air from the collapse of the Soviet Union exceeded the entire promised reductions, leaving the treaty essentially toothless."

Negotiators in Paris were trying to tackle global warming in the same way that has failed before, "by making promises that are individually expensive, will have little impact even in a hundred years and that many governments will try to shirk from."[55]

The world was giddy in December 2015 when two hundred countries announced the so-called Paris Agreement. *The Guardian* called it "the world's greatest diplomatic achievement."[56] Al Gore said it meant the end of "dirty energy."[57]

When the document was endorsed by 170 governments in April 2016, *The Guardian* said it signaled the end of the fossil fuel era.[58] French socialist president Francois Hollande said, "There is no turning back."[59]

Rich countries had agreed to hand over $100 billion every year starting in 2020 to poor countries to help them transform their economies. The deal set a target of limiting global warming to "well below" 3.6 degrees Fahrenheit by 2100, though pretty much all of it was supposed to be voluntary.

Each country was called upon to set "nationally determined contributions" and the agreement requires the goals to be "ambitious." Each five-year report should be more "ambitious" than the last.[60]

President Obama's position was that the Paris Agreement was an "executive agreement" and therefore did not require the consent of the Senate, which all treaties do. The idea was that the president can commit the United States to draconian reductions in energy use that would have a profound effect upon all sectors of the U.S. economy and upon all U.S. households by executive action and without the consent of the U.S. Senate. But according to UN and international law expert Steven Groves—then of the Heritage Foundation, now chief of staff to U.S. Ambassador to the UN Nikki Haley—the Paris Agreement is not a mere executive action and is in fact a treaty that must be submitted to the Senate for ratification.[61]

But the Obama administration was not about to submit the agreement to the Senate. Because it was nonbinding and there is no enforcement mechanism, the State Department under Secretary John Kerry insisted that it did not need the Senate's consent.

And that will likely be its undoing: the Paris Agreement is entirely voluntary, and there is no enforcement mechanism. There is little doubt that countries will hedge, will not meet their voluntary targets, will be accused of competitive advantage—and all of this will cause some countries to simply walk away.

The even better news for the United States is that new president Donald Trump is expected, as of this writing shortly after the election, to rescind President Obama's commitments under the agreement and withdraw the United States altogether from the Paris Agreement. This would cause a brouhaha at Turtle Bay and Brussels, but it would be a "yuge" boost for American industry.

Propping Up the Paris Agreement with Fraud

Another reason for withdrawing from the agreement was the news, which broke in early February 2017, that a paper produced by the National Oceanic and Atmospheric Administration had used fraudulent data in order to have a maximum impact on Barack Obama and the UK's Prime Minister David Cameron in advance of the Paris meeting. The report claimed that the "pause" or slowdown in global warming in the period after 1998 never existed and that temperatures had been rising even more rapidly than scientists had expected. This crucial report explained away the pesky "pause" in global warming.

But whistleblower John J. Bates produced "irrefutable evidence" that the paper was based on misleading and "unverified" data and not subjected to the typical rigorous checking that is standard for NOAA papers. He had objected to the publication of the paper but was overruled by his superiors.[62]

All the "climate change" agreements and conferences—and hundreds of millions of dollars in propaganda and advocacy—may not make much difference in global temperatures. But they do have other effects. The global warming scam inevitably enhances what's known as global governance, a lattice of agreements overseen by bureaucrats at the UN in New York and Geneva before whom sovereign states must appear every few years and report. The trend is, bit by bit, to give up pieces of national sovereignty to bodies that everyday Americans cannot see, let alone reach.

We see the same thing in human rights, where a half dozen treaty-monitoring bodies oversee "human rights" that most people have never heard of and that no government has ever agreed to. But there is no more powerful grip on a people than over their economy. Man-made catastrophic climate change is a vehicle for faceless bureaucrats to step in and save us—from our prosperity, from our economic freedom, from our power to make choices over our own lives. As we have seen, the empirical science supposedly supporting the global warming scam is shaky at best. The whole campaign is premised on scare tactics. And at what cost? Our economic freedom. And as we have also seen, the global warmists are so hell bent on shoving their alarmism down the throats of a recalcitrant public that they're willing to silence, demonize, and persecute anyone who exposes their shoddy "science."

But the news about global warming is actually good. Not only is the gradual warming that we are in fact seeing as the Earth recovers from the "Little Ice Age" actually a good thing for the planet, the economy, and the human race, but also the public has proven remarkably resistant to the global warming scare. Al Gore has become something of a joke. Everyone knows he is an utter hypocrite.[63] He owns a twenty-room house in Nashville that devoured 221,000 kilowatt-hours of energy in 2006.[64] His home in Santa Barbara has six fireplaces and nine bathrooms. He travels by private jet.[65] He wants to ration energy for us while he gulps it down greedily. In a two-part takedown published in *The American Prospect*, noted scholar Walter Russell Mead said of Gore, "It must be as perplexing to his many admirers as it is frustrating to himself that a man of Vice President Gore's many talents, great skills and strong beliefs is one of the most consistent losers in American politics."[66] Mead was talking about Gore's political career, to be sure, but also about his postpolitics career as a public policy huckster for calamitous climate change.

And after spending hundreds of billions of dollars, after scaring little school children half to death for going on thirty years, the global warming scam has achieved virtually nothing. With massive effort, they've succeeded in passing nonbinding, unenforceable agreements. And they haven't won over the public to their panic. Only a small percentage of Americans believe in catastrophic man-caused climate change. What we have seen is the utter failure of a crazy theory sold under the veneer of "science"—but lacking any basis in the real thing.

CHAPTER 11

Life on an Empty Planet

The next time you fly across the county, take a window seat and look down from thirty-five thousand feet. What you'll see may surprise you, given what you've heard all your life about overpopulation.

You've been taught since grade school that the world is dangerously overpopulated. And you probably note that things where you live are more crowded than they used to be: your commute is longer, those fields near your house are now subdivisions. You've been to New York, and you've seen pictures of Singapore and Mexico City. You just know that the world is dangerously overpopulated.

Panicking over a Problem That Doesn't Exist

But look down when you fly. Just look down.

What you will see is an empty country.

The effect is most pronounced at night. Fly from Boston to LA and you will spend hours over largely unoccupied country. For miles and miles at a time, you can search in vain for lights. You'll see a lone farm house here and there, a tiny town every once in a while. But for the most part it's empty spaces. The country is mostly dark.

Fly virtually anywhere in the world—South America, Europe, Asia, Africa, or Australia. Fly high, look down, and you'll see an empty planet.

The "scientific" population experts don't want us to believe our own eyes.

But what about these crowded, teeming populations? Well, they do exist, in certain pocketed urban areas. Fly into Mexico City. At night, you begin to see city lights a good thirty minutes before you land. It is disconcerting. Same with Sao Paolo, Jakarta, or other megacities with populations heading north of ten and twenty million. But urbanization is an altogether different problem from actual overpopulation of the planet—which is a myth. But you wouldn't be the first person to confuse those two very different things. In fact, it was urban crowding in India that first shocked John D. Rockefeller III into organizing and funding the modern population control movement.[1] He made the mistake of thinking a crowded city is the same thing as a crowded planet. Much mischief has come of that fundamental error.

Rockefeller commissioned a team of experts who in 1972 issued the Rockefeller Commission Report on "Population and the American Future."[2] It is the blueprint for everything that came afterward—the bribed and forced sterilizations of millions of poor women, the brutal one-child policy that has created a dangerous sex imbalance in China, and the implosion of populations virtually everywhere except for sub-Saharan Africa.

The Rockefeller report claimed that "an important group in our society, composed predominantly of young people, has been much concerned with population growth in recent years." These bien pensants believed that it was "highly desirable to avoid another baby boom," such as the one that came after World War II and drove a thriving economy through the 1960s. Singled out for opprobrium as enemies of "population stabilization" were our country's "addiction to growth" and our social institutions and laws that "often exert a pro-natalist effect."

The Rockefeller report complained about happy images of "family life and women's roles projected on television." Americans needed a better understanding of reproduction through sex education and more contraception—and the United States should legalize abortion.

One of the striking themes of the report is the purported need to target minority communities. Even today, UN population controllers especially target Africa. As the report explained, "Unwanted fertility falls most heavily on certain minority groups in our population. We have relevant data for blacks only, but this is *probably true* [emphasis added] for Mexican-Americans, Puerto Ricans, Indians, and others as well." Note that phrase "unwanted fertility." Who didn't want black people to be fertile? Presumably it wasn't the black Americans who were actually having the babies. It was the "scientific experts" who didn't want more black babies.

The public, they said, needed to be prepared "to welcome a replacement level of reproduction and some periods of reproduction below replacement."

The report called for massive governmental intervention and spending.[3] And in 1972–1973, Congress authorized $93 million for population research—close to the $100 million recommended by President Lyndon Johnson's Committee on Population and Family Planning. (Such numbers seem almost quaint these days; today the United States gives Planned Parenthood alone $500 million a year.)

It has been drilled into us that there are too many of us and that catastrophe necessarily follows our fecundity. And the incessant drip, drip, drip of anti-population (some would call it anti-*people*) propaganda has had a powerful effect. I grew up in a family of four children, something that seemed entirely normal in 1960s and 1970s America. But when I see a family with four children today, it seems like a troop. They take up so many seats at church! Even families with three children get snide comments from strangers. International agencies, national governments, and rich foundations have all launched massive programs to control population, to cajole and coerce men and women into having fewer children.

The classic period of population control—the 1970s and 1980s—saw massive sterilization programs in India in which both men and women were clearly coerced. Even the offer of a small amount of money or food is inherently coercive for poor people. And they weren't just bribed, browbeaten, and coerced. Women died. In fact, they are still dying. The *Wall Street Journal* reported deaths in a mass sterilization camp in India as recently as 2014.[4]

Overpopulation Overreaction

The Indian government held massive public rallies against "overpopulation." At one, a hundred thousand berated a man on stage who had dared to have more than two children.

Longtime Population Institute head Werner Fornos advocated the use of quinacrine, a chemical that burns the fallopian tubes, on poor women.

In Peru, it was reported that women were trading their fertility for bags of groceries.[5]

Such experiences led the Kenyan bishops to believe that millions of women were being sterilized without their knowledge through common vaccines against disease in 2015.[6]

Under the Chinese government's draconian population control program, couples are still being punished for unapproved pregnancies with losing their jobs, having their homes torn down, and forced abortions.

And the United Nations has cheered the whole way. More than that, UN agencies have been participants in these appalling human rights abuses. The UN Population Fund gave its highest award to the creator of the Chinese one-child policy.[7] Also leading the charge has been the U.S. government—primarily through the U.S. Agency of International Development—along with the development agencies of the European and Nordic countries.

And the modern population control movement has succeeded beyond its wildest dreams, creating a phenomenon that is wholly new in human history. We are witnessing a global decline in fertility, to rates so low that

UN experts are not sure where they will stop; a rapid aging of populations that is stalling economic growth and preventing governments from being able to protect their national interests; depopulation so severe that shrinking towns are being given over to wolves in parts of Germany; a global flight from marriage; and a war on baby girls with a concomitant demographic imbalance favoring males that is utterly new and profoundly dangerous. All of this is unprecedented, all of it is man-made, and all of it can be laid at the door of the "scientific" campaign against "overpopulation." And no one really knows what the ultimate result will be, or what we can do about it.

The story of the founding of the modern population control movement has been told and retold many times before, perhaps best by Columbia University scholar Matthew Connelly in *Fatal Misconception: The Struggle to Control World Population*.[8] John D. Rockefeller III went to India and was shocked at what he saw: the poverty and the crowds in the urban areas of India. He came away shocked and deeply worried that such massive numbers and such poverty would cause a radicalization of the populace, who would come to demand a greater share of the world's resources, hampering American development and perhaps threatening Americans' security, if unrest led to a radicalized Third World. The only answer, for everyone's sake, was to reduce their fertility rate, and quickly—by force if necessary.

Rockefeller, along with the Fords and the Hewletts and the Packards, founded something called the Population Council. Eventually Lyndon Johnson and Richard Nixon got involved, and then the United Nations too, and they all ended up spending hundreds of billions to convince first the Indians and then everyone else that they would be better off if their women had not six children but two—or even fewer. And if they couldn't be convinced, there would be hell to pay, in the form of reduced or withdrawn foreign aid.[9]

There is a little-known story about what happened after a July 1965 meeting between John D. Rockefeller III and the much-maligned Pope Paul VI.

In a letter following up on the meeting, Rockefeller warned Paul VI that the Church was on the wrong side of history. There was no stopping either history or the Rockefeller project: "If I may speak perfectly frankly, the Church will be bypassed on an issue of fundamental importance to its people and to the well-being of all mankind. The flooding tide (of population stabilization) cannot be stopped or even slowed, but it can be guided."[10]

Three years later, Pope Paul VI issued his controversial encyclical *Humanae Vitae*. It restated Catholic teaching against contraception and made certain prophetic pronouncements about what would happen if it became widely used. He warned specifically about how men and women could be coerced with "this power passing into the hands of public authorities" and "governments."[11] And in fact Rockefeller and his colleagues were planning exactly such coercion. Sexual Revolution scholar Jennifer Roback Morse wonders if Pope Paul VI was enlightened about inevitable governmental coercion by this meeting with the powerful John D. Rockefeller III.[12] Pope Paul VI, who could see around corners, no doubt knew exactly what Rockefeller and his pals were up to. For the people of the developing world, hell would follow.

Rockefeller failed to sell Paul VI on the anti-population crusade, but the participation of religious folk has been important to the population control movement for as long as it has existed. In fact, the movement was originally started by a cleric in the Church of England, who was also a political economist. Thomas Malthus postulated that an increase in the food supply leads to an increase in population. Rather than increasing their standard of living and wellbeing, people tend simply to increase their number, and famine and disease inevitably follow. Malthus argued that food production, which increases arithmetically, could never outpace population growth, which increases geometrically. The arguments against population have not changed a great deal from the time of Malthus, almost two hundred years ago.

As recently as 2014, Stanford University's Paul Ehrlich predicted that mankind would soon end up eating its dead: "Oh, it's moving in that direction with ridiculous speed."[13]

It was Ehrlich's book, *The Population Bomb*, published fifty years earlier, that scared the world half to death with wild predictions that the world would starve by the 1970s; that there would be four billion deaths, including sixty-five million Americans; and that by 2000 Great Britain would be no more than a "small group of impoverished islands inhabited by some 70 million hungry people."

Missing Man's Ingenuity

What both Malthus and Ehrlich missed was man's ingenuity. In particular, Ehrlich didn't reckon with a man named Norman Borlaug and Borlaug's manmade "Green Revolution."

After graduating with a Ph.D. in plant pathology and genetics from the University of Minnesota in 1942, Norman Borlaug decamped to Mexico, where he developed "semi-dwarf, high-yield, disease-resistant wheat." For most of his life he lived in the developing world, helping poor countries—notably India and Pakistan—with the techniques of high-yield agriculture. Some say he prevented a billion deaths from starvation. That would assume Ehrlich and the population alarmists were right, and that is a large assumption indeed. But the fact remains that much of the world relies on Borlaug's high-yield, low-pesticide dwarf wheat for basic sustenance.[14]

Paul Ehrlich had said it was a "fantasy" that India could ever feed itself. After Borlaug, by 1974, India was self-sufficient in the production of all cereals.[15] To this day, both India and Pakistan are among the top wheat-producing countries in the world.

Sadly, toward the end of his life, Borlaug ran into the environmentalist buzz saw. His "opponents" argued against bringing the Green Revolution to Africa where "inorganic fertilizers and controlled irrigation will bring new environmental stress to the one continent where the chemical-based approach to food production has yet to catch on."[16] Where Borlaug was stymied—in Africa—not a single country appears on the list of wheat-producing countries.

Ehrlich displayed his abundant foolishness in a famous bet he made with economist Julian Simon, who took issue with the notion of resource scarcity because of population growth. He challenged Ehrlich to pick a handful of raw material resources and wagered $10,000 that over a decade—1980 to 1990—the cost of each would go down, proving their abundance.

Ehrlich chose copper, chromium, nickel, tin, and tungsten, and during those ten years the cost of each declined. Ehrlich lost the bet.

But he never learned his lesson. He just kept trying to frighten mankind about its rapacious treatment of Mother Earth. In 2008, he predicted the "sixth extinction of thousands of species" unless people stop reproducing, eating beef, and driving cars.[17]

Along with other population alarmists, Erhlich founded the Millennium Alliance for Humanity and the Biosphere, which predicts global population could reach 296 billion in 150 years. An illustration on their website shows people literally falling off the earth.[18] These largely white academics are especially concerned about the African population, which they say will double in size in the next thirty years. They complain about the most densely populated countries—which just happen to be nonwhite: China, Indonesia, Nigeria, Japan, and India. They bemoan increased life expectancy, the decline in the death rate, the increasing use of fertility treatments, and the supposed lack of "family planning" around the world.

They deplore all this fecundity and increasing health. The results are bound to be food shortages and starvation and "easily spread disease." They point out, "The closer people become, the easier airborne illnesses are spread." They note increasing water contamination. They warn about man-made desertification—that is, the loss of arable land to desert because of water loss.

The oddest worry they warn about is the disappearance of nonrenewable resources like fossil fuels, particularly natural gas. Wait, isn't that supposed to be a good thing? Fossil fuels cause global warming.

These arguments are remarkably persistent. Ask any child attending a government-run school if the world has too many people and the answer will be yes.

Pestering the Poor to Limit Their Families

And rich guys are still in the game, big time. In 2009, a small group of the richest men in the world met in New York to keep the party going. Bill Gates, Warren Buffett, George Soros, Ted Turner, and David Rockefeller Jr. met to form what they're calling the "Good Club." These philanthropists intend to spend billions to find answers to "nightmarish" global concerns, chief among them overpopulation.[19]

Since that time, Bill Gates's Catholic wife Melinda has raised $2.6 billion to distribute a dangerous contraceptive called Depo-Provera to the brown-skinned women of the world.[20]

So, what has resulted from all this population control propaganda?

Twenty years ago, I attended an Expert Group Meeting at UN Headquarters in New York that explored the question, "How low can fertility rates go?" Even then, experts noticed that fertility rates were declining rapidly, perhaps too rapidly. At the time of the meeting, Japan was about to hit a milestone: it became the first country in history to have more people over the age of sixty than under the age of fifteen.

The population controllers' idea had been that fertility rates should decline to the replacement level, roughly 2.1 babies per woman, and then magically level off. Apparently, it never occurred to them that they could go too far. But that's exactly what has happened. In some places, fertility rates have plunged toward collapse and show no signs of slowing down. Fertility in the city of Bologna, Italy, for instance, has plunged below 1.0 child per woman.

The experts at the meeting I attended in the late nineties were demographers from around the world, representing universities, governments, and international agencies. They were alarmed, to put it mildly. Uniformly, their answer to the question was, "We do not know how low fertility rates can go." In the two decades since that conference, fertility rates across the world's populations have only gone lower.

Except in sub-Saharan Africa, every country in the world will soon be at sub-replacement fertility.

Success! The result of population alarmism has been fertility reduction and therefore a slowing of population growth. Which is, after all, what the population alarmists wanted. Some populations have actually begun to shrink, including in Bulgaria, Cuba, Germany, Poland, Russia, and Spain, though global population continues to expand[21]—not because of increased fertility but because of great steps in healthcare and nutrition and the resulting lengthening of life spans in recent decades. As demographer Nicholas Eberstadt says, "It's not that we are breeding like rabbits, it's that we are no longer dying like flies." Eberstadt says it's not a "population explosion, but a health explosion."[22]

Discovering Demographic Decline

Even the United Nations is predicting that global population will top out at ten billion in 2050 and then begin to decline.[23]

Because of low fertility coupled with longer lives, what's known as the demographic pyramid has turned upside down. Where once there was a huge number of young people supporting a shrinking number of oldsters there is now a shrinking number of youngsters supporting an increasing cohort of elderly. Some have called this phenomenon "demographic winter." Others have dubbed it "bare branches."[24]

It is something that the world has never seen before, and we really do not know what will happen next—except that an intergenerational competition for increasingly scarce resources has already begun. We are already seeing campaigns for killing the elderly and the sick.

Dangers of Declining Populations

Another observable consequence is less economic vibrancy. It is simply a fact that older populations slow down. They begin to retire.

They clip coupons, play golf, go on cruises. "Active seniors" may be running marathons and climbing mountains and doing yoga. But they're not making the economy hum—it's the younger cohort that does that. And the younger cohort is shrinking.

Consider China. A Chinese demographer came up with the epigram that China would "get old before it got rich."[25] China experienced the perfect storm of heavy-handed, rapid fertility reduction through forced abortion and the government's one-child policy; rapid aging; and economic modernization that is coming too late.

China is also a case study for several other deleterious effects of population collapse. The Chinese war on baby girls—many Chinese who were allowed only one child enforced their preference for a boy over a girl with sex-selective abortion and the abandonment of female infants—has resulted in a demographic skew favoring men over women. This comes with its own set of massive problems.

Back in the 1960s, headed toward a population of a billion or more, the Chinese were afraid of overpopulation. Working closely with the UN Population Fund, China instituted a one-child policy that forbade any couple from having more than a single child in their lifetime—this in a country that had hitherto revered large families. The UN assisted Chinese officials in using computers to track its people, their fertility, and all births. Anyone suspected of being pregnant a second time could be punished or imprisoned, have their house razed, and be forced into abortion.

China already had a cultural "son preference." Combine that with the one-child policy and the development of sonogram technology that reveals the child's sex before birth, and you have a recipe for "sex-selective" abortion—baby girls aborted on a massive scale.

Now consider that nature provides roughly 106 boys for every 100 girls. Nature provides more boys because boys are more likely to die than girls throughout the life cycle. But in some parts of China today, there are now between 117 and 150 boys for every 100 girls born. This is nature far out of wack. The result is that a substantial number of Chinese men face a life of forced bachelorhood. Eberstadt reports that China has changed "from a country where as of 2000 nearly all males (about 96%)

had been married by their early 40s to one in which nearly a quarter (23%) are projected to be never married as of 2040."[26]

There was a story in the *New York Times* a few years ago about how starving North Korean farmers were bartering their daughters to Chinese bachelors for food. Moreover, there is a growing and robust market for trafficked women and girls from neighboring Myanmar into China.[27]

According to Eberstadt, the war on baby girls has spread to other countries, including India, Pakistan, Hong Kong, and even parts of the United States. Except in South Korea, efforts to ban sex-selective abortions have largely failed. Such efforts are opposed by radical feminists, who view them not as protections for girls but as assaults on the sacred right to an abortion.

The Chinese have killed millions of baby girls and created a permanent bachelor class. And danger lurks in a world bereft of women. Consider how violent inner-city neighborhoods with large numbers of unattached young men are. Now multiply that phenomenon across the largest nation on Earth.

Unmarried men are more likely to live unhealthy lives, drink more, take drugs, engage in risky sexual behavior, engage in criminality, and be recruited into criminal gangs and even terror groups.[28] The bubble of young unmarried men may make Chinese policymakers more adventuresome, at least in the near term. These young single men will be spoiling for a fight. And Chinese leaders can read the demographic tea leaves. They see that an aging population may be unable to project Chinese power for much longer. Their pool of available soldiers will soon begin to shrink, and they know it. China has already become newly aggressive in recent years, threatening Taiwan, the Philippines, and Japan. It has even been spreading its largesse into Latin America in order to spread its influence. A decade ago I was at a conference in San José, Costa Rica, when I heard a massive cacophonous firework display near the hotel—so loud you would have thought we were under attack, being bombed. The hotel explained it was the opening night of a new multibillion-dollar soccer complex nearby, a gift to the Costa Rican people from the Chinese government. China is projecting power in any way it can, while it can.

The ability to project national power in the face of declining demography was the subject of the 2011 book *Population Decline and the Remaking of Great Power Politics*, edited by my C-Fam colleagues Susan Yoshihara and Douglas A. Sylva.[29] They looked at population aging in the United States, Europe, Russia, Japan, India, and China, and concluded that in the game of great-power politics the future looks bright only for the United States and India. Take Russia, for instance: the typical Russian eighteen-year-old is simply not healthy enough to put into the field as a soldier. Japan is so old it hardly has enough youngsters to draft. Moreover, because of the birth dearth, even a single death in uniform is a national tragedy covered in the news and followed by a day of mourning. A country that views a single death this way will not endure any significant losses in its national defense. It simply cannot withstand sustained conflict.

The harms and dangers unleashed on the world by the campaign to control "overpopulation" are legion. But is the world even overpopulated in the first place?

Consider a mental exercise that drives population alarmists crazy. Take seven billion people and fit them someplace. North America has an actual population density of a mere thirty-two people per square mile. Australia, where there is a robust population control movement, has a puny 6.4 people per square mile. Europe is at 134; South America, 73; Africa, 65; and Asia, the highest at 203. Now in New York City there are 26,403 people per square mile. So you could fit the entire world's population into the state of Texas and have the population density of New York City. When I pointed this out to longtime Population Institute head Werner Fornos, he wanted to know what you would do with all the pooh. That is certainly an interesting engineering problem. But there's an awful lot of available space for waste disposal in the rest of the world.

"Reproductive" Rebranding

Have the massive problems caused by population control—rapid aging, sex-selected abortion, demographic imbalance and societies without women, forced abortion—given the population controllers pause in their mission? On the contrary, these issues have only encouraged them to change their branding. "Population control" became "population stabilization." "Population stabilization" became "reproductive health" and "reproductive rights."

"Reproductive health" and "reproductive rights" are perhaps the most commonly used phrases in UN documents, with the possible exception of "peace." These terms were created by the sexual Left as euphemisms for abortion, but they also encompass other aspects of fertility regulation. Susan Yoshihara has written an extensive history of the development of "reproductive health" as a universal human rights norm in the *Ave Maria Law Review*. The phrase or variations thereof appear thousands of times in hundreds of documents and are intended both to advance a right to abortion and to persuade governments to adopt abortion and UN-style family planning programs. The basic idea is that fertility reduction will follow wherever "reproductive health" and "reproductive rights" are imposed or accepted.[30]

So successful has this campaign been that the world is awash in UN-style family planning. Pro-life aid workers will tell you that even when basic medicines are not available in crisis situations, condoms and devices like manual vacuum aspirators almost always are.[31] During the Serbian war during the Clinton administration, for example, when Kosovar refugees fled across the border into Albania, the UN Population Fund announced they were sending aid kits. These did not include a single Band-Aid or aspirin, but they did contain contraceptives and manual vacuum aspirators. UNFPA denied that the manual vacuum aspirators were used for abortions. However, when I traveled to Albania I interviewed medical personnel up and down the country who had been trained to use them as abortion devices in refugee tents, not exactly sterile or safe places.

While the world is awash in contraception, the UN is awash in euphemism, misdirection, and—above all—phony science.

"Reproductive health" stands in for abortion, which does the job of population control. Advocacy for "sustainable development" is used to block not just industrial development but also the spread of the Green Revolution cure malnutrition and starvation.

Unmasking "Unmet Need"

And then there's "unmet need"—one of the great frauds of the family planning debate, weasel words that come with a "scientific" imprimatur.

Abortion groups—International Planned Parenthood Federation and Marie Stopes International—say they need $9.4 billion to fulfill women's "unmet need" for "modern means of contraception."

As Rebecca Oas reports in *The New Atlantis*, "Visitors to New York's Times Square in September 2014 encountered a massive electronic billboard that said, 'Over 200 million women want access to contraception but can't get it.'" And a 2012 report coproduced by the UN Population Fund and the Alan Guttmacher Institute claimed 222 million women had this "unmet need." The 2014 edition of the same report increased that to 225 million women with an "unmet need for modern contraception." But as Oas points out, "The very concept of 'unmet need' is deeply flawed and routinely mischaracterized."[32]

This is not the first time that the United Nations has been caught using phony numbers to advance its "reproductive health" agenda. UN agencies used to say that five hundred (sometimes six hundred) thousand women per year were victims of maternal mortality. The only solution, of course, was "reproductive health" and "reproductive rights"—in other words, UN-style family planning and abortion. But those numbers were simply fictional. Joseph Chamie, longtime head of the Population Division of the United Nations, never used the five hundred thousand number because, he said, it could not be substantiated.[33] That did not stop UNICEF from using it regularly. But starting in 2011, researchers at the University of Washington and the UK medical journal *The Lancet* began to question those numbers.[34] Finally the United Nations relented: the number used now is three hundred thousand.[35] The about-face shows how elastic the claims of UN family planning advocates are.

The same players are involved in the equally phony proposition of "unmet need," and for the same reason: to advance the cause of fertility reduction and the spread of legal abortion.

Oas cites a "vast web" of entities promoting the purported "unmet need" for "reproductive health," including billion-dollar UN agencies, powerful abortion groups, and rich foundations like the one Bill Gates founded to lead a huge effort called FP2020, which is targeting sixty-nine countries with a pledge to fulfill the "unmet need" of 129 million "additional" women.[36] The coalition includes feminist groups and population control groups that have often been at loggerheads over the violation of human rights in the implementation of population control programs. But the thing that unites them all, Oas explains, is a purported "great global unmet need for contraception."

The UN's Millennium Development Goals measured the supposed "unmet need" for contraception by the number of women who are married, of reproductive age, sexually active, wishing to avoid pregnancy in the next two years, and not using a family planning method. As Oas explains, it "is not a simple measure of behavior (such as contraceptive prevalence) or personal interest (such as the desire to become pregnant or not within a specified length of time); rather, it is a policy construct that combines aspects of both." The assumption is that every woman who doesn't want to get pregnant but isn't using contraception must lack knowledge about or access to birth control.

But in fact, not using contraceptives may reflect a considered decision not to use them for many reasons: health, religion, dislike of side effects, infrequent or no sex, to name a few. Yet under the UN's rubric, even women who have made a sound decision to avoid contraception are said to have an "unmet need" for it. Oas points out that UN policy mavens have jiggered the data inputs in order to increase the numbers in other ways, too. Prior to 2003, "women were asked questions to determine the strength of their fertility intentions: How happy would they be, or how big a problem would it be, if they discovered they were pregnant in the near future?" No longer offering any nuance, the new question only gives them a yes or no option—Do you intend to get pregnant in the next two years? This naturally had the effect of increasing the number of women in the unmet need category.

Oas, who is now my colleague at C-Fam, did her research as an employee of an admittedly conservative research institute, one that is frequently at odds with UN policymakers on a whole host of issues. But she has picked up the baton on this issue from Harvard professor Lant Pritchett, who has been writing on this issue for more than twenty years. Pritchett has delivered blistering rebukes to the "unmet need" theory— usually to audiences of its proponents.

In 1996, he delivered a paper to the Johns Hopkins School of Hygiene and Public Health called bluntly "No Need for Unmet Need," which he pointed out was "neither a viable or a useful concept." Pritchett described "unmet need" as a "con game" ginned up by ideologues to pick the pockets of donor countries.

It is a failure as a concept because "there is no coherent sense in which the reported figure on 'unmet need' actually represents a need that is unmet." Strong words in the halls of academe and certainly in the halls of UN policy making. Pritchett pointed out that this supposed "need" is "attributed by others to women, not expressed by women themselves." He compared it to an unmet need for pork among Muslim and Jewish women or an unmet need for beef among Hindus. He said, "Such a use of the phrase 'need' would be misleading and unhelpful, if not downright offensive." He emphasized, however, that the issue is not religion but choice, and that women have by and large made a "knowing choice" not to use contraception.

He also debunked the notion that women around the world are uninformed about family planning and a wide range of contraceptive devices: "The data are clear that family planning knowledge is wide-spread" and that "in many cases ten times as many women know about contraception and where to obtain it than are actually using it."

Family planning advocates then argue that women cannot afford it. Remember the sorry countenance of Georgetown University law student Sandra Fluke, who complained that she needed taxpayers to pay for her contraception? (Otherwise the Pill would cost her nine dollars per month at Walmart!) But as Pritchett has shown, poor households will pay upward of 3 percent of their household income on tobacco. Certainly, they can afford the even smaller amount that contraception would cost.

Like Oas, Pritchett criticized the lack of any measure of the "intensity of the desire to avoid a child." If someone asked him if he wanted an icecream cone now, he might say no, but if someone handed him one, he might well say thank you very much and enjoy it.

Even more important, Pritchett argues,

> To classify this as a personal "need" ignores all other preferences the woman may have. She might not want a child but also, for some reason, might not want to use contraception (the bother, the side effects, whatever). Not allowing women to say whether or not they want contraception but classifying their "need" for contraception based on just one question about fertility does not allow women to speak for themselves. Many women classified with "unmet need" are not now using contraception and do not plan to use it even though it is available and they could afford it. I find saying these women have a "need" for contraception condescending in the extreme.[37]

And then there's the lie about "access" to contraception. International Planned Parenthood's Times Square billboard said that two hundred million women "wanted access to contraceptives but couldn't get it." But Oas points out, "According to data collected by the Alan Guttmacher Institute...from 51 country-level Demographic and Health Surveys between 2006 and 2013, in Africa, Asia, and Latin America and the Caribbean, only about 4 to 8 percent of married women aged 15 to 49 described as having 'unmet need' actually cited lack of access to contraceptives (including inability to afford them) as a reason for not using them."

Oas explains, "That means that in Africa, where 24 percent of married women are said to have an 'unmet need' (the highest rate of any region in the world), in fact just under 2 percent of surveyed married women actually have a self-reported lack of access to contraceptives."[38]

To put an even finer point on it, billions of dollars have been spent and will be spent to reach a vanishingly small number of women who may have a genuine desire for contraception but who cannot get it. This money could be spent elsewhere, such as in the provision of clean water, something that upwards of a billion people really do not have access to, and the lack of which really does kill them.

Almost everything you will hear from the United Nations and its allies about population, demography, and reproductive health comes cloaked in the authority of "science," "social science," and "scientific data." And almost every bit of it is ideological, skewed, or downright phony.

Would the world have sunk under the weight of billions more people if the United States and the United Nations had not intervened? In fact, fertility rates were already declining when the overpopulation scare got started.[39] Fertility rates have a habit of declining as education levels of women increase and as societies move from the farm to the city, from agriculture to industry. Even before industrialization, nineteenth-century France became the first country to reach what they call the "demographic transition," the point at which birth rates level off and begin to match death rates.

In a remarkable paper published by the Population Council in 1994, Lant Pritchett came to some startling conclusions that should have precluded the spending of those billions on family planning. The key determinant in family size—that is, the number of children a couple will have—is *the desire of the woman*: "Want a radical idea? Listen to the woman. She will tell you. In countries where fertility is high, women want more children. 'Excess' or 'unwanted' fertility plays a minor role in explaining fertility differences. Moreover, the level of contraceptive use, measures of contraceptive availability (such as 'unmet need'), and family planning effort have little impact on fertility after controlling for fertility desires."[40]

We do not know how the man-made demographic winter will play out. Japan is actually closing down little-used towns. You may recall the nuclear disaster in Fukushima, Japan, a few years ago. Rather than rebuild the nearby town, the Japanese have simply shuttered it, not out of safety concerns but because of a lack of population. There are reports that wolves have been sighted in abandoned towns in Germany. Twenty years ago, the demographers at UN headquarters did not know how low fertility can go. We still don't know. But we're about to find out. And it doesn't look pretty.

CHAPTER 12

Back Off, Man, I'm a Scientist

The day after Donald Trump's inauguration, feminists marched for "women's rights" on the National Mall in Washington, D.C. Within hours, "crowd scientists" from Manchester Metropolitan University in Britain were insisting that "three times as many attended the women's march as the Trump inauguration." And Obama's first inauguration had been three times larger than Trump's.[1]

These "crowd scientists" didn't just count noses; they used "sophisticated algorithms" and "a geometric analysis."[2] To adapt the line from Bill Murray in *Ghostbusters*, "Back off, man, we're scientists."

It will likely surprise no one that there is such a thing as "crowd science" and guys calling themselves "crowd scientists."

In February 2017, neuroscientists published a paper in *Current Biology* "proving" something called *misophonia*, a "disorder"—identified only in 2001—whereby sufferers have a hatred of sounds like chewing, eating, and loud breathing.[3] Something happens to a misophonia sufferer's frontal lobe when someone slurps his soup. It used to be a pet peeve, but now it's now a medical condition!

This anecdote demonstrates something that's wrong with science these days. Everyone wants to call what they do "science"—or at least to invoke "science" to support their claims.

Science is an inflated medium of exchange these days. It's the common currency of our age—you can hardly make an argument in the public square without a boatload of "studies" to back your claims—but its value has been eroded by the charlatans making obviously partisan and sometimes wild and contradictory "scientific" claims.

"Science" is used to shut the layman up. He's supposed to doff his cap to his scientific betters, to slink off mumbling "It doesn't make sense to me."

But the "science" we're all supposed to kowtow to is often more politics than real hard science. As we have seen again and again, the Left routinely uses dodgy data and skewed statistics in pursuit of some of the most truly unscientific projects in world history—from the bizarre campaign to define "gender" by feelings rather than biology, to the denial that growing human embryos are live human beings, to the hysterical rejection of genetically modified crops that would save millions from blindness and starvation, to the "overpopulation" scare that currently threatens to depopulate the planet.

Not all "science" is truly scientific. The fact that something goes by that name isn't a guarantee that there's anything truly scientific about it—not to mention, of its accuracy. Even when there's not obvious political pressure to skew results, scientists are human beings subject to the same temptations as the rest of us. And the iconic status of "science" in the world today, not to mention the fact that there are huge amounts of government money at stake, means that the rewards for dishonesty are enormous.

As *The Week's* Pascal-Emmanuel Gobry observes, "To most people, capital-S Science is the pursuit of capital-T Truth. It is a thing engaged in by people wearing lab coats and/or doing fancy math that nobody else understands...when people say 'science' what they really mean is magic or truth."[4]

No wonder there is rampant scientific fraud. And short of fraud, there is the tendency to publish only positive results—and superlative results at that.[5] The better the results, the more funding your project can garner, the more attractive your lab looks to top graduate students, and the more likely you are to get tenure and promotions. There is also the closed loop of friends praising the work of friends and groups of scientists chasing the same shiny thing that ultimately comes to nothing but nonetheless brings in accolades and cash, always cash.

And just as in any priest-ridden age, just as at any time when a class of people have been given enormous power, that power corrupts and those with the power are tempted to slip the leash, to wander far from their mission, to get involved in areas that are not their competence—in short, to meddle. Engineers pronounce on climate. Physicists pronounce on abortion. Chemists pronounce on transgenderism. And we, the simple folk in the pews, are supposed to fall into line because they are the scientists. Forget that their scientific knowledge does not extend so far as they want us to believe. *Yes, Father-Scientist, the seas will rise twenty feet unless I stop using chlorofluorocarbons. Forgive me, Father-Scientist, up until now I did not believe that a man could become a woman, but now I do. I will do penance and promise to sin no more.*

But, with all the power it has been given—indeed, taken—the Church of Science is a dirty business, emphasis on dirty. The barnacles of careerism have adhered to the Barque of Science. Start with the phonies and the fraudsters who in a better age would be laughed out of the room, but in our time are made rich and famous.

Take "Bill Nye the Science Guy."

The Smithsonian has a video on its website of "scientist" Bill Nye explaining the "science" of climate change. Now, anyone can talk about climate change. I do that in this book, but I do not hold myself out as a scientist. I do not speak from scientific credentials. Nye, however, does call himself a scientist, as do his many prominent fans. The *New York*

Post recently referred to Nye as one of the "top scientists" opposing Donald Trump.[6] He was one of the primary organizers of the March for Science in Washington, D.C., in late April 2017.[7] And as his fame has increased, he has become increasingly wacky. He called for parents who have "extra children" to be penalized.[8] On his new Netflix program, *Bill Nye Saves the World*, he presented *Crazy Ex-Girlfriend* sitcom star Rachel Bloom dancing and singing about her "sex junk," plumped for transgenderism, and explained how all sexuality is on a continuum.[9] Rather comically, it was revealed that on an old episode of *Bill Nye the Science Guy* he had told a little girl that her sex was determined by her chromosomes. This was conveniently edited out when the segment was shown on his new Netflix show.[10] It is so hard to keep up with the latest fashion in "science."

Bill Nye has a boatload of honorary doctorates from institutions like Johns Hopkins, Rensselaer Polytechnic, and Rutgers. But his lone earned credential is an undergraduate degree in mechanical engineering.[11] It appears that Nye spent at least a few years working in his field, at Boeing, but then left for a career in sketch comedy on a local show in Seattle called *Almost Live!* This was where Nye's character, "the Science Guy," came to life. The show won several Emmys, and eventually the character landed Nye on PBS and made him a breakout star.

Nye has become an icon of science, the CEO of the Planetary Society, no less—a highly influential NGO—and he is trotted out on talk TV to validate all manner of leftwing "scientific orthodoxy." He has gone so far as to suggest that it might be appropriate to throw "climate deniers" in jail.[12] Keep in mind, this man is a sketch comedian with an undergraduate degree in mechanical engineering.

Or take Neil deGrasse Tyson. He actually has an earned doctorate in astrophysics from Columbia University and has been director of the Hayden Planetarium at the American Museum of Natural History in New York City since 1996.[13] He is a real scientist—in the field of astrophysics. But Tyson opines endlessly on the dangers of and the catastrophic dangers to our planet from global warming. Astrophysics is not climate science. But we are only simple laymen. What do we know? Of course, an astrophysicist is qualified to speak on the science of climate. So is a mechanical engineer, a molecular biologist, or a paleontologist. Right?

Besides opining shamelessly beyond his competence, Tyson has also been caught saying some quite dubious things in his efforts to show how stupid journalists and congressmen can be about science. One hardly has to make things up to prove that point. But Tyson does make things up, and, when he's caught, he merely doubles down. Sean Davis of *The Federalist* website has called Tyson out for his claim that some congressman supposedly said his position had changed "360 degrees." Get it? See how dumb that is? The thing is, Tyson cannot prove that any congressman ever said that.

And for years, he has trotted out a headline meant to show how dumb journalists are: "Half the Schools in the District Are Below Average." See how mathematically illiterate that is? Only Tyson cannot show where this headline ever appeared, even when pressed by Davis at *The Federalist*. Has this diminished Tyson's credibility? Not one bit.[14]

But being a scientist means never ever saying you're sorry, especially when you play a scientist on TV—which brings us to Carl Sagan.

No one has been a bigger deal in "science" than Carl Sagan. Maybe Galileo or Einstein were bigger deals, but neither of them ever had his own show. But even Sagan—especially Sagan, who was an astronomer, cosmologist, astrophysicist, astrobiologist, and author—was not immune from opining far from his field, and sometimes quite stupidly so. Massive praise and TV can put a fella at risk for that.

In 1992, the readers of *Parade Magazine* voted Carl Sagan the smartest man in America.[15] Two years before, in that same magazine, this smartest man in America had slipped the leash of his scientific competence and lectured us on human embryology.[16] Sagan was an abortion advocate, and he wanted to demonstrate that the unborn child was not fully human. So he described a human embryo in the third week as "a little like a segmented worm. By the fourth week...it's recognizable as a vertebrate, its tube-shaped heart is beginning to beat, something like a gill arches of a fish or an amphibian have become conspicuous, and there is a pronounced tail. It looks like a newt or a tadpole."[17]

Sagan was relying on the catchy but long-discredited "ontogeny recapitulates phylogeny" theory of a nineteenth-century Darwinist named Ernst Haeckel, who had postulated that every human embryo must pass through various evolutionary stages: worm, fish, amphibian, finally human. Well before 1990, we knew what the stages of human embryonic development in utero actually look like—and it's not like a tadpole or a fish. What's more, it is well known that Haeckel doctored his own illustrations to reflect his erroneous theory. Sagan should have known these facts, but there is nothing quite like a scientist yoked firmly to ideology and making authoritative pronouncements outside the bounds of his field.

Like Tyson and Nye, Sagan possessed no special knowledge about climate science, but that didn't stop him from warning us that the burning oil fields in the 1991 Gulf War would "disrupt agriculture in much of South Asia."[18]

If scientists are priests, then physicist Stephen Hawking is an archbishop. He says, "There is a fundamental difference between religion, which is based on authority, [and] science, which is based on observation and reason. Science will win because it works."[19] How do we know? Because Archbishop Hawking says so. Hawking also said that we need to colonize space or we'll become extinct.[20] SCIENCE!

The current state of "science" is best described by Daniel Sarewitz in a remarkable essay in *The New Atlantis*, a journal published by the Ethics and Public Policy Institute in Washington, D.C. Sarewitz, who holds a doctorate in geological sciences from Cornell and runs the Consortium for Science Policy & Outcomes at the University of Arizona, describes what he calls "the big lie" about science: that "scientific progress on a broad front results from the free play of free intellects, working on subjects of their own choice, in the manner dictated by their curiosity of the unknown." Sarawitz attributes the "big lie" to Vannevar Bush, the MIT engineer and "architect of the nation's World War II research enterprise, which delivered the atomic bomb and helped advance microwave radar, mass production of antibiotics, and other technologies crucial to the Allied victory." *Time* magazine called Bush "the General of Physics."

Sarewitz not only calls this a lie, he calls it a "beautiful lie." This theory of how science works, coming from the lionized Bush, resulted in an explosion of federal funding for scientific research. "'Basic research' funding rose from $265 million in 1953 to $38 billion in 2012, a twentyfold increase when adjusted for inflation." At colleges and universities, it rose from $82 million to $24 billion, "a more than fortyfold increase when adjusted for inflation."

And what scientific discoveries have been made in this time? Plenty, but not from supposedly disinterested "basic research" by curious researchers whose discoveries just happened to converge in major scientific breakthroughs. No, the useful discoveries and advances in science over the past six decades have largely come not from "the free play of free intellects" described by Bush's "beautiful lie." To a large extent, they have come from the technological needs of the Department of Defense (DOD). Each of them—computers, genome sequencing, the discovery of gravitational waves, the discovery of flowing water on Mars, the modern jet engines, cell phones, the Internet, laser technology, satellites, GPS, digital imagery, nuclear power, and solar power—came from the need to solve problems, and not simply from a desire to increase knowledge and understanding.

Take the jet engine. During World War II jet engines had to be overhauled every hundred hours or so; they were forty-five times less efficient than piston engines. But military planners knew that jet engines were the wave of the future because of their combat performance, so the Air Force and Navy funded years of research and development to improve them. Then the Boeing Company took what it had learned in developing the jet-engine-powered fuel tanker for the Air Force and turned it into the Boeing 707, the first "truly safe and reliable commercial jet aircraft."

Do you like your iPhone? Of the thirteen areas of technological advances that were essential to its development, eleven—including the microprocessor, GPS, and the Internet—came from military investment in research and development.

Sarewitz reports, "The great accomplishments of the military-industrial complex did not result from allowing scientists to pursue 'subjects of their own choice, in the manner dictated by their curiosity,' but by channeling that curiosity toward the solution of problems that DOD wanted to solve." [21]

Scientific understanding advances most when it is tied to the needs of technology. Organic chemistry, for instance, originally grew out of the needs of dye making. Bacteriology advanced because of wine making.

But science has become increasingly untethered from technology, from problem solving, and from the real-world needs of the rest of us. The "beautiful lie" of Vannevar Bush seems to have finally triumphed.

How did we get here?

One could go back to the turn of the twentieth century, to H. G. Wells and his acolytes among American progressives, who were certain that men of science would lead us to utopia's sunny uplands in which the smelly men and women from the small towns would have no say. [22]

How it must have galled them when science was tied to the needs of the war machine in World War II. One of the tropes of the Left, repeated recently in a television series called *Manhattan*, is how the fascistic military bullied the artist-like scientists in the development of the atomic bomb.

In 1963, *Time* magazine chose fifteen American scientists as its Men of the Year: "Statesmen and savants, builders and even priests are their servants. Science is at the apogee of its power." [23] Journalist Ward Elliot said, "The land rang with calls for more Ph.Ds. to win all the wars we were fighting with a grand mobilization of expertise." [24]

That call for more Ph.D.s was answered by a veritable Mount Vesuvius of doctorates. In 1957, fewer than ten thousand earned doctorates had been awarded by American colleges and universities. By 2014, 54,074 were awarded, and the growth shows no sign of slowing down. [25] Just as the monasteries bulged with postulants in the Middle Ages, who wouldn't want to join the new priesthood?

This inflation of scientists has led to some counter-productive results. As of 2010, there were twenty-four thousand peer-reviewed scientific journals publishing something on the order of two million scientific papers each and every year. The importance of getting published and the importance of peer review cannot be overestimated for a scientific career. And the chances of fishy business in this competitive hothouse cannot be underestimated.

Get into a debate about virtually any public policy issue these days and refer to a study. Immediately your interlocutor will demand to know, *Was it peer reviewed*? If not, the study will be dismissed out of hand.

"Peer review" is practically a mantra and is one of the great scams of modern science. This is the process whereby a paper or a research proposal are turned over to experts in the field to review, comment on, and often give their thumbs up or thumbs down for publication or funding—supposedly based on the actual quality of the science in the study.

But in actual fact, peer review has become a way for the leftwing "consensus" to circle the wagons and shoot down any challenge to their agenda. Peer review has become a mug's game, an inside game. Science from outsiders is not welcome. This is exactly how "the science" stays "settled."

A paper on the dangers of abortion would never make it past peer review at the *New England Journal of Medicine*. Pro-life scientists know this, so why would they ever even submit such an article? When Lawrence Mayer and Paul McHugh wrote a survey of the scientific literature on sexual orientation and gender identity, they knew it couldn't go to any of the top-tier journals even though both men have been published in such journals. The material was too controversial. Instead it was published in *The New Atlantis*, a journal that is not peer reviewed and has even published articles critical of peer review.[26] The result is that their very fine paper was dismissed as "not peer reviewed." It was not even engaged by the Left.

The peer-review process has missed many papers for which the authors later won the Nobel Prize. George Akerlof's hugely influential paper *Market for Lemons*, for example, was rejected by three journals, yet he later won the 2001 Nobel Prize in economics. Paul Boyer, the winner of the 1997 Nobel Prize in chemistry, was rejected by *The Journal of Biological Chemistry.* Hans Kreb won the 1953 Nobel Prize in Medicine for his discovery of the citric acid cycle, but his work was rejected by the prestigious journal *Nature.*[27]

Speaking to the Second International Congress on Peer Review in Biomedical Publication in 1993, historian of science Horace Freeland Judson warned about "the vulnerability of peer-review to corruption." He addressed the enormous growth of the scientific enterprise, the relentless pressure to get funded, and the intrusion of politics.

So sketchy has the peer-review process become that Adam Marcus and Ivan Oransky founded a website called Retraction Watch that reports on nothing more than scandals in scholarly research. With Retraction Watch staff writer Cat Ferguson, they published "The Peer-Review Scam" on the website of *Nature,* describing massive fraud by researchers who used phony email accounts so that they could peer review their own papers—always favorably, of course: "In the past 2 years, journals have been forced to retract more than 110 papers in at least 6 instances of peer review rigging." The rigging included publications by the largest and most respected publishers of scholarly journals.[28]

The most spectacular case of peer-review rigging came to light in 2013 when the author of a paper under peer review for an outlet called the *Journal of Vibration and Control* received emails from two experts who were reviewing his paper. He was suspicious because authors are not supposed to hear directly from those reviewing their papers. The publisher contacted the reviewers, one of whom responded and said he had not sent the email and that he did didn't even work in the field. An investigation lasting more than a year revealed that sixty articles published by SAGE Publishing—the fifth largest producer of scholarly journals in the world—had to be withdrawn because of peer-review rigging. It turns out there was a ring of authors who were "both reviewing and citing each other at an anomalous rate." A central part of the problem is that many journals allow authors to suggest reviewers for their own papers and allow them to give only emails as contact information for reviewers. Obviously, it's quite easy to simply provide a phony email address. Hyung-In Moon, a medicinal plant researcher in South Korea, was caught by editors of a scholarly journal submitting phony emails for reviewers of his papers. They were going straight to him! Turns out he was reviewing his own papers.[29]

But it's not about just a few (or even many) dishonest "scientists." As Daniel Sarewitz writes, "the science world has been buffeted for nearly a decade by growing revelations that major bodies of scientific knowledge, published in peer-reviewed papers, may simply be wrong."[30]

Megan Scudellari reports on one stunning example. For twenty-five years, breast cancer researchers have been studying a cell line that has now been the subject of more than 650 published breast cancer studies. It turns out the cell line may not even be breast cancer after all, but a completely different kind of cancer.[31]

Equally troubling are the results of biotech firm Amgen's attempt to confirm published findings in fifty-three papers that were deemed "landmark" studies. They could confirm the findings of only six. As the scientific journal *Nature* said, "Even knowing the limitations of preclinical research, this was a shocking result."[32]

The chief scientific officer at the ALS Therapy Institute in Cambridge, Massachusetts, tested one hundred drugs for treating Lou Gehrig's Disease. Each of the drugs had been reported to have positive findings in published reports. He was unable to reproduce *any* of the positive findings.[33]

It is estimated that somewhere between 75 and 90 percent of all published studies in basic and preclinical biomedical research are not reproducible.[34] Consider that reproducibility is a cornerstone of science. Consider also that such nonreproducible research is likely cited over and over again, perhaps hundreds of times in peer-reviewed journals.

Sarewitz tells the story of patient rights' activist Fran Visco, who ran into a roadblock at the National Institutes of Health in the development of treatments for breast cancer. She found that breast cancer research was a closed loop of scientific professionals building their careers on, as she put it, "one gene or one protein" and not making any progress toward treatments, let alone cures. She ended up partnering with the Department of Defense and the Army—real problem solvers, not scientific navel gazers—who came up with "a new, biologically based targeted breast cancer therapy—a project that had already been turned down multiple times by NIH's peer-review system because the conventional wisdom was that targeted therapies wouldn't work. The DOD-funded studies led directly to the development of the drug Herceptin, one of the most important advances in breast cancer treatment in recent decades."[35]

Astrophysicist Alvin Weinberg, who was the administrator of Oak Ridge National Laboratory, elucidated the difference between what he called "Science and Trans-Science" in a 1972 article in *Science* magazine. As he pointed out, we are drawing public policy conclusions from observations that may seem "scientific" but quite simply aren't.

Weinberg was concerned with the relationship between scientific knowledge and decisions on social questions. He realizes that many issues "hang on the answers to questions which can be asked of science and yet cannot be answered by science." He proposed the term "transscientific for these questions since, though they are, epistemologically speaking, questions of fact and can be stated in the language of science, they are unanswerable by science; they transcend science." And he explored the problems that arise when a scientist is asked to provide "scientific" answers to public policy questions where only "trans-scientific" answers exist.

Weinberg used the example of the effects of low-level radiation. At the time of his article, the various standard-setting bodies allowed for exposure to 150 millirems of X-radiation. To test—for a result in which researchers could have 95 percent confidence—whether exposure to 150 millirems would increase the mutation rate by 0.5 percent would require an experiment on *8 trillion* mice. For 60 percent confidence, you would need only a hundred and ninety-five thousand mice. As Weinberg pointed out, "The number is so staggeringly large that, as a practical matter, the question is unanswerable by direct scientific investigation." And this problem is not confined to radiation; it applies to any environmental hazard: "One can never, with any finite experiment, prove that any environmental factor is totally harmless."

Weinberg went into the impossibility of predicting "extremely improbable events" like "a catastrophic reactor accident" or a devastating earthquake that would wash out the Hoover Dam. Scientists are called upon to make such predictions, but their forecasts cannot truly be called "scientific."

But Weinberg found even more concerning problems in the social sciences. Hard science is one thing: "In physics, if we know the initial position and velocity of a specific macroscopic object, and the forces acting upon it, we can predict its trajectory—not the trajectories on the average of many objects like this one, but the trajectory of this particular object. Thus, the physical sciences are capable of predicting particular macroscopic events precisely from the laws of nature and from the initial conditions."

Not so the social sciences, not so.

Weinberg explained, "The social sciences deal with classes, the individual members of which display wide variability, as well as being subject to the vagaries of consciousness." Social science simply cannot predict the behavior of an individual human being or a group of people with the same precision as a group.[36]

And yet the social scientists expect us to kowtow to their "scientific research" in the establishment of public policy. But we should know better. In fact, we have ample reason to know that even purported hard "science," such as the biology of nutrition, is not always a reliable guide.

How many times have we been told that a certain food is good and then bad and then good again? Full-fat milk is back on the good list, after years out of favor.[37] Salt is among the most hotly contested scientific—really, trans-scientific—questions on the planet. In 1972, a researcher told us, "The evidence that salt induces permanent and fatal hypertension is direct, quantitative, and unequivocal in the rat."[38] In 2012, the Centers for Disease Control and Prevention asserted that 100,000 people died every year because of too much salt in their diet.

But a 2011 meta-analysis of 167 randomized control trials[39] and thirteen population studies since 1950 found no clear connection between salt reduction and improved health.[40] Alas, how many men have suffered through under-seasoned steaks and green beans in all those years?

The bottom line is that "science" has slipped the leash, and somehow must be brought to heel. It must be put back in its place. Scientists are not priests; they are vendors—perhaps vendors of wonder, but vendors nonetheless. And perhaps we need far fewer than *fifty-four thousand* of them being launched upon the polis every single year.

Science has become a degraded currency. Its aura of authority has been used and abused to push every unscientific leftist fad from the Sexual Revolution to anti-fracking hysteria. And yet real, honest, non-political science has been an unexampled boon to the human race—lifting millions from privation and malady. We can't afford to leave science to the frauds, the fakers, and the Left. Or what will happen when we really need it?

Acknowledgments

In my work in public policy in New York and Washington, D.C., and places around the world, I am consistently charged with being "anti-science." My colleagues and I are repeatedly told that "the science is settled" on a whole host of issues—always in favor of the Left's agenda, whether on abortion and human sexuality, in bioethics debates, or on "climate change."

Couple this with the rather nasty politics of our time, and you have the specter of science becoming a new leftist religion, with conservative heretics being burned at least metaphorically at the stake.

Quite frankly, I have always been a tad skeptical about the claims made by scientists. One day salt is killing us, the next it is fine. The brontosaurus was real, then it wasn't, and now maybe it is. And all this uncertainty is fine. In fact, it's profoundly *un*scientific to claim that the facts are "settled" and thus beyond the scope of human inquiry.

So, I was greatly interested and grateful when Harry Crocker and Tom Spence of Regnery Publishing asked me to write a book about the phony science peddled by the Left and how science, properly understood, tends to support the positions advocated by conservatives. It is conservatives, after all, who live in the evidence-based community. I am grateful Harry and Tom were willing to take a chance on an untested book writer. I am profoundly grateful for the steady hand of my Regnery editor, Elizabeth Kantor, whom I have known and admired for years.

I am also grateful to the very helpful research assistance provided by Bethany Spare and my C-Fam colleague, Rebecca Oas. I am grateful to Jennifer Roback Morse and William "Matt" Briggs for reading and commenting on early chapters. Their advice was very helpful. Thanks also to Heather Hambleton for her very fine early reading and editing.

I also want to thank all the scientists and researchers who have bravely fought the leftwing zeitgeist simply by working in an honest and non-ideological way. I benefited greatly from the work of Paul McHugh of Johns Hopkins University, Mark Regnerus of the University of Texas, Brad Wilcox of the University of Virginia, Paul Sullins of the Catholic University of America, Robert Rector of the Heritage Foundation, and many others. I am especially grateful to the writers and editors connected to *The New Atlantis*, which I found to be indispensable to this project.

Thanks also to my C-Fam colleagues Lisa Correnti, Susan Yoshihara, Stefano Gennarini, and Marianna Orlandi for allowing me to be a ghost during the writing of this book.

Lastly, thanks to my wife, Cathy, and our children, Lucy and Gigi. Someone writing a book is not always the most pleasant person to be around. Thanks for your support and for your patience.

Notes

Introduction

1. https://twitter.com/iowahawkblog/status/664089892599631872?lang=en.
2. See Tom Bethell, *The Politically Incorrect Guide to Science* (Washington, DC: Regnery Publishing, 2005), 14–17.

Chapter 1

1. Amy Chozick, "Hillary Clinton Blames F.B.I. Director for Election Loss," *New York Times*, November 12, 2016, https://www.nytimes.com/2016/11/13/us/politics/hillary-clinton-james-comey.html?smprod=nytcore-iphone&smid=nytcore-iphone-share.
2. Jim Rutenberg, "A 'Dewey Defeats Truman' Lesson for the Digital Age," *New York Times*, November 9, 2016, http://www.nytimes.com/2016/11/09/business/media/media-trump-clinton.html.
3. Michael Cieply, "Stunned by Trump, the *New York Times* Finds Time for Some Soul-Searching," *Deadline*, November 10, 2016, http://deadline.com/2016/11/shocked-by-trump-new-york-times-finds-time-for-soul-searching-1201852490/.

4. Valerie Richardson, "Democratic Heads Roll After Video Shows Agitators Planted at Trump Rallies, *Washington Times*, October 18, 2016, http://www.washingtontimes.com/news/2016/oct/18/undercover-video-shows-democrats-saying-they-hire-/.

5. RealClearPolitics, General Election: Trump vs. Clinton Polling Data, http://www.realclearpolitics.com/epolls/2016/president/us/general_election_trump_vs_clinton-5491.html.

6. Jonathan Easley, "Pollsters Suffer Huge Embarrassment," *The Hill*, November 9, 2016, http://thehill.com/blogs/ballot-box/presidential-races/305133-pollsters-suffer-huge-embarrassment.

7. Larry Sabato, Kyle Kondik, and Geoffrey Skelley, "Our Final 2016 Picks," *Sabato's Crystal Ball*, University of Virginia Center for Politics, November 7, 2016, http://www.centerforpolitics.org/crystalball/articles/our-final-2016-picks/.

8. Josh Katz, "Who Will Be President?," *The Upshot* (blog), *New York Times*, last updated November 8, 2016, http://www.nytimes.com/interactive/2016/upshot/presidential-polls-forecast.html#other-forecasts.

9. Recall MSNBC commentator Chris Matthews gave him a "thrill right up my leg."

10. Nate Silver, "Clinton Probably Finished Off Trump Last Night," *FiveThirtyEight* (blog), October 20, 2016, http://fivethirtyeight.com/features/clinton-probably-finished-off-trump-last-night/.

11. David Weigel, "State Pollsters, Pummeled by 2016, Analyze What Went Wrong," *Washington Post*, December 30, 2016, https://www.washingtonpost.com/news/post-politics/wp/2016/12/30/state-pollsters-pummeled-by-2016-analyze-what-went-wrong/?utm_term=.ef8aa93b9119.

12. Steven Shepard, "GOP Insiders: Trump's Overhaul Won't Succeed," *The Politico Caucus* (blog), August 19, 2016, http://www.politico.com/story/2016/08/donald-trump-reset-insiders-caucus-227177.

13. Ibid.

Chapter 2

1. Laura Mowat, "Transgender Man Gives Birth to His Own Baby in World First," *Express*, September 28, 2016, http://www.express.co.uk/news/world/714481/Transgender-man-gives-birth-OWN-BABY-world-first.

2. Abigail Jones, "Free Tampons and Pads Are Making Their Way to U.S. Colleges, High Schools, and Middle Schools," *Newsweek*, September 9, 2016, http://www.newsweek.com/free-tampons-pads-us-schools-496083.

3. Petula Dvorak, "Transgender at Five," *Washington Post*, May 19, 2012, https://www.washingtonpost.com/local/transgender-at-five/2012/05/19/gIQABfFkbU_story.html?utm_term=.2801318b8b27.

4. Alan B. Goldberg and Joneil Adriano, "'I'm a Girl': Understanding Transgender Children," ABC News, April 27, 2007, http://abcnews.go.com/2020/story?id=3088298&page=1.

5. Joshua Terry, "'Modern Family' Will Feature Transgender Child Actor," *Variety*, http://variety.com/2016/tv/news/modern-family-transgender-actor-jackson-millarker-1201870412/.

6. "R. Kelly's Youngest Child Comes Out as Transgender," *In Touch Weekly*, June 9, 2014, http://www.intouchweekly.com/posts/r-kelly-s-youngest-child-comes-out-as-transgender-39152.

7. "Dear Colleague Letter on Transgender Students," U.S. Department of Justice Civil Rights Division, U.S. Department of Education Office for Civil Rights, https://www2.ed.gov/about/offices/list/ocr/letters/colleague-201605-title-ix-transgender.pdf.

8. Edward Whelan, "Fourth Circuit Inflicts Sex Change on Title IX— Part 2," Bench Memos, *National Review*, April 25, 2016, http://www.nationalreview.com/bench-memos/434535/fourth-circuit-transgender-ruling.

9. Ariane de Vogue, "Meet Gavin Grimm, the Transgender Student at the Center of Bathroom Debate," *CNN Politics*, September 8, 2016, http://www.cnn.com/2016/09/08/politics/transgender-bathroom-issues-gavin-grimm/index.html.

10. It is a common oddity that boys who identify as girls almost inevitably take names resembling those of strippers, always "Stormi" never Susan.

11. Lindsey Bever, "Transgender Girl Scout Stands Up to Bully Who Wouldn't Buy Cookies 'from a Boy in a Dress,'" Morning Mix, *Washington Post*, February 2, 2016, https://www.washingtonpost.com/news/morning-mix/wp/2016/02/02/transgender-girl-scout-stands-up-to-bully-who-wouldnt-buy-cookies-from-a-boy-in-a-dress/.

12. Phoebe Jackson-Edwards, "Eight-Year-Old Boy Learns How to Do 'Drag' Makeup after Begging His Mother for a Tutorial—and a Selfie of the Results Is Sweeping the Internet," *Daily Mail*, January 7, 2016,

http://www.dailymail.co.uk/femail/article-3388302/Eight-year-old-boy-learns-drag-makeup-begging-mother-book-tutorial-selfie-results-sweeping-internet.html?ITO=applenews.

13. American Psychiatric Association, *Diagnostic and Statistical Manual of Mental Disorders* [hereafter *DSM-5*] (Arlington, VA: American Psychiatric Association, 2013), https://psychiatry.org/psychiatrists/practice/dsm.

14. American Psychological Association, "Answers to Your Questions about Transgender People, Gender Identity and Gender Expression," pamphlet, http://www.apa.org/topics/lgbt/transgender.pdf.

15. Judith Butler, *Gender Trouble: Feminism and the Subversion of Identity* (London: Routledge, 1990), 6.

16. "Facebook Diversity" (web page), https://www.facebook.com/facebook diversity/photos/a.196865713743272.42938.105225179573993/5675 87973337709/.

17. *DSM-5*, 452, http://dx.doi.org/10.1176/appi.books.9780890425596. dsm14.

18. Ibid.

19. American Psychiatric Association, "Gender Dysphoria," *DSM-5*, 455.

20. Jesse Singal, "How the Fight over Transgender Kids Got a Leading Sex Researcher Fired," Science of Us, *New York Magazine*, February 7, 2016, http://nymag.com/scienceofus/2016/02/fight-over-trans-kids-got-a-researcher-fired.html.

21. Mary Hasson, "Threatening Violence, Trans Activists Expel Un-PC Research at Medical Conference, *The Federalist*, February 17, 2017, http://thefederalist.com/2017/02/27/threatening-violence-trans-activists-expel-un-pc-research-medical-conference/.

22. Mayer and McHugh, "Sexuality and Gender...Part Three: Gender Identity," n. 74, http://www.thenewatlantis.com/publications/part-three-gender-identity-sexuality-and-gender#_ftn74.

23. Austin Ruse, "Mother Can't Stop Doctor from Mutilating Autistic Daughter Who Wants to Be a Transgender Boy," *Breitbart*, June 29, 2016, http://www.breitbart.com/big-government/2016/06/29/hold-mother-cant-stop-doctor-from-mutilating-autistic-daughter-who-wants-to-be-a-boy/.

24. Lawrence S. Mayer and Paul R. McHugh, "Sexuality and Gender: Findings from the Biological, Psychological, and Social Scientists," *The New Atlantis*, 50, special report, three parts, Fall 2016.

25. Samantha Allen, "The Right's Favorite Anti-LGTB Doctor Strikes Again," *The Daily Beast*, http://www.thedailybeast.com/articles/2016/08/23/the-right-s-favorite-anti-lgbt-doctor-strikes-again.html.

26. Mayer and McHugh, "Sexuality and Gender."

27. Mayer and McHugh, "Sexuality and Gender...Part Three: Gender Identity," n. 34, http://www.thenewatlantis.com/publications/part-three-gender-identity-sexuality-and-gender#_ftn34.

28. J. Michael Bostwick and Kari A. Martin, "A Man's Brain in an Ambiguous Body: A Case of Mistaken Gender Identity," *American Journal of Psychiatry* 164, no. 10 (2007): 1499–1505, http://dx.doi.org/10.1176/appi.ajp.2007.07040587.

29. Eva-Katrin Benz et al., "A Polymorphism of the CYP17 Gene Related to Sex Steroid Metabolism Is Associated with Female-to-Male but not Male-to-Female Transsexualism," *Fertility and Sterility* 90, no. 1 (2008): 56–59, http://www.fertstert.org/article/S0015-0282(07)01228-9/fulltext.

30. Lauren Hare et al., "Androgen Receptor Repeat Length Polymorphism Associated with Male-to-Female Transsexualism," *Biological Psychiatry* 65, no. 1 (2009): 93–96, https://www.ncbi.nlm.nih.gov/pmc/articles/PMC3402034/.

31. Harald J. Schneider, Johanna Pickel, and Günter K. Stalla, "Typical Female 2nd–4th Finger Length (2D:4D) Ratios in Male-to-Female Transsexuals—Possible Implications for Prenatal Androgen Exposure," *Psychoneuroendocrinology* 31, no. 2 (2006): 265–269, http://www.psyneuen-journal.com/article/S0306-4530(05)00177-0/abstract.

32. Robert Sapolsky, "Caught between Male and Female," *Wall Street Journal*, December 6, 2013, http://www.wsj.com/articles/SB10001424052702304854804579234030532617704.

33. Mayer and McHugh, "Sexuality and Gender...Part Three: Gender Identity," n. 53, http://www.thenewatlantis.com/publications/part-three-gender-identity-sexuality-and-gender#_ftnref53.

34. Ibid.

35. Hsiao-Lun Ku et al., "Brain Signature Characterizing the Body-Brain-Mind Axis of Transsexuals, *PLoS One* 8, no. 7 (2013), http://journals.plos.org/plosone/article?id=10.1371/journal.pone.0070808.

36. Ibid.

37. Ferris Jabr, "Cache Cab: Taxi Drivers' Brains Grow to Navigate London's Streets," *Scientific American*, December 8, 2011, https://www.scientificamerican.com/article/london-taxi-memory/.

38. Mayer and McHugh, "Sexuality and Gender...Part Three: Gender Identity."

39. Ibid.

40. Gary J. Gates, "How Many People Are Lesbian, Gay, Bisexual and Transgender?" The Williams Institute, April 2011, https://williams institute.law.ucla.edu/wp-content/uploads/Gates-How-Many-People-LGBT-Apr-2011.pdf.

41. Mayer and McHugh, "Sexuality and Gender...Part Three: Gender Identity."

42. Paul McHugh, "Transgender Surgery Isn't the Solution," *Wall Street Journal*, May 13, 2016, http://www.wsj.com/articles/paul-mchugh-transgender-surgery-isnt-the-solution-1402615120.

43. Sari L. Reisner et al., "Mental Health of Transgender Youth in Care at an Adolescent Urban Community Health Center: A Matched Retrospective Cohort Study," *Journal of Adolescent Health* 56, no. 3 (2015): 274–279, http://dx.doi.org/10.1016/j.jadohealth.2014.10.264.

44. Anne P. Haas, Philip L. Rodgers, and Jody Herman, "Suicide Attempts among Transgender and Gender Non-Conforming Adults: Findings of the National Transgender Discrimination Survey," Williams Institute, UCLA School of Law, January 2014, http://williamsinstitute.law.ucla.edu/wp-content/uploads/AFSP-Williams-Suicide-Report-Final.pdf.

45. Mayer and McHugh, "Sexuality and Gender...Part Two: Sexuality, Mental Health Outcomes, and Social Stress," n. 71, http://www.thenewatlantis.com/publications/part-two-sexuality-mental-health-outcomes-and-social-stress-sexuality-and-gender#_ftnref71.

46. Mayer and McHugh, "Sexuality and Gender...Part Three: Gender Identity."

47. Cecilia Dhejne et al., "Long-Term Follow-Up of Transsexual Persons Undergoing Sex Reassignment Surgery: Cohort Study in Sweden," *PLoS One* 6, no. 2 (2011), http://journals.plos.org/plosone/article?id=10.1371/journal.pone.0016885.

48. Lawrence S. Mayer and Paul R. McHugh, "Sexuality and Gender: Findings from the Biological, Psychological, and Social Scientists," *The New Atlantis* 50, special report, three parts, Fall 2016

49. David Batty, "Sex Changes Are Not Effective, Say Researchers," *The Guardian*, July 30, 2004, https://www.theguardian.com/society/2004/jul/30/health.mentalhealth.

50. Walt Heyer, "Regret Isn't Rare: The Dangerous Lie of Sex Change Surgery's Success," *Public Discourse*, June 17, 2016, http://www.thepublicdiscourse.com/2016/06/17166/.

51. Singal, "How the Fight over Transgender Kids Got a Leading Sex Researcher Fired."

52. Tari Hanneman, "Johns Hopkins Community Calls for Disavowal of Misleading Anti-LGBTQ 'Report,'" Human Rights Campaign, October 6, 2016, http://www.hrc.org/blog/johns-hopkins-community-calls-for-disavowal-of-misleading-anti-lgbtq-report.

53. *The New Atlantis*, "Lies and Bullying from the Human Rights Campaign," press release, October 10, 2016, http://www.thenewatlantis.com/docLib/20161010_TNAresponsetoHRC.pdf.

54. Michelle Goldberg, "What Is a Woman?," American Chronicles, *New Yorker*, August 4, 2014, http://www.newyorker.com/magazine/2014/08/04/woman-2.

55. Alan Murphy, "Transgender Fighter Fallon Fox Sends Opponent to Hospital," #WHOATV, September 15, 2014, http://whoatv.com/transgender-fighter-fallon-fox-sends-opponent-to-hospital/.

56. "'It's not Fair': Transgender Student's Success in Girls Track Causes Backlash," *Fox News Insider*, June 7, 2016, http://insider.foxnews.com/2016/06/07/nattaphon-wangyot-transgender-athlete-wins-all-state-honors-girls-track-and-field.

57. Daniel Harris, "The Sacred Androgen: The Transgender Debate," *Antioch Review* 74, no. 1 (2016), http://review.antiochcollege.org/sacred-androgen-transgender-debate-daniel-harris.

Chapter 3

1. Judith Reisman, Kinsey: *Crimes and Consequences*: *The Red Queen and the Grand Scheme*, 3d. rev. ed. (Hartline Marketing, 2001); Judithe Reisman, *Sexual Sabotage: How One Mad Scientist Unleashed a Plague of Corruption*

and Contagion on America (WND, 2010); Judith Reisman, et al., *Kinsey, Sex and Fraud: The Indoctrination of a People* (Vital Issues, 1990).

2. Alfred Kinsey, *Sexual Behavior in the Human Male* (Bloomington: Indiana University Press, 1948).

3. Robert Reilly, *Making Gay Okay: How Rationalizing Homosexuality Is Changing Everything* (San Francisco: Ignatius Press, 2014).

4. Frank Newport, "Americans Greatly Overestimate Percent Gay, Lesbian in U.S.," *Gallup*, May 21, 2015, http://www.gallup.com/poll/183383/americans-greatly-overestimate-percent-gay-lesbian.aspx.

5. Brian Ward, James Dahlhamer, Adena Galinsky, and Sarah Joesti, "Sexual Orientation and Health among U.S. Adults: National Health Interview Survey, 2013," *National Health Statistics Reports* 77, July 15, 2014, http://www.cdc.gov/nchs/data/nhsr/nhsr077.pdf.

6. United Methodist Church, "Data Services," http://www.umc.org/gcfa/data-services.

7. The three markers for homosexuality are generally understood to be sexual attraction, sexual behavior, and self-identity.

8. Michel Foucault, *History of Sexuality* (Paris: Éditions Gallimard, 1976).

9. Michael W. Hannon, "Against Heterosexuality," *First Things*, March 2014, https://www.firstthings.com/article/2014/03/against-heterosexuality.

10. Brief for Richard Hodges et al. as Amicus Curiae, Obergefell v. Hodges, 576 U.S. __ (2015), https://www.supremecourt.gov/Obergefell Hodges/AmicusBriefs/14-556_Prof_Daniel_N_Robinson.pdf.

11. Jeffrey B. Satinover, "The 'Trojan Couch': How the Mental Health Associations Misrepresent Science," National Association for Research and Therapy of Homosexuality, https://www.scribd.com/document/69609293/The-Trojan-Couch-Satin-Over.

12. Ibid.

13. Evelyn Hooker, The Adjustment of the Male Overt Homosexual, http://www.tandfonline.com/doi/abs/10.1080/08853126.1957.10380742.

14. Franklin A. Robinson Jr., "Guide to the Lesbian, Gay, Bisexual, Transgender (LGBT) Collection, NMAH.AC.1146," Smithsonian Institution National Museum of American History Archives Center, Smithsonian Institution, 55–58.

15. Evelyn Hooker, "Reflections of a 40-Year Exploration: A Scientific View on Homosexuality," *American Psychologist* 48, no. 4 (1993): 450–53.

16. Satinover, "The 'Trojan Couch.'"

17. Ibid.

18. Charles W. Socarides, "Sexual Politics and Scientific Logic: The Issue of Homosexuality," *Journal of Psychohistory*, 19: (1992), 307–29.

19. James Martin, "John Jay Report: On Not Blaming Homosexual Priests," *America*, May 17, 2011, http://www.americamagazine.org/content/all-things/john-jay-report-not-blaming-homosexual-priests.

20. *James Obergefell, et al., vs. Richard Hodges*, https://www.apa.org/about/offices/ogc/amicus/obergefell-supreme-court.pdf.

21. Lisa M. Diamond, "New Paradigms for Research on Heterosexual and Sexual-Minority Development, "*Journal of Clinical Child and Adolescent Psychology* 32, no. 4 (2003): 492, http://www.tandfonline.com/doi/abs/10.1207/S15374424JCCP3204_1.

22. Andrea L. Solarz, ed., *Lesbian Health: Current Assessment and Directions for the Future* (Washington, DC: National Academy Press, 1999), 22–33.

23. "Exclusively heterosexual/Predominantly heterosexual, only incidentally homosexual/predominantly heterosexual/but more than incidentally homosexual/Equally heterosexual and homosexual/Predominantly homosexual, but more than incidentally heterosexual/Predominantly homosexual, only incidentally heterosexual/Exclusively homosexual," Kinsey, *Sexual Behavior in the Human Male.*

24. Edward Laumann et al., *The Social Organization of Sexuality* (Chicago: University of Chicago Press, 2000).

25. David Nimmons, "Sex and the Brain," *Discover*, March 1994, http://discovermagazine.com/1994/mar/sexandthebrain346.

26. Steve Connor, "The 'Gay Gene' Is Back on the Scene," *Independent*, November 1, 1995, http://www.independent.co.uk/news/the-gay-gene-is-back-on-the-scene-1536770.html.

27. Ibid. Kelly Servick, "Study of Gay Brothers May Confirm X Chromosome Link to Homosexuality," *Science*, November 17, 2014, http://www.sciencemag.org/news/2014/11/study-gay-brothers-may-confirm-x-chromosome-link-homosexuality.

28. Jennifer Abbasi, "Could Scientists Have Found a Gay Switch?,"
     Popular Science, December 13, 2012, http://www.popsci.com/science/
     article/2012-12/being-born-gay-isnt-your-genes-its-them.
29. Lawrence S. Mayer and Paul R. McHugh, "Sexuality and Gender:
     Findings from the Biological, Psychological, and Social Scientists," *The
     New Atlantis* 50, special report, three parts, Fall 2016, http://www.
     thenewatlantis.com/publications/number-50-fall-2016.
30. Mayer and McHugh, "Sexuality and Gender…Part One: Sexual
     Orientation," http://www.thenewatlantis.com/publications/part-one-
     sexual-orientation-sexuality-and-gender.
31. Ibid.
32. J. Michael Bailey, Michael P. Dunne, and Nicholas G. Martin, "Genetic
     and Environmental Influences on Sexual Orientation and Its Correlates
     in an Australian Twin Sample," *Journal of Personality and Social
     Psychology* 78, no. 3 (2000): 534, https://genepi.qimr.edu.au/
     contents/p/staff/CV261Bailey_UQ_Copy.pdf.
33. David Bierbach et al., "Homosexual Behaviour Increases Male
     Attractiveness to Females," *Biology Letters* 9, no. 1 (2013), http://rsbl.
     royalsocietypublishing.org/content/9/1/20121038.
34. Alex Witchel, "Life after 'Sex,'" *New York Times*, January 19, 2012,
     http://www.nytimes.com/2012/01/22/magazine/cynthia-nixon-wit.html.
35. Austin Ruse, "Powerful Leftist Group Sues to Close Jewish Counseling
     Service for Gays," *Breitbart*, May 29, 2015, http://www.breitbart.com/
     big-government/2015/05/29/powerful-leftist-group-sues-to-close-
     jewish-counseling-service-for-gays/.
36. Brief for Obergefell et al. as Amicus Curiae, Obergefell v. Hodges, 576
     U.S. __ (2015), https://www.apa.org/about/offices/ogc/amicus/
     obergefell-supreme-court.pdf.
37. Robert L. Spitzer, M.D., "Can Some Gay Men and Lesbians Change
     Their Sexual Orientation? 200 Participants Reporting a Change from
     Homosexual to Heterosexual Orientation," *Archives of Sexual
     Behavior* 32: 5 (October 2003): 402–17
38. Ibid.
39. Ibid.
40. Gerard van den Aarweg, "Frail and Aged, a Giant Apologizes,"
     Mercatornet, May 31, 2012, https://www.mercatornet.com/articles/
     view/frail_and_aged_a_giant_apologizes.

41. Private lecture, C-Fam Newport Colloquium, August 2013.
42. "Add Health: The National Longitudinal Study of Adolescent to Adult Health," Carolina Population Center, the University of North Carolina, http://www.cpc.unc.edu/projects/addhealth.
43. Lisa M. Diamond and R. C. Savin-Williams, "Explaining Diversity in the Development of Same-Sex Sexuality among Young Women," *Journal of Social Issues* 56 (2000): 297–313.
44. *Obergefell vs.* Hodges, https://www.supremecourt.gov/ObergefellHodges/AmicusBriefs/14-556_Dr_Paul_McHugh.pdf.
45. Linda D. Garnets and Letitia Anne Peplau, "A New Look at Women's Sexuality & Sexual Orientation," *CSW Update*, December 2006.
46. Joseph P. Stokes et al., "Predictors of Movement toward Homosexuality: A Longitudinal Study of Bisexual Men," Journal of Sex Research 34: 3 (1997): 304, http://www.tandfonline.com/doi/abs/10.1080/0022449970 9551896?src=recsys.
47. Ibid.
48. Nigel Dickson et al., "Same Sex Attraction in a Birth Cohort: Prevalence and Persistence in Early Adulthood," *Social Science and Medicine* 56: 8 (2003): 1607–15, http://www.sciencedirect.com/science/article/pii/S0277953602001612.
49. American Psychological Association, "Just the Facts about Sexual Orientation and Youth: A Primer for Principals, Educators, and School Personnel," http://www.apa.org/pi/lgbt/resources/just-the-facts.pdf.
50. "11 Ridiculous, Strange, and Terrifying Gay Conversion Therapy Methods for 'Curing' Homosexuality," Huffington Post, October 31, 2011, http://www.huffingtonpost.com/2011/10/31/11-conversion-therapy-methods-curing-homosexuality_n_1068103.html.
51. "The Psychology behind Homosexual Tendencies (Part 1)," *Zenit*, December 5, 2005, https://zenit.org/articles/the-psychology-behind-homosexual-tendencies-part-1/.
52. Satinover, "The 'Trojan Couch.'"
53. Jeffrey Satinover, "The Complex Interaction of Genes and Environment: A Model for Homosexuality," Catholic Resource Education Center, 1995, http://www.catholiceducation.org/en/marriage-and-family/sexuality/the-complex-interaction-of-genes-and-environment-a-model-for-homosexuality.html.

54. Emily F. Rothman, Deinera Exner, and Allyson L. Baughman, "The Prevalence of Sexual Assault Against People Who Identify as Gay, Lesbian, or Bisexual in the United States: A Systematic Review," *Trauma, Violence, and Abuse* 12, no. 2 (2011): 55–66, http://dx.doi.org/10.1177/1524838010390707.

55. Judith P. Andersen and John Blosnich, "Disparities in Adverse Childhood Experiences among Sexual Minority and Heterosexual Adults: Results from a Multi-State Probability-Based Sample," *PLoS One* 8, no. 1 (2013): http://dx.doi.org/10.1371/journal.pone.0054691.

56. It should be noted that the gay establishment bristles at any mention of a gay "lifestyle" or a gay "agenda." Such terms are considered bigoted.

57. M. L. Walters, et al., "The National Intimate Partner and Sexual Violence Survey: 2010 Findings on Victimization by Sexual Orientation," Centers for Disease Control, https://www.cdc.gov/violenceprevention/pdf/nisvs_sofindings.pdf.

58. "Sexually Transmitted Diseases," Centers for Disease Control, http://www.cdc.gov/msmhealth/STD.htm.

59. "National Gay Men's HIV/AIDS Awareness Day," *Morbidity and Mortality Weekly Report*, September 25, 2015, https://www.cdc.gov/mmwr/preview/mmwrhtml/mm6437a1.htm.

60. Material on Dale O'Leary's research was adapted from Austin Ruse, *Their Sexual Proclivities Are Killing Them*, Crisis Magazine, January 29, 2016, http://www.crisismagazine.com/2016/their-sexual-proclivities-are-killing-them-and-costing-us-billions.

61. Dale O'Leary, *The Syndemic of AIDS and STDS among MSM*, *Linacre Quarterly*, February 2014 https://www.ncbi.nlm.nih.gov/pmc/articles/PMC4034619/

62. Ibid.

63. Ibid.

64. Conor Habib, "Rest Stop Confidential," *Salon*, March 29, 2012. http://www.salon.com/2012/03/29/rest_stop_confidential/.

65. "Chem Sex Revealed: Part One," Beige, February 18, 2014, http://www.beigeuk.com/2014/02/chem-sex-revealed-part-one/.

66. O'Leary, "The Syndemic of AIDS and STDs."

67. Mark Oppenheimer, "Married, with Infidelities," *New York Times*, June 30, 2011, http://www.nytimes.com/2011/07/03/magazine/infidelity-will-keep-us-together.html.

Chapter 4

1. Dick Cavett, "Lillian, Mary and Me," *New Yorker*, December 16, 2002, http://www.newyorker.com/magazine/2002/12/16/lillian-mary-and-me.

2. "Beginning of Pregnancy Controversy," *Wikipedia*, last updated November 16, 2016, https://en.wikipedia.org/wiki/Beginning_of_pregnancy_controversy.

3. "Who Was Alan Guttmacher?" (Frequently Asked Questions), Guttmacher Institute, https://www.guttmacher.org/guttmacher-institute-faq#5.

4. Rachel Benson Gold, "The Implications of Defining when a Woman Is Pregnant," *Guttmacher Policy Review* 8, no. 2 (2005), https://www.guttmacher.org/about/gpr/2005/05/implications-defining-when-woman-pregnant.

5. K. Putnam, "The Death of 'Life Begins at Conception,'" NFPAware, February 25, 2015, http://nfpaware.com/2015/02/the-death-of-life-begins-at-conception/.

6. Chikako Takeshika, *The Global Biopolitics of the IUD: How Science Constructs Contraceptive Users and Women's Bodies*, (Massachusetts Institute of Technology Press, 2012), 108.

7. James Barron, "Christopher Tietze, Physician and Authority on Pregnancy," Obituaries, *New York Times*, April 5, 1984, http://www.nytimes.com/1984/04/05/obituaries/christopher-tietze-physician-and-authority-on-pregnancy.html.

8. Gold, "The Implications of Defining when a Woman Is Pregnant."

9. Christopher M. Gacek, "Conceiving 'Pregnancy': U.S. Medical Dictionaries and Their Definitions of 'Conception' and 'Pregnancy,'" *Insight* (a publication of the Family Research Council), April 2009, http://downloads.frc.org/EF/EF09D12.pdf.

10. "The Carnegie Stages," http://www.embryology.ch/anglais/iperiodembry/carnegie02.html.

11. Thanks to my C-Fam colleague, Dr. Rebecca Oas, for her insights here.

12. *Buck v. Bell*, 274 U.S. 200 (1927).

13. Margaret Sanger, "The Tragedy of the Accidental Child," *Birth Control Review* April 1919, 5–6, https://www.nyu.edu/projects/sanger/webedition/app/documents/show.php?sangerDoc=223981.xml.

14. Karl Menninger, "Psychiatric Aspects of Contraception," *Pastoral Psychology* 5: 9 (December 1954), 27–33, http://link.springer.com/article/10.1007/BF01567181.

15. Ibid.

16. Hans Forssman and Inga Thuwe, "One Hundred and Twenty Children Born after Application for Therapeutic Abortion Refused," *Acta Pyschiatrica Scandinavica* 42, no. 1 (1966): 71–88.

17. Sara McLananan and Gary Sandefur, "Growing Up with a Single Parent: What Hurts, What Helps," *New England Journal of Medicine*, April 6, 1995, 196.

18. "Population and the American Future: The Report of the Commission on Population Growth and the American Future" ("The Rockefeller Commission Report"), Center for Research on Population and Security, http://www.population-security.org/rockefeller/001_population_ growth_and_the_american_future.htm.

19. James W. Prescott, "Abortion or the Unwanted Child: A Choice for a Humanistic Society" *Humanist* 35: 2 (March–April 1975), 11–15.

20. James W. Prescott, curriculum vitae, http://www.violence.de/prescott/ cv.html.

21. Henry P. David, Born Unwanted: Long-Term Development Effects of Denied Abortion, Journal of Social Issues, Volume 48, Issue 3: 163–81.

22. Henry P. David with Deborah McFarlane, Population and Reproductive History Oral History Project, Smith College, 2005

23. *Doe v. Bolton*, 410 U.S. 179 (1973), https://supreme.justia.com/cases/ federal/us/410/179/.

24. "Abortion Statistics: United States Data and Trends," National Right to Life Committee, April 2017, http://www.nrlc.org/uploads/factsheets/ FS01AbortionintheUS.pdf.

25. For a more in-depth look at poverty, see chapter 8.

26. Child Trends Databank, *Births to Unmarried Women*, 2015, http:// www.childtrends.org/indicators/births-to-unmarried-women/.

27. George A. Akerlof and Janet Yellen, "An Analysis of Out-of-Wedlock Births in the United States," Brookings Institution, 1996, https://www. brookings.edu/research/an-analysis-of-out-of-wedlock-births-in-the- united-states/.

28. Ibid.

29. *Child Abuse Prevention Act of 1973: Hearings on S. 1191, Before the Subcommittee on Children and Youth of the Committee on Labor and Public Welfare*, 93rd Cong. (1973), http://files.eric.ed.gov/fulltext/ ED081507.pdf.

30. Child Trends Databank, *Child Maltreatment*, 2016, http://www.childtrends.org/indicators/child-maltreatment/.

31. P. K. Coleman, et al., "Associations between Voluntary and Involuntary Forms of Perinatal Loss and Child Maltreatment among Low-Income Mothers," *Acta Paediatrica* 94, no. 10 (2005): 1476–1483, https://www.ncbi.nlm.nih.gov/pubmed/16299880.

32. John R. Lott Jr. and John E. Whitley, "Abortion and Crime: Unwanted Children and Out-of-Wedlock Births," Yale Law and Economics Research Paper 254, April 30, 2001, https://papers.ssrn.com/sol3/papers.cfm?abstract_id=270126.

33. Steven D. Levitt and Stephen J. Dubner, *Freakonomics: A Rogue Economist Explores the Hidden Side of Everything* (New York: William Morrow, 2005).

34. "Uniform Crime Reporting Statistics," Federal Bureau of Investigations, http://www.ucrdatatool.gov/Search/Crime/State/StatebyState.cfm.

35. Ibid.

36. Ibid.

37. Oliver Roeder, Lauren-Brooke Eisen, and Julia Bowling, "What Caused the Crime Decline?," Brennan Center for Justice, https://www.brennancenter.org/sites/default/files/analysis/What_Caused_The_Crime_Decline.pdf.

38. John Lott and John Whitley, "Abortion and Crime: Unwanted Children and Out-of-Wedlock Births," John M. Olin Center for Studies in Law, Economics, and Public Policy Working Papers no. 2545, 2001, http://digitalcommons.law.yale.edu/cgi/viewcontent.cgi?article=1018&context=lepp_papers.

39. Chinué Turner Richardson Elizabeth Nash, "Misinformed Consent: The Medical Accuracy of State-Developed Abortion Counseling Materials," Guttmacher Institute, October 23, 2006, https://www.guttmacher.org/gpr/2006/10/misinformed-consent-medical-accuracy-state-developed-abortion-counseling-materials.

40. "Abortion and Breast Cancer Risk," American Cancer Society, https://www.cancer.org/cancer/cancer-causes/medical-treatments/abortion-and-breast-cancer-risk.html.

41. American Congress of Obstetricians and Gynecologists, "Induced Abortion and Breast Cancer Risk," 434 (June 2009), http://www.acog. org/Resources-And-Publications/Committee-Opinions/Committee-on-Gynecologic-Practice/Induced-Abortion-and-Breast-Cancer-Risk.

42. Collaborative Group on Hormonal Factors in Breast Cancer, "Breast Cancer and Hormone Replacement Therapy: Collaborative Reanalysis of Data from 51 Epidemiological Studies of 52,705 Women with Breast Cancer and 108,411 Women without Breast Cancer," Lancet 350:9089 (November 15, 1997): 1484, https://www.ncbi.nlm.nih.gov/pubmed/10213546.

43. "Abortion, Miscarriage, and Breast Cancer Risk: 2003 Workshop," National Cancer Institute, https://www.cancer.gov/types/breast/abortion-miscarriage-risk.

44. "Abortion and the Risk of Breast Cancer: Information for the Adolescent Woman and Her Parents," American College of Pediatricians, December 2013, http://www.acpeds.org/the-college-speaks/position-statements/health-issues/abortion-and-the-risk-of-breast-cancer-information-for-the-adolescent-woman-and-her-parents.

45. Mads Melbye et al., "Induced Abortion and the Risk of Breast Cancer," *New England Journal of Medicine* 336 (1997): 81–85, http://www.nejm.org/doi/full/10.1056/NEJM199701093360201#t=article.

46. Melbye et al., "Induced Abortion and the Risk of Breast Cancer."

47. M. Segi et al., "An Epidemiological Study on Cancer in Japan," *GANN* (Japanese Journal of Cancer Research) 48, Suppl. (1957): 1–63.

48. B. MacMahon et al., "Age at First Birth and Breast Cancer Risk," *Bulletin of the World Health Organization* 48, no. 2 (1970): 209–21.

49. APA Task Force on Mental Health and Abortion, Report of the APA Task Force on Mental Health and Abortion (Washington, DC: APA, 2008), http://www.apa.org/pi/women/programs/abortion/executive-summary.pdf.

50. Priscilla K. Coleman, "Abortion and Mental Health: Quantitative Synthesis and Analysis of Research Published 1995–2009," *British Journal of Psychiatry* 199 (2011): 180–86, http://bjp.rcpsych.org/content/bjprcpsych/199/3/180.full.pdf.

51. D. C. Reardon et al., "Psychiatric Admissions of Low-Income Women Following Abortion and Childbirth," *Canadian Medical Association Journal* 168, no. 10 (2003): 1253–1256, https://www.ncbi.nlm.nih.gov/pubmed/12743066.

52. Lawrence B. Finer et al., "Reasons U.S. Women Have Abortions: Quantitative and Qualitative Perspectives," *Perspectives on Sexual Health* 37, no. 3 (September 2005), https://www.guttmacher.org/sites/default/files/pdfs/journals/3711005.pdf, quoting data from the Guttmacher Institute.

53. Charlotte Lozier Institute, "History of Fetal Tissue Research and Transplants," July 27, 2015, https://lozierinstitute.org/history-of-fetal-tissue-research-and-transplants/.

54. Center for Medical Progress website, http://www.centerformedical progress.org.

55. Tanya Lewis, "Growing Human Kidneys in Rats Sparks Ethical Debate," CBS News, January 21, 2015, http://www.cbsnews.com/news/growing-human-kidneys-in-rats-sparks-ethical-debate/.

56. Maureen L. Condic, "What We Know about Embryonic Stem Cells," *First Things*, January 2007, https://www.firstthings.com/article/2007/01/what-we-know-about-embryonic-stem-cells.

57. The Witherspoon Council, "The Stem Cell Debates: Lessons for Science and Politics, *The New Atlantis*, Winter 2012, http://www.thenewatlantis.com/publications/the-stem-cell-debates-lessons-for-science-and-politics.

58. Ibid., n. 5, http://www.thenewatlantis.com/publications/the-stem-cell-debates-lessons-for-science-and-politics#_ftn5.

59. David Montgomery, "Rush Limbaugh on the Offensive against Ad with Michael J. Fox," *Washington Post*, October 24, 2006, http://www.washingtonpost.com/wp-dyn/content/article/2006/10/24/AR2006102400691.html.

60. Ron Reagan's Speech to the Democratic National Convention, *New York Times*, July 27, 2004, http://www.nytimes.com/2004/07/27/politics/campaign/ron-reagans-speech-to-the-democratic-national-convention.html.

61. Email exchange with the author, November 21, 2016.

62. Eryn Brown, "Geron Exits Stem Cell Research," *Los Angeles Times*, November 15, 2011, http://articles.latimes.com/2011/nov/15/news/la-heb-geron-stem-cells-20111115.

63. Luke Timmerman, "Stem Cell Transplant Startup with Harvard Tech, Magent Therapeutics, Gets $48.5M," *Forbes*, November 16, 2016,

http://www.forbes.com/sites/luketimmerman/2016/11/16/stem-cell-transplant-startup-with-harvard-tech-magenta-therapeutics-gets-48-5m/#46672adc296c.

64. "Ron Reagan's Speech to the Democratic National Convention," *Washington Post*, July 27, 2004, http://www.nytimes.com/2004/07/27/politics/campaign/ron-reagans-speech-to-the-democratic-national-convention.html?_r=0.

65. President's Council on Bioethics, "Alternative Sources of Pluripotent Stem Cells," white paper, May 2005, https://bioethicsarchive.georgetown.edu/pcbe/reports/white_paper/text.html.

66. Donald Landry and Howard Zucker, "Embryonic Death and the Creation of Human Embryonic Stem Cells," *Journal of Clinical Investigation* 114:9 (2004): 1184–86, http://www.jci.org/articles/view/23065/pdf.

67. As a side note, the scientist, Dr. Shinya Yamanaka was looking at a human embryo under a microscope at a friend's fertility clinic and had a eureka moment that changed his life: "When I saw the embryo, I suddenly realized there was such a small difference between it and my daughters," said Dr. Yamanaka, forty-five, a father of two and now a professor at the Institute for Integrated Cell-Material Sciences at Kyoto University. "I thought, we can't keep destroying embryos for our research. There must be another way." Martin Fackler, "Risk Taking Is in His Genes," *New York Times*, December 11, 2007, http://www.nytimes.com/2007/12/11/science/11prof.html.

68. "HB2254: Requiring Doctors to Inform Women of Fetal Pain—Key Vote," Vote Smart, https://votesmart.org/bill/1183/3410/requiring-doctors-to-inform-women-of-fetal-pain#.WOkLlxiZPBI.

69. Ashley Fantz, "Utah Passes 'Fetal Pain' Abortion Law Requiring Anaesthesia," CNN, March 29, 2016, http://www.cnn.com/2016/03/29/health/utah-abortion-law-fetal-pain/.

70. Susan Lee, Henry J. Peter Ralston, and Eleanor A. Drey, "Fetal Pain: A Systematic Multidisciplinary Review of the Evidence," Journal of the American Medical Association 294, no. 8 (2005): 947–954, http://jamanetwork.com/journals/jama/fullarticle/201429.

71. Doctors on Fetal Pain website, http://www.doctorsonfetalpain.com/scientific-studies/.

72. Ibid.

73. Denise Grady, "Study Authors Didn't Report Abortion Ties," *New York Times*, August 26, 2005, http://www.nytimes.com/2005/08/26/health/study-authors-didnt-report-abortion-ties.html.

74. Nick Cannon: Planned Parenthood Is Nothin' but Population Control," TMZ, November 26, 2016, http://www.tmz.com/2016/11/26/nick-cannon-planned-parenthood-population-control/.

75. Charlotte Allen, "Planned Parenthood's Unseemly Empire," *Weekly Standard*, October 22, 2007, http://www.weeklystandard.com/article/15326.

76. Rachael Larimore, "The Most Meaningless Abortion Statistic Ever," *Slate*, May 7, 2013, http://www.slate.com/blogs/xx_factor/2013/05/07/_3_percent_of_planned_parenthood_s_services_are_abortion_but_what_about.html.

77. Lydia Saad, "Americans Choose 'Pro-Choice' for the First Time in Seven Years," Gallup, May 29, 2015, http://www.gallup.com/poll/183434/americans-choose-pro-choice-first-time-seven-years.aspx.

78. "42 U.S. Code § 289g–2: Prohibitions Regarding Human Fetal Tissue," Legal Information Institute, Cornell University Law School, https://www.law.cornell.edu/uscode/text/42/289g-2.

79. Cheryl Wetzstein, "Fewer Abortion Clinics in Minority Communities: Study," *Washington Times*, July 10, 2014, http://www.washingtontimes.com/news/2014/jul/10/fewer-abortion-clinics-in-minority-communities-stu/.

Chapter 5

1. International Planned Parenthood Foundation, *Healthy, Happy and Hot: A Young Person's Guide to Their Rights, Sexuality and Living with HIV* (London: IPPF, 2010), http://www.ippf.org/sites/default/files/healthy_happy_hot.pdf.

2. Centers for Disease Control, "Reported Cases of STDs on the Rise in the U.S.," press release, November 17, 2015, https://www.cdc.gov/nchhstp/newsroom/2015/std-surveillance-report-press-release.html.

3. Centers for Disease Control, "2015 STD Surveillance Report," press release, October 19, 2016, https://www.cdc.gov/nchhstp/newsroom/2016/std-surveillance-report-2015-press-release.html.

4.   Terrence McKeegan, "Sex Toys on Display at the World Youth Conference," Friday Fax, Center for Family and Human Rights, September 2, 2010, https://c-fam.org/friday_fax/sex-toys-on-display-at-the-world-youth-conference/.

5.   Austin Ruse, "A New Devastating Critique of the Global Sexual Revolution," *Crisis Magazine*, May 6, 2016, http://www.crisis magazine.com/2016/a-new-devastating-critique-of-the-global-sexual-revolution; E. Michael Jones, *Libido Dominandi: Sexual Liberation & Political Control* (South Bend: St. Augustine Press, 2005).

6.   E. Michael Jones, *Libido Dominandi: Sexual Liberation & Political Control* (South Bend: St. Augustine Press, 2005).

7.   Ibid.

8.   Ibid.

9.   Among the best treatments of the Cultural Marxists is Michael Walsh's *Devil Pleasure Palace: The Cult of Critical Theory and the Subversion of the West* (New York: Encounter Books, 2015).

10.   Wilhelm Reich, *The Function of the Orgasm*, trans. Vincent R. Carfagno (New York: Farrar, Straus, Giroux, 1972).

11.   Christopher Turner, "Wilhelm Reich: The Man Who Invented Free Love," *The Guardian*, July 8, 2011, https://www.theguardian.com/books/2011/jul/08/wilhelm-reich-free-love-orgasmatron.

12.   Ibid.

13.   Ibid.

14.   Judith Reisman, *Kinsey Crimes and Consequences: The Red Queen and the Grand Scheme* (Hartline Marketing, 2001).

15.   Roy Porter, "Alfred's Brush with Pleasure," *Times Higher Education*, November 14, 1997, https://www.timeshighereducation.com/books/alfreds-brush-with-pleasure/157174.article; James H. Jones, *Alfred Kinsey: A Public/Private Life*, (W.W. Norton & Company, October, 1997).

16.   Alfred Kinsey et al., *Sexual Behavior in the Human Male* (St. Louis: W. B. Saunders, 1948).

17.   Alfred Kinsey et al., *Sexual Behavior in the Human Female* (St. Louis: W. B. Saunders, 1953).

18.   Kinsey et al., *Sexual Behavior in the Human Male*.

19.   Judith Reisman, *Sexual Sabotage: How One Mad Scientist Unleashed a Plague of Corruption and Contagion on America* (Washington, DC: WND Books, 2010), 21.

20. Kinsey et al., *Sexual Behavior in the Human Male.*

21. Lymari Morales, "U.S. Adults Estimate That 25% of Americans Are Gay or Lesbian," Gallup poll, May 27, 2011, http://www.gallup.com/poll/147824/Adults-Estimate-Americans-Gay-Lesbian.aspx.

22. David Spiegelhalter, "Is 10% of the Population Really Gay?," The Observer, *The Guardian*, April 5, 2015, https://www.theguardian.com/society/2015/apr/05/10-per-cent-population-gay-alfred-kinsey-statistics.

23. Ibid.

24. Brian Ward, James Dahlhamer, Adena Galinsky, and Sarah Joestl, "Sexual Orientation and Health among U.S. Adults: National Health Interview Survey, 2013," *National Health Statistics Report* 77, July 15, 2014, https://www.cdc.gov/nchs/data/nhsr/nhsr077.pdf.

25. J. Bancroft, "Alfred C. Kinsey and the Politics of Sex Research," *Annual Review of Sex Research 15* (2004): 1–39.

26. Mary Vespa, "America's Biggest Problem? Fearless Dr. Mary Calderone Says It's 'Fear of Sex,'" *People*, January 21, 1980, http://people.com/archive/americas-biggest-problem-fearless-dr-mary-calderone-says-its-fear-of-sex-vol-13-no-3/.

27. UNESCO, *International Technical Guidance on Sexuality Education* (Paris: UNESCO, 2009), http://unesdoc.unesco.org/images/0018/001832/183281e.pdf.

28. "The Yogyakarta Principles," http://www.yogyakartaprinciples.org.

29. "The Principles in Action," website, http://www.ypinaction.org.

30. Mary Eberstadt, "Is Pornography the New Tobacco?," *Policy Review*, April/May 2009, Hoover Institution, http://www.hoover.org/research/pornography-new-tobacco.

31. Ibid.

32. https://www.justice.gov/criminal-ceos/citizens-guide-us-federal-law-obscenity.

33. "Your Child's Immunizations: Human Papillomavirus Vaccine," Kids Health, last updated October 2016, http://kidshealth.org/en/parents/hpv-vaccine.html.

34. Centers for Disease Control, "HIV among Gay and Bisexual Men," last updated September 30, 2016, https://www.cdc.gov/hiv/group/msm/index.html.

Chapter 6

1. Eric Ripert, *32 Yolks: From My Mother's Table to Working the Line* (New York: Random House, 2016), 22.
2. American Psychological Association, *Lesbian and Gay Parenting* (Washington, DC: American Psychological Association, 2005), https://www.apa.org/pi/lgbt/resources/parenting-full.pdf.
3. "What Does the Scholarly Research Say about the Wellbeing of Children with Gay or Lesbian Parents?," *What We Know*, project of Columbia Law School, June 2016 (updated), http://whatweknow.law.columbia.edu/topics/lgbt-equality/what-does-the-scholarly-research-say-about-the-wellbeing-of-children-with-gay-or-lesbian-parents/.
4. Simon R. Crouch et al., "Parent-Reported Measures of Child Health and Wellbeing in Same-Sex Parent Families," *BMC Public Health* 14, no. 635 (2014), http://bmcpublichealth.biomedcentral.com/articles/10.1186/1471-2458-14-635.
5. Lindsay Bever, "Children of Same-Sex Couples Are Happier and Healthier than Peers, Research Shows," *Washington Post*, July 7, 2014, https://www.washingtonpost.com/news/morning-mix/wp/2014/07/07/children-of-same-sex-couples-are-happier-and-healthier-than-peers-research-shows/.
6. Lisa Belkin, "What's Good for the Kids," *New York Times Magazine*, November 5, 2009, http://www.nytimes.com/2009/11/08/magazine/08fob-wwln-t.html.
7. Ibid.
8. Sandhya Somashekhar, "How Kids Became the Strongest Argument for Same-Sex Marriage," *Washington Post*, June 24, 2015, https://www.washingtonpost.com/politics/how-kids-became-the-strongest-argument-for-same-sex-marriage/2015/06/24/98955632-18fe-11e5-ab92-c75ae6ab94b5_story.html?utm_term=.0814daef8245.
9. Lawrence S. Mayer and Paul McHugh, "Sexuality and Gender: Findings from the Biological, Psychological, and Social Sciences," *The New Atlantis*, 50, (Fall 2016).
10. Ibid.
11. Paul Sullins, "Emotional Problems among Children with Same-Sex Parents: Difference by Definition," *British Journal of Education, Society and Behavioral Science* 7: 2 (2015), 99–120.

12.   Sara McLanahan and Gary Sandefur, *Growing Up with a Single Parent* (Cambridge, MA: Harvard University Press, 1994); Sara McLanahan, "Parent Absence or Poverty: Which Matters More?," in *Consequences of Growing Up Poor*, ed. Greg Duncan and Jeanne Brooks-Gunn (New York: Russell Sage, 1994), 35–48; David Popenoe, *Life Without Father* (Cambridge, MA: Harvard University Press, 1996); Bruce Ellis et al., "Does Father Absence Place Daughters at Special Risk for Early Sexual Activity and Teenage Pregnancy?," *Child Development* 74 (2003): 801–821; Sara McLanahan, Elisabeth Donahue, and Ron Haskins, "Introducing the Issue," The Future of Children 15 (2003): 3–12; Mary Parke, "Are Married Parents Really Better for Children?," *Couples and Marriage Research and Policy* brief (Washington, DC: Center for Law and Social Policy, 2003); Barbara Schneider, "Family Structure and Children's Educational Outcomes," Institute for American Values, Research Brief no. 1, November 2005; Wilcox et al. (2005); Elizabeth Marquardt, *Between Two Worlds: The Inner Lives of Children of Divorce* (New York: Crown, 2005).

13.   Mark Regnerus, *The New Family Structures Study*," University of Texas at Austin, http://www.prc.utexas.edu/nfss/.

14.   Ana Samuel, "The Kids Aren't All Right: New Family Structures and the 'No Differences' Claim," *Public Discourse*, June 14, 2012, http://www.thepublicdiscourse.com/2012/06/5640/.

15.   Regnerus, *The New Family Structures*.

16.   Philip Blumstein and Pepper Schwartz, "American Couples: Money, Work, Sex," *American Journal of Sociology* 90: 3, 669–71.

17.   Paul Sullins, "Invisible Victims: Delayed Onset Depression among Adults with Same-Sex Parents," *Depression Research and Treatment*, article 2410392 (2016), https://www.hindawi.com/journals/drt/2016/2410392/.

18.   Ibid.

19.   Nathaniel Frank, "The Latest Gay Parenting Study Is a Dishonest, Gratuitous Assault on LGBTQ Families," Slate, July 12, 2016, http://www.slate.com/blogs/outward/2016/07/12/new_gay_parenting_study_is_a_dishonest_assault_on_lgbtq_families.html.

20.   Emma Green, "Using 'Pseudoscience' to Undermine Same-Sex Parents," *The Atlantic*, February 19, 2015, https://www.theatlantic.com/politics/archive/2015/02/using-pseudoscience-to-undermine-same-sex-parents/385604/.

21. Zack Ford, "Conservatives Seize on Hugely Flawed Study about Same-Sex Parents," ThinkProgress, February 10, 2015, https://thinkprogress.org/conservatives-seize-on-hugely-flawed-study-about-same-sex-parents-bd797734bf40.

22. Emma Green, "Using 'Pseudoscience' to Undermine Same-Sex Parents, *The Atlantic*, February 19, 2015, https://www.theatlantic.com/politics/archive/2015/02/using-pseudoscience-to-undermine-same-sex-parents/385604/.

23. Andrew Rosenthal, "After the Riots; Quayle Says Riots Sprang from Lack of Family Values," *New York Times*, May 20, 1992, http://www.nytimes.com/1992/05/20/us/after-the-riots-quayle-says-riots-sprang-from-lack-of-family-values.html?pagewanted=all.

24. Bill Carter, "Back Talk from 'Murphy Brown' to Dan Quayle," *New York Times*, July 20, 1992, http://www.nytimes.com/1992/07/20/arts/back-talk-from-murphy-brown-to-dan-quayle.html.

25. Barbara Dafoe Whitehead, *The Problem of Divorce* (New York: Knopf, 1997).

26. Ibid.

27. David Popenoe, *Families Without Fathers: Fathers, Marriage, and Children in American Society* (New Brunswick, NJ: Transaction Publishers, 2009).

28. Ibid.

29. Jessie Bernard, *The Future of Marriage*, 2nd ed. (New Haven, CT: Yale University Press, 1982).

30. Google Scholar, as of May 4, 2017.

31. Ibid., 29, 30.

32. Ibid.

33. Ibid.

34. Ibid., 47.

35. Ibid.

36. The State of Our Unions, Marriage in America 2009, (University of Virginia).

37. Barbara Dafoe Whitehead, *The Problem of Divorce* (New York: Knopf, 1997).

38. Ibid., 54.

39. Randy Olson, "144 Years of Marriage and Divorce in One Chart," Randal S. Olson, June 15, 2015, http://www.randalolson.com/2015/06/15/144-years-of-marriage-and-divorce-in-1-chart/.

40. Ibid.

41. Michelle L. Evans, "Wrongs Committed During a Marriage: The Child that No Area of the Law Wants to Adopt," *Washington and Lee Law Review* 465 (2009), http://scholarlycommons.law.wlu.edu/wlulr/vol66/iss1/11/.

42. David Popenoe, *Families without Fathers: Fathers, Marriage, and Children in American Society* (New Brunswick, NJ: Transaction Publishers, 2009).

43. Ibid.

44. Ibid.

45. Ibid.

46. Ibid.

47. Nicholas Eberstadt, "The Global Flight from the Family," *Wall Street Journal*, February 21, 2015, https://www.wsj.com/articles/nicholas-eberstadt-the-global-flight-from-the-family-1424476179.

48. Ibid.; "The Future of Marriage and the Family," The Boisi Center for Religion and American Public Life Symposium on Religion and Politics, reading packet 5, 2015, https://www.bc.edu/content/dam/files/centers/boisi/pdf/S15/Boisi%20Center%20Symposium%20Reading%20Packet%205.pdf.

49. W. Brad Wilcox and Laurie DeRose, *Childrearing in the Age of Cohabitation*, Foreign Affairs, February 14, 2007, https://www.foreignaffairs.com/articles/2017-02-14/ties-bind; W. Brad Wilcox and Laurie DeRose, *The Cohabitation-Go-Round: Cohabitation and Family Instability Across the Globe*, World Family Map, 2017, http://worldfamilymap.ifstudies.org/2017/files/WFM-2017-FullReport.pdf.

50. Sarah McLanahan and Christopher Jencks, "Was Moynihan Right?," *Education* Next 15, no. 2 (Spring 2015), http://educationnext.org/was-moynihan-right/.

51. "Poverty Rates for Families with Children," Family Facts, http://www.familyfacts.org/charts/329/poverty-rates-are-higher-among-single-mother-families-regardless-of-rac.

52. Sara McLanahan, "The Consequences of Single Motherhood," *The American Prospect*, Summer 1994, http://prospect.org/article/consequences-single-motherhood.

53. Brad Wilcox, "The Kids Are Not Really Alright: It's Worse to Be Raised by a Single Mother, Even If You're Not Poor," Slate, July 20, 2012, http://www.slate.com/articles/double_x/doublex/2012/07/single_motherhood_worse_for_children_.html.

54. Ibid.

55. Mary Eberstadt, *Home-Alone America: The Hidden Toll of Day Care, Behavioral Drugs, and Other Parent Substitutes* (New York: Sentinel, Penguin Group, 2004).

56. Ibid, 106.

57. Ibid.

58. Jason DeParle, "Two Classes, Divided by 'I Do,'" *New York Times*, July 14, 2012, http://www.nytimes.com/2012/07/15/us/two-classes-in-america-divided-by-i-do.html.

59. Jason DeParle, "Two Classes in America, Divided by 'I Do,'" *New York Times*, July 14, 2012, http://www.nytimes.com/2012/07/15/us/two-classes-in-america-divided-by-i-do.html?_r=1&pagewanted=all.

60. Sara McLanahan, "Diverging Destinies: How Children Are Faring under the Second Demographic Transition," Project Muse 41, no. 4 (November 2004): 607–27, http://muse.jhu.edu/article/175402.

61. J. D. Vance, *Hillbilly Elegy: A Memoir of a Family and Culture in Crisis* (New York: Harper, 2016).

62. Steven Stack and J. Ross Eshleman, "Marital Status and Happiness: A 17-Nation Study," *Journal of Marriage and Family* 60, no. 2 (May 1998): 527–36, https://researchconnect.wayne.edu/en/publications/marital-status-and-happiness-a-17-nation-study.

63. Ibid.

64. David Blanchflower and Andrew Oswald, "Well-Being over Time in Britain and the USA," *Journal of Public Economics* 88 (2004): 1359–1386, https://www.dartmouth.edu/~blnchflr/papers/jpube.pdf.

65. Linda Waite and Maggie Gallagher, *The Case for Marriage: Why Married People Are Happier, Healthier and Better Off Financially*, 10th ed. (New York: Broadway Books, 2001).

66. Tim Wadsworth, "Sex and the Pursuit of Happiness: How Other People's Sex Lives Are Related to Our Sense of Well-Being," *Social Indicators Research* 116, no. 1 (March 2014), http://link.springer.com/article/10.1007/s11205-013-0267-1.

67. Some of these studies are collected at Marripedia, http://marripedia.org.

68. Jessica Hamzelou, "World's First Baby Born with New '3-Parent' Technique," *New Scientist*, September 26, 2007, https://www.newscientist.com/article/2107219-exclusive-worlds-first-baby-born-with-new-3-parent-technique/.

Chapter 7

1. "California Proposition 65 List of Chemicals," https://en.wikipedia.org/wiki/California_Proposition_65_list_of_chemicals.

2. "Proposition 65: By the Numbers," Center for Accountability in Science, August 2015, https://www.accountablescience.com/?research=proposition-65-by-the-numbers.

3. William Saletan, "Unhealthy Fixation," *Slate*, July 15, 2015, http://www.slate.com/articles/health_and_science/science/2015/07/are_gmos_safe_yes_the_case_against_them_is_full_of_fraud_lies_and_errors.html.

4. Ibid.

5. Ibid.

6. Ibid.

7. David R. Schubert, "The Problem with Nutritionally Enhanced Plants," Journal of Medicinal Food 11, no. 4 (2008): 601–05, http://online.liebertpub.com/doi/pdf/10.1089/jmf.2008.0094.

8. Saletan, "Unhealthy Fixation."

9. Ibid.

10. Ibid.

11. Ibid.

12. Ibid.

13. Ibid.

14. Schubert, "The Problem with Nutritionally Enhanced Plants."

15. Saletan, "Unhealthy Fixation."

16. "Micronutrient Deficiences: Vitamin A Deficiency," World Health Organization, http://www.who.int/nutrition/topics/vad/en/; "Vitamin

A Deficiency–Related Disorders," Golden Rice Project, http://www. goldenrice.org/Content3-Why/why1_vad.php.

17. Sarah Nell Davidson, "Forbidden Fruit: Transgenic Papaya in Thailand," *Plant Physiology* 147: 2 June 2008), 487–93.

18. Saletan, "Unhealthy Fixation."

19. Ibid.

20. Ibid.

21. Ibid.

22. Ibid.; Tom Philpott, "No, GMOs Didn't Create India's Farmer Suicide Problem, But . . .," *Mother Jones*, September 30, 2015, http://www. motherjones.com/tom-philpott/2015/09/no-gmos-didnt-create-indias-farmer-suicide-problem; Keith Kloor, "The GMO-Suicide Myth," *Issues in Science and Technology* 30:2 (Winter 2014), http://issues.org/30-2/keith/.

23. Imre S. Otvos, Holly Armstrong, and Nicholas Conder, "Safety of Bacillus thuringiensis var. kurstaki Applications for Insect Control to Humans and Large Mammals," paper presented at the 6th Pacific Rim Conference on the Biotechnology of Bacillus thuringiensis and Its Environmental Impact, Victoria, British Columbia, 2005, http://www. erudit.org/livre/pacrim/2005/000211co.pdf.

24. Warren E. Leary, "Just How Distressing Is Lactose Intolerance?," *New York Times*, July 12, 1995, http://www.nytimes.com/1995/07/12/ garden/just-how-distressing-is-lactose-intolerance.html.

25. The story of DDT is well told by Robert Zubrin in *Merchants of Despair: Radical Environmentalists, Criminal Pseudo-Scientists, and the Fatal Cult of Antihumanism* (New York: Encounter Books, 2013) and in "The Truth about DDT and *Silent Spring*," *The New Atlantis*, September 27, 2012, http://www.thenewatlantis.com/publications/the-truth-about-ddt-and-silent-spring.

26. Rachel Carson, *Silent Spring* (New York: Houghton Mifflin, 1962).

27. Zubrin, *Merchants of Despair*; Zubrin, "The Truth about DDT."

28. Ibid.; Zubrin, Merchants of Despair.

29. J. Gordon Edwards, "DDT: A Case Study in Scientific Fraud," Journal of American Physicians and Surgeons, 9: 3 (fall 2004).

30. U.S. Environmental Protection Agency, "Consolidated DDT Hearing: Hearing Examiner's Recommended Findings, Conclusions, and Orders," report prepared by Edmund M. Sweeney, April 25, 1972, http://www.thenewatlantis.com/docLib/20120926_SweeneyDDT decision.pdf.

31. Zubrin, Merchants of Despair; Zubrin, "The Truth about DDT."
32. Ibid.; Zubrin, Merchants of Despair.
33. John Stossel, "Excerpt: 'Myths, Lies, and Downright Stupidity,'" ABC News, http://abcnews.go.com/2020/Stossel/story?id=1898820&page=1.
34. Kent Hill, letter to the editor, *The Hill*, February 12, 2017, https://web.archive.org/web/20060331190237/http://www.hillnews.com/thehill/export/TheHill/Comment/LetterstotheEditor/111505.html.
35. USAID, "USAID Support for Malaria Control in Countries Using DDT," http://pdf.usaid.gov/pdf_docs/PDACH948.pdf.

Chapter 8

1. "The 100 Largest U.S. Charities," Forbes, http://www.forbes.com/companies/feeding-america/.
2. Robert Egger, "5 Myths about Hunger in America," *Washington Post*, http://www.washingtonpost.com/wp-dyn/content/article/2010/11/19/AR2010111906872.html.
3. US Department of Agriculture Economic Research Service, Definitions of Food Security, https://www.ers.usda.gov/topics/food-nutrition-assistance/food-security-in-the-us/definitions-of-food-security.aspx.
4. William L. Hamilton et al., *Household Food Security in the United States in 1995*, report prepared for US Department of Agriculture Food and Consumer Service, September 1997, http://www.fns.usda.gov/sites/default/files/SUMMARY.PDF.
5. Mark Nord, Alisha Coleman-Jensen, Margaret Andrews, and Steven Carlson, *Household Food Security in the United States, 2009*, US Department of Agriculture Economic Research Service, Economic Research Report no. 108, November 2010, p. 5, http://www.ers.usda.gov/media/122550/err108_1_.pdf.
6. Robert Rector, *Reducing Hunger and Very Low Food Security*, Heritage Foundation, February 2016, https://thf-reports.s3.amazonaws.com/2016/Rector_Testimony_02112016.pdf.
7. Ibid.
8. Ibid.
9. Ibid.
10. Ibid.
11. Ibid
12. Ibid.

13. Rector, *Reducing Hunger.*

14. "President Johnson's Special Message to Congress: The American Promise," March 15, 1965, http://www.lbjlibrary.org/lyndon-baines-johnson/speeches-films/president-johnsons-special-message-to-the-congress-the-american-promise/.

15. Gordon M. Fisher, "The Development and History of the U.S. Poverty Thresholds—a Brief Overview," U.S. Department of Health and Human Services, January 1, 1997, https://aspe.hhs.gov/history-poverty-thresholds.

16. Robert Sheffield and Robert Rector, "The War on Poverty After 50 Years," Heritage Foundation, September 15, 2014, http://www.heritage.org/research/reports/2014/09/the-war-on-poverty-after-50-years.

17. Annie Lowrey, "Changed Life of the Poor: Better Off, but Far Behind," *New York Times,* April 30, 2014, http://www.nytimes.com/2014/05/01/business/economy/changed-life-of-the-poor-squeak-by-and-buy-a-lot.html.

18. Rector and Sheffield, "The War on Poverty."

19. Jordan Weissmann, "Why Poverty Is Still Miserable, Even if Everyone Can Own an Awesome Television," *Slate,* May 1, 2014, http://www.slate.com/blogs/moneybox/2014/05/01/why_poverty_is_still_miserable_cheap_consumer_goods_don_t_improve_your_long.html.

20. Ibid.

21. C. T. Windham, B. W. Wyse, and R. G. Hansen, "Nutrient Density of Diets in the USDAI Nationwide Food Consumption Survey, 1977–1978: I. Impact of Socioeconomic Status on Dietary Density," Journal of the American Dietetic Association 82, no. 1 (January 1983): 28–43.

22. Robert Sheffield and Robert Rector, "Understanding Poverty in the United States: Surprising Facts About America's Poor," Heritage Foundation, September 13, 2011, http://www.heritage.org/poverty-and-inequality/report/understanding-poverty-the-united-states-surprising-facts-about.

23. Robert Rector and Jamie Hall, "Did Welfare Reform Increase Extreme Poverty in the United States?," Heritage Foundation issue report, April 21, 2016, http://www.heritage.org/research/reports/2016/08/did-welfare-reform-increase-extreme-poverty-in-the-united-states.

24. Ibid.

25. William Julius Wilson, "'$2.00 a Day,' by Kathryn J. Edin and H. Luke Shaefer," *New York Times,* September 2, 2015, https://www.nytimes.com/

2015/09/06/books/review/2-00-a-day-by-kathryn-j-edin-and-h-luke-shaefer.html.

26. Charles Kenny, "Taking Aim at the GOP's War on the Poor," *Bloomberg*, September 30, 2013, http://www.bloomberg.com/news/articles/2013-09-30/taking-aim-at-the-gops-war-on-the-poor.

27. Wilson, "'$2.00 a Day.'"

28. Rector and Hall, "Did Welfare Reform Increase Extreme Poverty?"

29. Ibid.

30. Ibid.

31. Ibid.

32. "Policy Basics: Introduction to the Supplemental Nutrition Assistance Program," Center on Policy and Budget Priorities, March 24, 2016, http://www.cbpp.org/research/policy-basics-introduction-to-the-supplemental-nutrition-assistance-program-snap.

33. Fox News Insider, "Shocking: Fox News Reporting Interview with Unabashed Surfer Receiving Food Stamps," August 10, 2013, http://insider.foxnews.com/2013/08/10/shocking-fox-news-reporting-interview-unabashed-surfer-receiving-food-stamps.

34. Kay S. Hymowitz, "The Black Family: 40 Years of Lies," *City Journal*, Summer 2005, http://www.city-journal.org/html/black-family-40-years-lies-12872.html.

35. Ibid.

36. Ibid.

37. Robert Hill, *The Strengths of the Black Family* (National Urban League, New York, 1972).

38. Kay S. Hymowitz, "The Black Family: 40 Years of Lies," *City Journal*, Summer 2005, http://www.city-journal.org/html/black-family-40-years-lies-12872.html.

39. Annie Lowrey, "Can Marriage Cure Poverty?," *New York Times Magazine*, February 4, 2014, http://www.nytimes.com/2014/02/09/magazine/can-marriage-cure-poverty.html.

Chapter 9

1. "Yoko Ono, Jimmy Fallon, and Sean Lennon Sing 'Don't Frack My Mother,'" *Huffington Post*, July 17, 2012, http://www.huffingtonpost.com/2012/07/17/yoko-ono-jimmy-fallon-sean-lennon-frack-mother_n_1680464.html.

2. Lydia O'Connor, "Celebrities Demand Obama, State Officials Ban Fracking Now," *Huffington Post*, November 19, 2013, http://www.huffingtonpost.com/2013/11/19/celebrity-fracking-video_n_4304689.html.

3. Susan L. Brantely and Anna Meyendorff, "The Facts on Fracking," *New York Times*, March 13, 2013, http://www.nytimes.com/2013/03/14/opinion/global/the-facts-on-fracking.html.

4. "Marcellus Shale," http://geology.com/articles/marcellus-shale.shtml.

5. "Eagle Ford Shale: News, Marketplace, Jobs," http://eaglefordshale.com.

6. US Geological Survey, "USGS Estimates 20 Billion Barrels of Oil in Texas' Wolfcamp Shale Formation," press release, November 15, 2016, https://www.usgs.gov/news/usgs-estimates-20-billion-barrels-oil-texas-wolfcamp-shale-formation.

7. John Wihby, "Pros and Cons of Fracking: 5 Key Issues," *Yale Climate Connections*, May 27, 2015, http://www.yaleclimateconnections.org/2015/05/pros-and-cons-of-fracking-5-key-issues/.

8. Josh Fox, *Hyper Real America*, play in two acts, http://www.internationalwow.com/newsite/scripts/HyperRealAmerica.pdf, accessed February 14, 2017.

9. Peter Applebome, "The Light is Green, and Yellow, on Drilling," *New York Times*, July 27, 2008, http://www.nytimes.com/2008/07/27/nyregion/27towns.html.

10. Mike Markham, complaint report, Colorado Oil and Gas Conservation Commission, May 23, 2008, http://cogcc.state.co.us/cogis/ComplaintReport.asp?doc_num=200190138.

11. Steven and Shyla Lipsky v. Durant, Carter, Coleman, LLC et al., No. CV11-0798 (43rd Tex. Feb. 6, 2012), http://www.eenews.net/assets/2013/11/25/document_ew_01.pdf.

12. "*FrackNation*," *Wikipedia*, last updated February 8, 2017, https://en.wikipedia.org/wiki/FrackNation.

13. Mark H. Schofield, "What Would George Washington Do about Fracking," *Science Progress*, November 22, 2011, https://scienceprogress.org/2011/11/what-would-george-washington-do-about-fracking/.

14. Phelim McAleer and Ann McElhinney, *FrackNation* (2013), http://fracknation.com/.

15. Ibid.

16. Josh Fox, *The Sky is Pink*, short film, June 20, 2012, https://vimeo.com/44367635.

17. https://www.yahoo.com/news/experts-fracking-critics-bad-science-161729688.html.

18. http://www.theblaze.com/news/2012/07/23/major-fracking-concerns-lack-scientific-backing-basically-not-using-science/.

19. Ibid.

20. Ibid.

21. United States House of Representatives Committee on Energy and Commerce Minority Staff, "Chemicals Used in Hydraulic Fracturing," April 2011, http://www.conservation.ca.gov/dog/general_information/Documents/Hydraulic%20Fracturing%20Report%204%2018%2011.pdf.

22. John Wihbey, "Pros and Cons of Fracking: 5 Key Issues," Yale Climate Connections, May 27, 2015, http://www.yaleclimateconnections.org/2015/05/pros-and-cons-of-fracking-5-key-issues/.

23. US Environmental Protection Agency, *Assessments of the Potential Impacts of Hydraulic Fracturing for Oil and Gas on Drinking Water Resources*, draft report, June 2015, https://www.epa.gov/sites/production/files/2015-07/documents/hf_es_erd_jun2015.pdf.

24. Federal Energy Regulatory Commission, North American LNG Import/Export Terminals, https://www.ferc.gov/industries/gas/indus-act/lng/lng-approved.pdf.

25. Andrew Higgins, "Russian Money Suspected behind Fracking Protests," *New York Times*, November 30, 2014, http://www.nytimes.com/2014/12/01/world/russian-money-suspected-behind-fracking-protests.html?_r=0; Robert Zubrin, "Putin's Anti-Fracking Campaign," *National Review*, May 5, 2014, http://www.nationalreview.com/article/377201/putins-anti-fracking-campaign-robert-zubrin.

Chapter 10

1. Jeffrey M. Jones, "In U.S., Concern about Environmental Threats Eases," Gallup, March 25, 2015, http://www.gallup.com/poll/182105/concern-environmental-threats-eases.aspx.

2. "Climate Change: Basic Information," Environmental Protection Agency, https://www.epa.gov/climatechange/climate-change-basic-information.

3. Al Gore, *An Inconvenient Truth: The Planetary Emergency of Global Warming and What We Can Do about It* (2006).

4. J. T. Houghton, et al., eds, "Climate Change 2001: The Scientific Basis," Intergovernmental Panel on Climate Change (IPCC), https://www.ipcc.ch/ipccreports/tar/wg1/pdf/WG1_TAR-FRONT.PDF.

5. Christopher Monckton, "Hockey Stick? What Hockey Stick? How Alarmist 'Scientists' Falsely Abolished the Mediaeval Warm Period," September 2008, http://www.webcommentary.com/docs/monckton_what_hockey_stick.pdf.

6. Anthony Esolen, "How Dark Were the Dark Ages?," January 26, 2015, Prager University, January 26, 2015, https://www.prageru.com/courses/history/how-dark-were-dark-ages.

7. Monckton, "Hockey Stick?"

8. Stephen McIntyre and Ross R. McKitrick have done substantial work in pointing out problems with Michael Mann's "hockey stick". A collection of their work can be found here at http://www.rossmckitrick.com/paleoclimatehockey-stick.html.

9. Ibid.

10. Ibid

11. Monckton, "Hockey Stick?"

12. Jonathan H. Adler, "Making Defamation Law Great Again: Michael Mann's Suit May Continue," *Washington Post*, December 22, 2016, https://www.washingtonpost.com/news/volokh-conspiracy/wp/2016/12/22/making-defamation-law-great-again-michael-manns-suit-may-continue/.

13. National Oceanic and Atmospheric Administration, "History of Earth's Temperature since 1880," Climate.gov, January 16, 2015, https://www.climate.gov/news-features/videos/history-earths-temperature-1880.

14. John P. Rafferty and Stephen P. Jackson, "Little Ice Age (LIA)," *Encyclopedia Britannica*, March 18, 2016, https://www.britannica.com/science/Little-Ice-Age.

15. William Briggs has a Ph.D. in mathematical statistics and has been a professor at the Cornell Medical School and a meteorologist with the National Weather Service. His most recent book is Uncertainty: The Soul of Modeling, Probability & Statistics (Springer, 2016).

16. Roy W. Spencer, "What Causes el Nino Warmth?," Roy Spencer, Ph.D., January 1, 2016, http://www.drroyspencer.com/2016/01/what-causes-el-nino-warmth/.

17. "Global Temperature Page," Watts Up with That?, https://wattsupwiththat.com/global-temperature/.

18. "Global Warming Standstill/Pause Increases to "a New Record Length: 18 Years 6 Months," Climate Depot, June 2, 2015, http://www.climatedepot.com/2015/06/03/global-warming-standstillpause-increases-to-a-new-record-length-18-years-6-months/.

19. We are in an inter-glacial period now, with another glaciation expected when the orbit changes a bit more; we're talking on the order of hundreds of centuries. Interview with William Briggs.

20. "Are CO_2 Levels Increasing?," Skeptical Science, July 8, 2015, http://www.skepticalscience.com/co2-levels-airborne-fraction-increasing.htm.

21. "Geological Timescale: Concentration of CO_2 and Temperature Fluctuations," Watts Up with That?, July 7, 2008, https://wattsupwiththat.files.wordpress.com/2013/06/co2_temperature_historical.png.

22. Interview of William Briggs by the author.

23. David Kreutzer, et al., "The State of Climate Science: No Justification for Extreme Policies," Heritage Foundation, April 22, 2016, http://www.heritage.org/research/reports/2016/04/the-state-of-climate-science-no-justification-for-extreme-policies#_ftnref27.

24. Stefano Gennarini, "Vatican Prelate Responds to Critics of Climate Conference, Blames Tea Party and Oil Business," Turtle Bay and Beyond, May 18, 2015, https://c-fam.org/turtle_bay/vatican-prelate-blasts-critics-of-climate-conference/.

25. Joseph Bast and Roy Spencer, "The Myth of the Climate Change '97%,'" Climate Change Dispatch, December 2, 2015, http://climatechangedispatch.com/wsj-the-myth-of-the-climate-change-97/.

26. D.R. Legates, et al., Science & Education 24(2015): 299, doi:10.1007/s11191-013-9647-9.

27. Adler, "Making Defamation Law Great Again."

28. Mark Steyn, *A Disgrace to the Profession*, (Stockade Books, 2015).

29. Monckton, "Hockey Stick?"

30. "Polar Bear Declines Have Not Been Harmed by Sea Ice Declines in Summer—the Evidence," Polar Bear Science, August 18, 2013,

https://polarbearscience.com/2013/08/18/polar-bears-have-not-been-harmed-by-sea-ice-declines-in-summer-the-evidence/.

31. Ibid.
32. Phelim McAleer, "Inconvenient Questions to Al Gore," Youtube, December 14, 2009, https://www.youtube.com/watch?v=fooYtalS9Gc.
33. "Polar Bear," National Wildlife Federation, http://www.nwf.org/Wildlife/Wildlife-Library/Mammals/Polar-Bear.aspx.
34. "The State of Climate Science."
35. Craig Boudreau, "Global Warming Expedition Stopped in Its Tracks by Arctic Sea Ice," Daily Caller, July 20, 2016, http://dailycaller.com/2016/07/20/global-warming-expedition-stopped-in-its-tracks-by-arctic-sea-ice/#ixzz4EyFJfll0.
36. John Turner, "Research Ship Trapped in Antarctic Ice Because of Weather, Not Climate Change," *The Guardian*, January 3, 2014, https://www.theguardian.com/world/2014/jan/03/antarctica-ice-trapped-academik-shokalskiy-climate-change.
37. Jeff Dunetz, "Ship Abandons Global Warming Research Due to EXCESSIVE ICE," MRCTV, July 23, 2015, http://www.mrctv.org/blog/worst-ice-conditions-20-years-force-ice-breaker-stop-global-warming-study-and-help-ships-stuck-ice.
38. John Vidal "'Extraordinarily Hot' Arctic Temperatures Alarm Scientists," *The Guardian*, November 22, 2016, https://www.theguardian.com/environment/2016/nov/22/extraordinarily-hot-arctic-temperatures-alarm-scientists.
39. James Hansen et al., "Perception of Climate Change," PNAS, March 29, 2012, http://www.pnas.org/content/109/37/E2415.full.pdf.
40. "Infographic: Extreme Weather and Climate Change," Union of Concerned Scientists, http://www.ucsusa.org/global_warming/science_and_impacts/impacts/extreme-weather-climate-change.html#.WEbHyHeZOqQ.
41. "What Does Winter Weather Reveal about Global Warming?," Nature America, February 11, 2010, https://www.scientificamerican.com/podcast/episode/what-does-winter-weather-reveal-abo-10-02-11/.
42. "Explaining Extreme Events from a Climate Perspective," American Meteorological Society, https://www.ametsoc.org/ams/index.cfm/publications/bulletin-of-the-american-meteorological-society-bams/explaining-extreme-events-from-a-climate-perspective/.

43. P. J. Webster et al., "Changes in Tropical Cyclone Number, Duration, and Intensity in a Warming Environment," *Science* 309: 5742 (September 16, 2005), 1844–46, http://science.sciencemag.org/content/309/5742/1844. full?sid=85ac3b49-c42e-4b10-b52e-300fc12c6390.

44. Patrick Michaels, "Global Warming and Hurricanes: Still No Connection," September 16, 2005, https://friendsofscience.org/assets/ files/documents/Patrik_Michaels_hurricane.pdf

45. Marlo Lewis, "Revisiting Gore's Katrina Innuendo," Competitive Enterprise Institute, January 29, 2016, https://cei.org/blog/revisiting-gore's-hurricane-prediction.

46. "Monthly and Annual U.S. Tornado Summaries," NOAA's National Weather Service, 2017, http://www.spc.noaa.gov/climo/online/monthly/ newm.html.

47. Becky Oskin, "Terrifying Tornado Clusters on the Rise", LiveScience, October 16, 2014, http://www.livescience.com/48316-tornados-cluster-more-often.html.

48. Patrick J. Michaels and Paul C. "Chip" Knappenberger, "Climate Models and Climate Reality: A Closer Look at a Lukewarming World," Cato Institute, December 15, 2015, https://object.cato.org/sites/cato. org/files/pubs/pdf/working-paper-35_2.pdf.

49. Roger Pielke, "My Unhappy Life as a Climate Heretic," *Wall Street Journal*, December 2, 2016, https://www.wsj.com/articles/my-unhappy-life-as-a-climate-heretic-1480723518.

50. Ibid.

51. Ibid.

52. Kevin Dayaratna, et al., "Consequences of Paris Protocol: Devastating Economic Costs, Essentially Zero Environmental Benefits," Heritage Foundation, April 13, 2016, http://www.heritage.org/research/ reports/2016/04/consequences-of-paris-protocol-devastating-economic-costs-essentially-zero-environmental-benefits.

53. Ibid.

54. Bjorn Lomborg, "Paris Climate Promises Will Reduce Temperatures by Just 0.05 °C in 2100 (Press Release), November 2015, http://www. lomborg.com/press-release-research-reveals-negligible-impact-of-paris-climate-promises.

55. Ibid.

56. Fiona Harvey, "Paris Climate Change Agreement: The World's Greatest Diplomatic Success," *The Guardian*, December 13, 2015, https://www.theguardian.com/environment/2015/dec/13/paris-climate-deal-cop-diplomacy-developing-united-nations.

57. John Vidal and Adam Vaughan, "Paris Climate Agreement May Signal End of Fossil Fuel Era," *The Guardian*, December 12, 2015, https://www.theguardian.com/environment/2015/dec/13/paris-climate-agreement-signal-end-of-fossil-fuel-era.

58. Suzanne Goldenberg and Arthur Nelson, "World Governments Vow to End Fossil Fuel Era at UN Climate Signing Ceremony, *The Guardian*, April 22, 2016, https://www.theguardian.com/environment/2016/apr/22/un-climate-change-signing-ceremony.

59. Ibid.

60. "Chapter XXVII: Environment; 7 d. Paris Agreement," United Nations Treaty Collection, https://treaties.un.org/pages/ViewDetails.aspx?src=TREATY&mtdsg_no=XXVII-7-d&chapter=27&clang=_en.

61. Steven Groves, "The Paris Accord Is a Treaty That Should Be Submitted to the Senate," The Heritage Foundation, March 15, 2016, http://www.heritage.org/research/reports/2016/03/the-paris-agreement-is-a-treaty-and-should-be-submitted-to-the-senate.

62. John Bates, "Climate Scientists versus Climate Data," February 2, 2017, Climate Etc., https://judithcurry.com/2017/02/04/climate-scientists-versus-climate-data/.

63. Alan Moore, "The Top 12 Celebrity Climate Hypocrites," MRC TV, March 1, 2016, http://www.mrctv.org/blog/top-12-climate-hypocrites?page=0,3.

64. Jake Tapper, "Al Gore's 'Inconvenient Truth,'? A $30,000 Utility Bill," ABC News, February 26, 2007, http://abcnews.go.com/Politics/GlobalWarming/story?id=2906888&page=1.

65. Lauren Beale, "Al Gore, Tipper Gore Snap Up Montecito-Area Villa," *Los Angeles Times*, April 28, 2010, http://articles.latimes.com/2010/apr/28/home/la-hm-hotprop-gore-20100428.

66. Walter Russell Mead, "The Failure of Al Gore: Part One," *American Interest*, June 24, 2011, http://www.the-american-interest.com/2011/06/24/the-failure-of-al-gore-part-one/.

Chapter 11

1. Rebecca Williams, "The Rockefeller Foundation, the Population Council, and Indian Population Control," Rockefeller Archive Center Research Reports Online , 2010, http://rockarch.org/publications/resrep/williams.pdf.
2. "Population and the American Future: The Report of the Commission on Population Growth and the American Future," Rockefeller Commission, 1972, http://www.population-security.org/rockefeller/001_population_growth_and_the_american_future.htm.
3. "Population and the American Future."
4. Shanoor Seervai, "Deaths Put Spotlight on India's Sterilization 'Camps,'" *Wall Street Journal*, November 13, 2014, http://www.wsj.com/articles/doctor-detained-for-sterilization-deaths-in-india-1415871780.
5. Population Research Institute, "Peru: UNFPA Supported Fujimori's Forced Sterlization Campaigns," July 22, 2002, https://www.pop.org/content/peru-unfpa-supported-fujimoris-forced-sterilization-campaigns.
6. Gregory Warner, "Catholic Bishops in Kenya Call for a Boycott of Polio Vaccines," *Goats and Soda* (NPR blog), August 9, 2015, http://www.npr.org/sections/goatsandsoda/2015/08/09/430347033/catholic-bishops-in-kenya-call-for-a-boycott-of-polio-vaccines.
7. Stephen Moore, "Don't Fund UNFPA Population Control," *Washington Times*, May 9, 1999, available at https://www.cato.org/publications/commentary/dont-fund-unfpa-population-control.
8. Connelly, *Fatal Misconception*.
9. National Security Memorandum 200, https://pdf.usaid.gov/pdf_docs/PCAAB500.pdf.
10. Jennifer Roback Morse, "Blessed Paul VI, Prophet and Pope: His Views on Same Sex Marriage Are Being Upheld by Pope Francis," *Christian Post*, October 29, 2014, http://www.christianpost.com/news/blessed-paul-vi-prophet-and-pope-his-views-on-same-sex-marriage-are-being-upheld-by-pope-francis-128821/.
11. Stefano Gennarini, "Paul VI and Rockefeller III," *Turtle Bay and Beyond* (blog), Center for Family and Human Rights, October 30, 2014, https://c-fam.org/turtle_bay/paul-vi-v-john-d-rockefeller-iii/.
12. Morse, "Blessed Paul VI."
13. http://www.forbes.com/sites/timworstall/2014/05/23/paul-ehrlich-predicts-cannibalism-plot-finally-and-irretrievably-lost/#6eeb6ed139e0.

14. Gregg Easterbrook, "Forgotten Benefactor of Humanity," *The Atlantic*, January 1997, http://www.theatlantic.com/past/issues/97jan/borlaug/borlaug.htm.

15. Ibid.

16. Ibid.

17. David Biello, "*Population Bomb* Author's Fix for Next Extinction: Educate Women," *Scientific American*, August 12, 2008, https://www.scientificamerican.com/article/sixth-extinction/.

18. Jeremy Alder, "The Effect of Overpopulation on Public Health," infographic, http://www.mphonline.org/overpopulation-public-health/, accessed February 11, 2017.

19. Paul Harris, "They're Called the Good Club—and They Want to Save the World," *The Guardian*, May 30, 2009, https://www.theguardian.com/world/2009/may/31/new-york-billionaire-philanthropists.

20. Lisa Correnti, "Gates Foundation Suspected of Forcing Dangerous Contraceptives on Africans," *Friday Fax*, Center for Family and Human Rights, November 19, 2015, https://c-fam.org/friday_fax/gates-foundation-suspected-of-forcing-dangerous-contraceptive-on-africans/.

21. "Population Decline," Wikipedia, https://en.wikipedia.org/wiki/Population_decline.

22. Nicholas Eberstadt, "Not a Population Explosion but a 'Health Explosion,'" *New York Times*, October 16, 2011, http://www.nytimes.com/roomfordebate/2011/10/16/fewer-babies-for-better-or-worse/not-a-population-explosion-but-a-health-explosion.

23. "The World Population Prospects: 2015 Revision," United Nations Department of Economic and Social Affairs," July 29, 2015, http://www.un.org/en/development/desa/publications/world-population-prospects-2015-revision.html.

24. Steven E. Smoot, "Demographic Winter: The Decline of the Human Family," DemographicBomb.com, http://www.demographicbomb.

25. Benjamin Shobert, "China Will Get Old Well before It Gets Rich," CNBC, October 10, 2013, http://www.cnbc.com/2013/10/10/china-will-get-old-well-before-it-gets-rich.html.

26. Austin Ruse, "The Dangers of a World without Women," *Breitbart*, January 18, 2015, http://www.breitbart.com/national-security/2015/01/18/the-dangers-of-a-world-without-women/.

27. Jonah Fisher, "Sold in Myanmar and Trafficked to China," BBC News, January 111, 2015, http://www.bbc.com/news/world-asia-30272273.

28. Joseph Henrich, Robert Boyd, and Peter J. Richerson, "The Puzzle of Monogamous Marriage," *Philosophical Transactions of the Royal Society B* 367, no. 1589 (2012), http://rstb.royalsocietypublishing.org/content/367/1589/657.

29. Susan Yoshihara and Douglas A. Sylva, *Population Decline and the Remaking of Great Power Politics* (Washington, DC: Potomac Books, 2011).

30. Susan Yoshihara, "Lost in Translation: The Failure of the International Reproductive Rights Norm," *Ave Maria Law Review* 11, no. 2 (2013), https://c-fam.org/wp-content/uploads/Lost-in-Translation.pdf.

31. Portable abortion devices also used to finish miscarriages.

32. Rebecca Oas, "Is There an 'Unmet Need' for Family Planning?," *The New Atlantis*, Spring/Summer 2016, http://www.thenewatlantis.com/publications/is-there-an-unmet-need-for-family-planning.

33. Private conversation with the author.

34. Margaret C. Hogan, et al., "Maternal Mortality for 181 Countries, 1980–2008: A Systematic Analysis of Progress towards Millennium Development Goal 5," *Lancet*, http://thelancet.com/journals/lancet/article/PIIS0140-6736(10)60518-1/fulltext.

35. "Trends in Maternal Mortality: 1990 to 2008," World Health Organization, UNICEF, UNFPA, The World Bank, http://apps.who.int/iris/bitstream/10665/44423/1/9789241500265_eng.pdf

36. "FP 2020," http://www.familyplanning2020.org.

37. Lant H. Pritchett, "No Need for Unmet Need," presentation at the Johns Hopkins School of Hygiene and Public Health, Hopkins Population Seminar Series, February 12, 1996, https://www.hks.harvard.edu/fs/lpritch/Population%20-%20docs/noneedforunmetneed_hopkins.pdf.

38. Oas, "Is There an 'Unmet Need' for Family Planning?"

39. Max Roser, "Fertility," Our World in Data, https://ourworldindata.org/fertility/.

40. Lant H. Pritchett, "Desired Fertility and the Impact of Population Policies," Population and Development Review 20: 1 (March 1994), 2.

Chapter 12

1. Tim Wallace and Alicia Parlapiano, "Crowd Scientists Say Women's March in Washington Had 3 Times as Many People as Trump's Inauguration, *New York Times*, January 22, 2017, https://www.nytimes.com/interactive/2017/01/22/us/politics/womens-march-trump-crowd-estimates.html.

2. "How Many People Were at Trump's Inauguration?," Manchester Metropolitan University, January 23, 2017, http://www.mmu.ac.uk/news/news-items/5037/.

3. Sukhbinder Kumar et al., "The Brain Basis for Misophonia," *Current Biology*, February 2, 12017, http://www.cell.com/current-biology/fulltext/S0960-9822(16)31530-5.

4. Pascal-Emmanuel Gorby, "Big Science is Broken," *The Week*, April 18, 2016, http://theweek.com/articles/618141/big-science-broken.

5. Daniel Sarewitz, "Saving Science," *The New Atlantis*, Spring/Summer, 2016, http://www.thenewatlantis.com/publications/saving-science.

6. Mara Slegler, "Top Scientists Stand Up to Trump," Page Six, January 27, 2017, http://pagesix.com/2017/01/27/top-scientists-stand-up-to-trump/?_ga=2.255237387.283294335.1493928609-1121561173.1493928404.

7. "March for Science: Bill Nye Rallies Thousands in DC amid Threat of Trump Budget Cuts," Fox News, April 22, 2017, http://www.foxnews.com/politics/2017/04/22/march-for-science-bill-nye-rallies-thousands-in-dc-amid-threat-trump-budget-cuts.html.

8. Chris Perez, "Bill Nye: Should We Penalize Parents for Having 'Extra' Kids?," *New York Post*, April 26, 2017, http://nypost.com/2017/04/26/bill-nye-should-we-penalize-parents-for-having-extra-kids/.

9. Crazy Cod, "My Sex Junk—Rachel Bloom—Bill Nye Saves the World, Youtube, April 23, 2017, https://www.youtube.com/watch?v=Wllc5gSc-N8.

10. Alex Griswold, "'Bill Nye' Episode on Netflix Omits Segment on Saying Chromosomes Determine Gender," Free Beacon, May 3, 2017, http://freebeacon.com/culture/netflix-edits-bill-nye-episode-remove-segment-chromosomes-determine-gender/.

11. "Bill Nye," Wikipedia, https://en.wikipedia.org/wiki/Bill_Nye.

12. "Bill Nye, the Science Guy, Is Open to Criminal Charges and Jail Time for Climate Change Dissenters," *Washington Times*, April 14, 2016, http://www.washingtontimes.com/news/2016/apr/14/bill-nye-open-criminal-charges-jail-time-climate-c/.

13. "Neil deGrasse Tyson (profile)," Hayden Planetarium, http://www.
    haydenplanetarium.org/tyson/profile.
14. Sean Davis, "Neil Tyson's Final Words on His Quote Fabrications: 'My
    Bad,'" *The Federalist*, October 2, 2014, http://thefederalist.com/2014/
    10/02/neil-tysons-final-words-on-his-quote-fabrications-my-bad/
15. Kevin Williamson, "Nobody @#$%&*! Loves Science," *National
    Review*, July 7, 2014, https://www.nationalreview.com/nrd/
    articles/380742/nobody-loves-science.
16. Ibid.
17. Ibid.
18. Ibid.
19. Ki Mae Huessner, "Steven Hawking on Religion: Science Will Win,"
    ABC News, June 7, 2010, http://abcnews.go.com/WN/Technology/
    stephen-hawking-religion-science-win/story?id=10830164.
20. "Stephen Hawking: Man Must Colonise Space or Die Out," *The
    Guardian*, August 9, 2010, https://www.theguardian.com/
    science/2010/aug/09/stephen-hawking-human-race-colonise-space.
21. Daniel Sarewitz, "Saving Science," *The New Atlantis*, Spring/Summer
    2016, http://www.thenewatlantis.com/publications/saving-science.
22. Fred Siegel, *The Revolt Against the Masses: How Liberalism Has
    Undermined the Middle Class* (New York: Encounter Books, 2015).
23. Ibid
24. Ibid.
25. National Science Foundation, *Doctorate Recipients from U.S.
    Universities: 2014* (Washington, DC: National Science Foundation,
    2015), https://www.nsf.gov/statistics/2016/nsf16300/digest/nsf16300.pdf.
26. Lawrence S. Mayer and Paul R. McHugh, "Sexuality and Gender:
    Findings from the Biological, Psychological, and Social Sciences," *The
    New Atlantis*, Fall 2016, http://www.thenewatlantis.com/publications/
    executive-summary-sexuality-and-gender.
27. Fiona MacDonald, "8 Scientific Papers That Were Rejected Before
    Going On to Win a Nobel Prize," *Science Alert*, August 19, 2016,
    http://www.sciencealert.com/these-8-papers-were-rejected-before-
    going-on-to-win-the-nobel-prize.
28. Cat Ferguson, Adam Marcus, and Ivan Oransky, "Publishing: The
    Peer-Review Scam," *Nature*, November 26, 2014, http://www.nature.
    com/news/publishing-the-peer-review-scam-1.16400.

29. Ibid.
30. Sarewitz, "Saving Science."
31. Megan Scudellari, "A Case of Mistaken Identity," *The Scientist*, September 16, 2008, http://www.the-scientist.com/?articles.view/articleNo/26748/title/A-case-of-mistaken-identity/.
32. C. Glenn Begley and Lee M. Ellis, "Drug Development: Raise Standards for Preclinical Cancer Research," *Nature* 483 (March 2012), http://www.nature.com/nature/journal/v483/n7391/full/483531a.html.
33. Steve Perrin, "Preclinical Research: Make Mouse Studies Work," *Nature*, March 26 2014, http://www.nature.com/news/preclinical-research-make-mouse-studies-work-1.14913.
34. C. Glenn Begley and John P. A. Ioannidis, "Reproducibility in Science: Improving Standards for Basic and Preclinical Research," *Circulation Research* 116, no. 1 (2015): 116–126, http://circres.ahajournals.org/content/116/1/116.
35. Sarewitz, "Saving Science."
36. Alvin M. Weinberg, "Science and Trans-Science," Science, July 1972, Vol. 177, Issue 4945, pp 211 http://science.sciencemag.org/content/177/4045/211.
37. Markham Heid, "Why Full-Fat Dairy May Be Healthier Than Low-Fat," *Time*, March 5, 2015, http://time.com/3734033/whole-milk-dairy-fat/.
38. Ronal Bayer, David Merritt Johns, Sandro Galea, *Salt And Public Health*: *Contested Science and the Challenge of Evidence-Based Decision Making*, http://content.healthaffairs.org/content/31/12/2738.full.
39. Niels Albert Graudal et al., "Effects of Low Sodium Diet versus High Sodium Diet on Blood Pressure, Renin, Aldosterone, Catecholamines, Cholesterol, and Triglycerides," Database of Systematic Reviews, Cochrane Library, http://onlinelibrary.wiley.com/doi/10.1002/14651858.CD004022.pub3/abstract.
40. Sarewitz, "Saving Science."

Index